MW00454251

SEMIOTEXT(E) FOREIGN AGENTS SERIES

Originally published as *L'inverno è finito: scritti sulla trasformazione negata 1989–1995*. © 1996 Antonio Negri.
© This edition 2013 by Semiotext(e).

All rights reserved. No part of this book may be reproduced, stored in a retrieval system, or transmitted by any means, electronic, mechanical, photocopying, recording, or otherwise, without prior permission of the publisher.

Published by Semiotext(e)
2007 Wilshire Blvd., Suite 427, Los Angeles, CA 90057
www.semiotexte.com

Special thanks to John Ebert, Glen Milstein and Brett Phares.

Cover art by Claude Lévêque, *Mon Repos aux Tuileries*, 2007.
Installation in situ, Jardin des Tuileries, FIAC, Galerie Kamel Mennour, Paris.
Tube Citroën, lustre, réverbères parisiens. Collection de la Ville de Paris
© ADAGP Claude Lévêque. Courtesy the artist and kamel mennour, Paris.

Back Cover Photography by Marco Dotti
Design by Hedi El Kholti

ISBN: 978-1-58435-121-4
Distributed by The MIT Press, Cambridge, Mass. and London, England
Printed in the United States of America

THE WINTER IS OVER

WRITINGS ON TRANSFORMATION DENIED, 1989–1995

Antonio Negri

Edited by Giuseppe Caccia

Introduction by Jason E. Smith

Translated by Isabella Bertoletti, James Cascaito, and Andrea Casson

\<e\>

Rochester, MN Public Library

Contents

Jason E. Smith

To Build a Fire, or Striking the Metropolis

Often, in trying to make an image of historical time, we turn to the heavens. It is well-known that the term *revolution* entered our political imaginary through the idiom of astronomy. Our fumbling attempts to get a handle on the irreversibility of an historical event needed recourse to the perfectly described circles of heavenly bodies, returning ever to their assigned places in the sky. The inversion proper to this type of figuration, casting the crisp cuts of historical breaks in the language of natural pulsations, their rises and falls, their ebbs and flows, their heatings up and coolings down, has haunted recent political sequences—or, rather, our attempt to map them—in particular, with some of the more determinant historical phases and punctuations of the past forty years being painted in climactic terms: the paradoxical heat of Italy's 1969 *Hot Autumn* is echoed in the recent popular rebellions of the *Arab Spring*. The shape of historical time is in this way folded back onto the thumping circuits of natural cycles: birth and death, slumber and awakening, surging and retreating waves. The pattern of the seasons have a special power to concentrate this cyclical imagery. When Saint Just wrote in his journals—at the beginning of 1794—that *the revolution is frozen*, he was forecasting a long winter whose frost was just beginning to settle over Europe. Our own historical period, defined by the falling off of the intense conflictuality of the period stretching from 1968 to 1977, can be thought of as still another long winter. When Félix Guattari spoke of the 1980s as "the winter years," he was not only describing a defeat and retreat of the antagonistic forces that consolidated themselves in the previous decade, he was also underlining the existential fallout of this withdrawal, the libidinal collapse into a kind of historical, and not simply psychic, depression, an hibernal rut. These winters can only be waited out, underground. A surviving remnant huddles close together sheltered from the snap of the bone-chilling historical winds, bent over and blowing lightly on—to keep alive—the cinder and ash left over from the last summer's fire.

There can be winters within winters as well. The title of Antonio Negri's *The Winter Is Over: Writings on Transformation Denied* refers in fact to two winters, to two historical time scales. Collecting essays and short interventions written during the period between 1989 and 1995, this title evokes the period coming after the collapse or suppression of the Italian Autonomia movement in the late 1970s, a time of massive state repression, prison and exile for Negri among others, as one winter embedded within the longer, secular freeze of the Soviet 20th century that comes to an end during this same period. The winter years of the 1980s are defined by these essays as an historical parenthesis marked in Italy by the emergence of Berlusconi in the field of electoral politics and by the triumph of what is called "weak thought" in Italian philosophy, and on a geopolitical scale by the foundering of the Soviet bloc and its state capitalist ("really existing socialist") satellites, various foreign incursions by the U.S. and the West (Iraq, Kosovo), and the formation of a European polity and economic configuration today coming apart at the seams. The hibernal period that takes hold in the late 1970s is not, however, simply a season among others, in a local historical cycle, but the terminal phase of a much larger arc. The capitalist response to the conflicts of the late 1960s and early 1970s was a profound restructuration that entailed, or was occasioned by, the decomposition of the workers' movement whose first riotous phase—the so-called *time of riots*—gave rise to the bloody defeats of the European rebellions of 1848 and to the formation of an organized, international movement in the second half of the 19th century. The winter that settles over Europe and the globe during the late 1970s and 1980s (the first frost having appeared as early as 1973) is therefore not one winter among others: it marks the end of the line for a cycle of struggles that developed and deepened over the course of a century and a half, a spiraling movement marked by local ebbs and flows but whose general movement was one of expansion and intensification. The winter referred to in Negri's title is first and foremost *this* winter, the epochal transformation induced by the capitalist restructuration of the 1970s that puts to rout the consolidated forces of the workers' movement. And it is with the wave of strikes in France in December 1995 that, as Negri's opening essay to the collection ("A New Public") makes clear, the discontent of the winter years begins to melt away, and the first shoots of an antagonistic new spring peek through.

The ice breaks in 1995 because, for Negri, the public sector strikes that hit Paris and France at the end of that year announced a new cycle of struggles founded on a fundamental principle: the involution of the spheres of production and circulation, a new topology of antagonism that foregrounds the *metropolis* as the privileged site of contemporary struggles. The wave of strikes that

Negri discusses began as a seemingly defensive response to a government proposal to roll back pension benefits among workers in the transportation sector. But the strikes quickly spread to other sectors, primarily in spheres tasked with providing services that contribute to the reproduction of the capitalist class relation: education and hospitals, as well as workers in telecommunications, the postal service and even the energy sector. But it was in the transportation sector—railways, subways—that the struggles took their most visible form, in part because of the response of the *users* of these services. While the government strategy was to split the users off from the striking workers, encouraging them to perceive the latter as adopting a defense of privileges denied those in the private sector, the response was the opposite: by the hundreds of thousands, users of these services organized and improvised forms of transportation (including the most primitive: walking, biking, hitchhiking) that made the perpetuation of the strikes possible. Oriented by the slogan *All together!—Tous ensemble!*—these strikes represented, according to Negri, a novel form of struggle in the history of worker antagonism. The users of these services, in organizing their own transportation during this prolonged strike, have in fact *co-produced* the strike, were themselves on strike. And this strike, which brought together service workers and users of services in a single, sustained action—the paralysis of a city—was a strike no longer localized, as in the classical form, at a point of production (the factory, say) that could be separated from the texture of social life, from the tissue of the metropolitan fabric. Where the classical form of the strike implies a separation between the production of value and the reproduction of the society, between the fabrication and the circulation of commodities—between the factory and the city—the service sector strikes of 1995 had a *diffuse* spatial character, *embracing the whole of societal life*, becoming *part of everyday reality*. Negri coins a name for this conflictual figure, a form that will shape and define the nature of conflicts to come in a new cycle of struggles: *to the dictionary of strikes invented by the proletariat in struggle (sectoral strikes, general strikes, wildcat strikes, sit down strikes, etc. . . .) we now have to add a new term, the metropolitan strike.*

In the history of working-class insurgency it has always been the case, Negri underlines, that the *ability to block the circulation of commodities has been fundamental* and that railway workers in particular have had a special place in this history. A fundamental condition for the classical general strike: workers, denied transportation, cannot go to work. But while the form of the transportation strike remains superficially the same in 1995, the paralysis it induces has a different valence, touches a different nerve. The strategic significance of these networks of transportation and communication was italicized by the capitalist restructuration of the 1970s, with its fragmentation of the production process through outsourcing, the dissolution of worker identity, the casualization of work, the supplementation of wages with private debt, the corresponding explosion of the financial sector, and perhaps most importantly with its total integration of the spheres of capitalist production and circulation. The increasing importance of containerization, supply-chain management, just-in-time and pull production (Toyota, Walmart) combined with the increasing inaccessibility of the point of production—either relocated, in a new a global division of labor, to East Asia or itself distributed across global supply chains—signals, for Negri, that the sphere of circulation is no longer simply one moment in the total process of capitalist valorization, but *the global form that structures production itself.* To strike capital in the sphere of circulation, that is, not at an increasingly unlocatable point of production but in the metropolis, the site where life and work tend to pass over into one another, their difference effaced, will be a fundamental vector of contemporary struggles. To attack the global form of production is to *affect the entire chain of production.*

In fact, Negri's approach to the metropolitan strike underlines two fundamental novelties playing themselves out in it. In addition to the involution of the different segments of the valorization process, the paradigmatic nature of the public sector strikes of 1995 is also found in the fact that the services suspended during this episode are themselves not simply produced by the workers who provide them, but are co-produced by the users of the services themselves. And it is this intrinsically *public* (or what Negri would today call *common*) character of this form of work that is implicitly recognized, according to Negri, by those users who went *on strike* with the transportation workers. What Negri suggests—and this is the leap his reading of the strikes makes—is that the *immaterial* and *interactive* character of the labor performed in the service sector constitutes the global form of an increasingly interactive and even *democratic* form of production in a post-industrial or post-Fordist environment. Emergent in these struggles is therefore a form of publicness that would be antagonistic both to the state (historically the provider of these very services) and to a capitalist command that is increasingly *parasitic* and predatory in its rela-tion to the self-organized sociality and co-operation exhibited in immaterial labor. It is in this democratic co-production of public services that it will be necessary, in turn, to seek out a properly democratic form of politics. Or instead: to insist that the figure of the anti-state public that briefly exhibited itself in this provisional suspension, in this shutting down of the post-Fordist city, names the very indistinction between the economic and the political, between the democracy of production and the political form of democracy.

In an unsigned text published in the April 1962 issue of the *Internationale Situationniste*, *The Bad Days Will End*, the authors identify the uncertain emergence of a new cycle of struggle that mirrors, in its frenetic capacity for destruction, the larval phases of the 19th century workers' movement. Just as the riotous days that accompanied the initial implantation of mechanized production—primitive forms of automation replacing human labor—were characterized by direct, violent attacks on the *machines of production*, the early 1960s according to the S.I. were witnessing similar tactics not in factories or at the point of production, but in the city itself: a *wave of vandalism against the machines of consumption*. A series of incidents is cited. In Naples, workers lay siege to a streetcar garage, light buses on fire and, in confrontations with police throughout the city, shatter shop windows and neon signs. In France, miners inexplicably attack twenty-one automobiles parked in front of their workplace and belonging to their fellow employees. In Belgium, during a general strike, workers destroy the machines used in the production of the newspaper *La Meuse*. In each case what takes place are acts of destruction that are, we are told, incomprehensible from the point of view of classical, *demands-based* forms of struggle: not only because these actions do not take the form of a work stoppage or strike meant to leverage or pressure wage-increases, but because their site is no longer the site of work but of the space and time of non-work (transportation, communications). In these first acts of insubordination, which echo the machine-breaking of the early 19th century, we see the still illegible signs of a new cycle of struggles that has as its target the spectacular city and the *new poverty* that is its crucial feature. Instead of striking at the point of production—or in addition to this classical tactic from the first cycle of workers' struggles—the contemporary period will instead be defined by a lashing out into the city itself: the *metropolis* and its networks and infrastructures, its capacities for communicating commodities, bodies and information.

The attacks on the streetcars, buses, automobiles and *apparatuses of information* identified in the early 1960s by the S.I. will in turn be echoes in the struggles that emerge in Italy after the exhaustion (or expansion) of the factory-based struggles in 1969's Hot Autumn. The slogan *Prendiomoci la città!*—*Let's take the city!*—emerged in the early 1970s to group together a range of proletarian practices that proliferated in the urban fabric itself, outside the factory struggles that had themselves become, for the classical organs of the workers' movement, increasingly hard to manage. The wildcat strikes of FIAT nevertheless gave way to a diffuse form of struggle centered in and on the metropolitan infrastructure, a shift of the site of antagonism away from struggles around the wage to an array of tactics intervening in the spheres of circulation and reproduction. Perhaps the most important of these novel forms of conflict were the auto-reduction practices that unilaterally determined, based on a proletarian assessment of worker needs, the price of certain public services often administered by the state (housing, energy, public transport). This tactic mirrored in its one-sidedness the worker assertion of the wage as an *independent variable*, defined not by productivity or market rationality but by an independent assessment by workers them-selves of the levels of wages necessary to reproduce, and perhaps overcome, the capitalist class relation. But this measured attack on public services—organized self-reduction of prices rather than the pure and simple torching of the machines of consumption—was always necessarily accompanied, in certain parts of the city and among certain milieus, by the direct expropriation of commodities, the organized and immediate consumption of—looting, setting fire to—goods no longer mediated by exchange and money. To take the city necessarily meant not only a move away from the factory, the wage, and the figure of the strike, it also signaled a cer-tain abandonment of the workers movement and its strategic framework. To speak of a *diffuse* form of struggle meant the deployment of a range of tactics that were disseminated outside of any recognizable strategic horizon, without any consideration of a fatal weak link. To take the city meant then not to seize the city at its crucial chokepoints, in order to overturn an existing form of power and reformat a city now managed by its former plebs. To take the city is simply to render it untakeable, a diffuse, unconcerted pro-duction of the *ungovernable*.

While Guy Debord and the S.I. did not consistently use the term metropolis to refer to the spectacular city, Debord's reference to a *managed territory* that reformats all of the classical distinctions inherited from Marxism that structure our analysis of class antagonism (production, consumption, distribution, circulation, reproduction). Marx once remarked that the key to opening up a communist future was the abolition of the opposition between the city and countryside, between the urban proletariat and the rural peasantry. It was in fact capitalism itself in its mature—or late—form that pulled off this abolition in a negative form and integrated these poles into a single, total circuit dedicated to the self-valorization of capital.

It is, however, the specifically Italian form of Marxism called *operaismo* that offered the most powerful theorization of this new metropolitan integration of the historically opposed spheres. Mario Tronti first developed the thesis of the *social factory* to theorize the way that the contemporary social whole had been paradoxically subordinated to one moment of its total process, the factory; it was Antonio Negri who, taking this thesis a step further, saw in the capitalist metropolis not a paradoxical dialectic of part and whole—in which the social or urban totality is subsumed beneath a key part of that whole, the point of production, and restructured in view of capitalist valorization—but rather the total convergence of the productive capacities of the factory and the sociality as such. This meant that the metropolis came to name not simply a particularly complex topological tension between factory and society but the diffusion of production across the social whole itself, in such a way that the separation between the times and space of work and those of the reconstitution of labor-power become increasingly eclipsed. The figure of the worker that corresponds to this spatial redistribution and integration of the moments of capitalist valorization was in turn retheorized by Negri as the *socialized* worker who on the one hand comes to be exploited outside the formerly defined space-time of the wage and work, and on the other hand is increasingly capable of self-organizing its own productive capacities outside the mediation of capital. It is precisely this figure of the socialized worker that re-emerges, according to Negri, in the transportation and public sector strikes in late 1995. It is this worker—the striking workers in the transportation sector, but also the users of those same services, the co-producers of those services and the strikes that bring them to a halt—that, for Negri, are beginning to build the fire that will liquidate the forms of domination and social control implemented in the Winter Years.

Reading *The Winter Is Over* today, at a distance of almost two decades, compels us to consider the way in which these important landmarks—the struggles of the 1960s and 1970s as well as the strikes of 1995—find a contemporary resonance. Our own time can be defined in large part by the global crisis of capitalism in 2007–08, and by the forms of struggles that have emerged in response to this crisis, whether they be the riots in Athens and London in 2008 and 2011, the anti-austerity struggles across Europe, the Arab Spring of 2011 going forward, or the occupy movement in the US. Specifically, we must consider the way in which contemporary conflicts seem, for many of us that invested in the struggles of a newly militant, if precarious and disoriented, global proletariat to be concentrating themselves not at the point of production—itself no longer a point, but distributed globally along intricate and precarious supply webs—but in the sphere of circulation. What this displacement of struggles has meant in certain cases is the rise of novel forms of struggle that rhyme with tactics—occupation, blockade, commodity riot—that recall the *time of riots* preceding the workers' movement (as the S.I. already suggested in 1962). It is for this reason that the most important conceptual transformation developed by Negri in *The Winter Is Over* is his use of the term *metropolitan strike* to capture the novelty of these new forms of struggle that nevertheless echo more archaic tactics, returning spectrally from the deep, pre-workers' movement past to haunt and animate the present. The task facing us is that of measuring the adequacy of both of the terms combined in this formulation for conceiving the site and form of these struggles. For if the name *metropolis* is able, it seems, to registers the restructuration of the capitalist valorization circuitry engineered over the course of the past four decades, integrating the spheres of production and circulation to the point of rendering each inseparable from the other, and leaving each equally exposed to proletarian and worker intervention, the term *strike* on the other hand seems to narrowly subsume the forms, often desperate, of current worker and proletarian struggles under the sign of the classical figuration of class conflict, centered as always on the wage-form and its possible overcoming. The question these tactics, whether they take the form of occupying urban sites, blockading ports, or the riotous and direct expropriation of commodities without passing through the mediation of money, pose to and for us is whether the concept of the strike is flexible enough to capture these forces and energies. Should we still speak of a strike when many of the forms contemporary metropolitan antagonism take involve the freezing or shutting down of various forms of transportation and supply and the direct seizure of space and goods? To what extent should we instead retire this term in an epoch no longer defined by struggles around wages, struggles that no longer have as their horizon the seizure of the means of production in view of worker management of production, and are not even always undertaken by workers (as was the case in the recent port shutdowns during Occupy Oakland)? And what would it mean, today, to take the city, when the city is now the metropolitan concentration of apparatuses and infrastructure to some extent inseparable from the valorization of capital?

In their 1962 text heralding the coming end of the *bad days*—
a pronouncement echoed in Negri's declaration that *winter* is
over—the S.I. declared that these riotous days in which the *ravages*
of the 1950s youth rebellion were married to the *vandalism* of
workers striking the metropolis would eventually, and necessarily,
be transformed *into a positive project*, ultimately *reconverting* the
machines of consumption into forces capable of expanding *the real
power of* men. This is why they could speak of a new *cycle* of
struggles: the larval forms of conflict always take a violent, even
criminal, form whose value lies not in the destruction they undertake but in the quality of insubordination they articulate. The
time of riots eventually wises up, and the machine-breaking and
commodity riots necessarily follow an arc that, with an increasing
degree of theoretical and strategic comprehension, will seek not to
demolish this machinery so much as seize and repurpose it in
view of founding another society, another world, another life, one
no longer serving the ends of capitalist accumulation and the
compulsions of its *real abstractions*. By 1973, however, Debord—
in the film version of his *Society of the Spectacle*—had come to
believe, it seems, that the contemporary capitalist city, whose
exemplary figure is that of a Paris now *assassinated*, that just such
a reconversion of the metropolis had come to be impossible. If the
fundamental project of the S.I. in its earliest phases was one of
seizing the machines and means of capitalist accumulation in view
of constructing and *collectively dominating* the environment, the
built environment of the Paris of the 1970s was to the contrary so
unsalvageable that it was good—or so the film, in its intertexts
and imagery, suggests—only for the fire. Cruelly alluding to the
recent arson of a poorly-built middle school that killed 16 children
and four adults, Debord asserts that shabby scenery of the

metropolis is rebuilt so constantly and so shoddily, in the interests of both profit and repressive control, that it can only be an *incitement to vandalism* and unavoidably *produces arsonists*: the décor of capitalism in its spectacular stage is as *flammable as a French middle school*. His next and final film, made five years later, will of course be called *In girum imus nocte et consumimur igni*: we turn around in the night and are consumed by fire.

The unsalvageability of the metropolis envisioned by Debord in the 1970s—in fact, a self-immolating metropolis will be paired with a *sick planet*, pollution destroying the unbuilt environment in turn—can likely be chalked up to the pessimism we associate with his later, post-S.I. trajectory. If it envisions, in hyperbolic form, a nihilistic solution to the intractable impasses that structure the environments we move in and through, these force fields built out of an array of apparatuses that pull and push us through them, it perhaps has the virtue of posing the question of whether contemporary struggles, oriented as they are toward an increasingly global metropolitan mesh, should truly envisage seizing these increasingly unoriented spaces, in view of building a new city and a new life. The sting of its bleakness at the very least offers a counterpoint, however implausible, to any scenario that sees contemporary urban struggles as directed simply toward the reappropriation of the capitalist infrastructure that encircles us, a making ours of its built environments, its energy infrastructure, its supply chains and information networks.

It may be, however, that each of these scenarios should in turn be bracketed by a different question altogether, one posed by the most unlikeliest of visionaries, Eric Hobsbawm. In a short text that implicitly offers a guide to future *urbanists* and communist militants of the 21st century, he asks a question that has never been formulated in the history of the city: *Suppose, then, we construct the ideal city for riot and insurrection. What will it be like?* How to build a properly insurrectionary city, ideal for riot? Such a question traces the horizon that forms along the distant edges of the contemporary metropolitan strike.

THE WINTER IS OVER

Prologue

Beppe Caccia has put together a series of materials (articles, speeches, documents) which I have edited in the last few years, having found them among so many other materials in my files and in various magazines and collections of writings. In order to organize this collection, the editor made a bet with me that he would find some coherencies, or at least some significant continuities of discourse, not only among the individual pieces, which he grouped into four chapters (movements, cultural statements, political statements on world events and on the Italian crisis), but also within the chapters themselves. Since these were materials edited on various occasions, while pursuing different contract writing assignments (political, cultural and even simply mercenary: to live, I write), Beppe's bet was arduous as I saw it. Moreover, because of the rules of the game which had been imposed, he was not able to take into consideration, nor even to clip extracts from, the philosophical books or the sociological research which I have published during recent years:[1] ranging from *Il potere costituente* (Milan, 1993) to *Spinoza sovversivo* (Rome, 1994); from *Il lavoro di Dioniso* (Rome, 1995) to my research on the businesses of short-term employment (*Des entreprises pas comme les autres*, Paris, 1994), on the field of immaterial labor (*Ministero del Piano*, Paris, 1991), on the new form of services

(*Ministero del Lavoro*, Paris, 1993), on communication networks and on information highways (*France-Telecom*, 1995). And yet, even within these limits, as I reread the collection, I must admit that a certain homogeneity can be recognized in this work. To my surprise, I give my heartfelt thanks to the editor.

The publisher (whom I must also thank for the attention he has given to the work of a "bad teacher" banned by the scientific and political realms of the *Bel Paese*[2] and the editor have asked me, in any case, to give, in the preface to this book, a brief illustration of the devices that control the continuity of a non-continuous discourse. They do not know how difficult it is to illustrate, *ex post*, a coherence that, *ex ante*, could only perhaps exist; and if they do know, they have not mentioned it. It is not by chance that the shared disdain has fallen definitively and rightly upon every thought that interprets a historical teleology. Nevertheless, given that we live a shared reality and that we reason by utilizing shared concepts, it happens that our cognitive desires, be they configured within the realm of sociological analysis, philosophical criticism or political rhetoric, end up being compared with each other in a positive way and, at times, in such a way as to fulfill themselves, within the realm of historical reality. Within this field of comparison, and in the historical realization of the desire that animates the research, we find not only its coherence and meaningful continuity, but also the truth of the act of researching.

For this reason, it seems useful to me, in response to the incitation of the publisher, to introduce these past writings, not going back over them again for the second time, but placing them, instead, in comparison with an event of great importance in my actual experience: the social struggles that developed in France in December of 1995. In fact, I believe that my research, in its diverse forms, has taken part in that collective effort which has produced, communally, that explosion of resistance and of desire that constitute precisely the December struggles. An enormous event: the masses imagined it, desired it and made it work. The masses, once again, the active and creative multitude. But in this spider web of thought and desire into which I place my work, it is not narcissism that calls the shots: no, it is the invitation to those who read my work to understand that their intellectual commitment to action is only true when they think, and continue to think, and to live only in the desire to make themselves part of the movement of the radical transformation of reality. Thus, what follows is an essay, still unpublished, in which, outside of the presupposed immediate description of events, I seek to read the implicit meaning of the struggles: of the events which took place in France in December, of what I am searching for in the articles gathered together here. And good luck to all of us. Because when the masses think, the intellectual dies.

---

1. The following books mentioned in this preface are available in English:

Il potere costituente (Milan, 1993). *Insurgencies: Constituent Power and the Modern State*, translated by Maurizia Boscagli. Minneapolis: University of Minnesota Press, 2010.

Spinoza sovversivo (Rome, 1994). *Subversive Spinoza: (Un)contemporary Variations*, edited by Timothy S. Murphy; translated by Timothy S. Murphy, Michael Hardt, Ted Stolze and Charles T. Wolfe. Manchester: Manchester University Press, 2004.

Il lavoro di Dioniso (Rome, 1995). Hardt, Michael and Antonio Negri. *Labor of Dionysus: A Critique of the State-Form*. Minneapolis: University of Minnesota Press, 1994.

2. *Beautiful country*, i.e., Italy. TN.

Preface to the American Edition of
The Winter Is Over

Is the winter really over? I find that, in my life, I have asked myself this question at least two or three times.

The first time, without a doubt, was when the experience of 1968 broke out. For me, it had already exploded in 1966–1967, when, for the first time, my comrades had autonomously, outside of the framework of the unions, gotten the workers in the factories of Marghera to go on strike: 30,000 strong. A *quasi*-general strike, declared by an entirely informal organization, a strike which threw bosses, journalists and politicians into a burst of anger, just as it stunned the unions and the population at large. It was actually possible to revolt! So, the winter was over—the winter of post-war (reactionary, under the yoke of NATO) reconstruction which had followed the end of World War II; the winter of sterile reforms and of government coalitions aimed at preventing any credible opposition (from the left, from the Italian Communist Party); the winter which could neutralize any desire for change; the winter in which the bourgeoisie dominated, bribing workers to sell their souls to the consumer culture and corrupting their traditions with unprecedented intensity. But this rupture within the capitalist system was short-lived. The stability of the markets and of governance swiftly suffocated the spirit of 1968. That historic event continued to inspire multiple narratives and a sense of nostalgia, but the struggles themselves waned. There was no longer any joy; the weather had turned gray again.

Then, the winter seemed to be over once again, in 1977, when, in Italy, a strange movement took the leading role in social struggles and imposed its own agenda upon governments. This agenda consisted of the undoing of the standard work day: eight hours on the job, eight hours with family, eight hours of sleep, a Fiat 500 car, to be washed every Sunday; and the labor class turned into a middle class. This equilibrium fell apart, and, for a good while, there was cause to celebrate. Wages were no longer sufficient simply for survival, but for actually enjoying life. We destroyed the concept of the factory as the central, lugubrious site of production and as the symbol of capitalist domination. The repression was brutal. The winter—which seemed to have ended—was then imposed, for a number of years, even in spring-time, in summer and in the fall. Many of us ended up in jail, many others were strung out on drugs; the majority were forced back to work … and, hoping to free themselves of this new reality, would often turn to freelance productive or commercial ventures, reject-ing factory wages and endeavoring to live a life of temporary employment which would allow for some added freedom. Illu-sions? Yes, of course: the winter was not over.

Again in the Nineties, we did not feel that the winter had really ended. But we hoped, nonetheless, that it had. In this book, here translated in English, this observation and this hope turn into a critique of the ten-year period between 1985 and 1995, years characterized by repression not only on the part of the police and the criminal justice system, but also by ideological and political repression. The Soviet Union had collapsed. In the Nineties the

bourgeois world seemed to rejoice in its own survival of that collapse. The Soviet Union had ceased to exist. The "brief (20th)
century" had ended. There was something mysterious about this
collapse: the fact that there had been no war, no hysterical and/or
pathological reactions, was a surprise to everybody. Was it possible,
in that unexpected situation, in that non-death-dealing void, to re-
think the mission of communist liberation? It seemed to us that it
was possible. It seemed to us that we were facing a renewed crisis
even in the Western world. Had the Western world not been listening, since 1917, to Red Square, which stood for resistance, at one
and the same time, to fascism and to capitalism? Hadn't capitalism
held it all together not only because of its fear of communism, but
also because of a kind of osmosis with it? Would Keynes and the
New Deal ever have been possible without Lenin and Soviet planning? And when the socialist system had become corrupted, didn't
its bureaucratic and state corruption correspond to the corruption
prevalent in the Western world of business and marketing, all of
which was safeguarded by the state monopoly on violence? Furthermore, hadn't the West, for all intents and purposes, been deprived of
that source of necessary exploitation provided by the colonial world?
And America's imperial dominance, which was starting to take
shape in its solitary and delusional autonomy: wouldn't it soon be
plagued by new crises and by new revolutionary insurgencies? That's
exactly what happened. And quickly. It took no time at all to see
that American hegemony was weakening and deteriorating. No one
would have foreseen this before the collapse of Soviet communism.
But that's what happened. Today we can verify this decline with a
great deal of accuracy.

In this last instance, at the closing of the 20th century, it
was no illusion to talk about a "winter that was over," about a

historical phase in the hegemony of capitalism and in the repression of revolutionary movements that had finally come to an end. And yet, this pronouncement does not seem satisfactory. In the book that is here translated into English, I endeavored to interpret the entirety of the transformations that had taken shape, after 1968 had burst forth, on the cultural and political horizon of the West, with particular attention to what was happening in Europe. The articles contained in this book capture the obstruction of the transformation that had been launched in 1968 and the return of political hope after the collapse of the Soviet Union. These writings are reflections which follow the birth of new networks of social production and of new subjects of living labor (from within the information technology revolution). They interpret the affirmation of "weak thought" as being the mourning on the part of the socialists for their failed revolution; as the softening of critical thought confronted by a transformation of reality which sought to renew the crises of the century; as the beginning of the end of American hegemony, with the Gulf War; and, finally, as an initial stage of reflection upon that grotesque stain left upon the fabric of the history of Italy, personified by Berlusconi—as a corrupt summary of the series of events that I had been outlining up to this point.

However, was the winter really over, or were we, instead, faced with a sort of transfiguration of that winter, with a kind of cold season, a season provoking new sensations, with a winter that returns after the ice has melted—after the revolutionary aspirations of the 20th century had not only been pathetically recognized in the failure of the world of "really-existing socialism," but also, and above all, in the inability to express, articulate, or even dream of those revolutionary aspirations? There was a moment when we felt that way. But the justifications presented to support this opinion were too primitive. It appeared that information technologies had replaced every methodology for searching for the truth; it appeared that wars were no longer the loathsome events which centuries of experience had taught us to recognize, but were, rather, a dutiful homage to "human rights." And then we were told that progress, which is difficult to peg, had to be, nonetheless, guided and enjoyed by the richest nations. In other words, we were told—by way of a sort of divine decree—that good things happen to those who least deserve them … something which did not last long, because the peoples and movements (in Latin America, for instance) showed us just the opposite; that is, that only a democracy of the multitudes was productive. Then, Western propagandists added that Islamic populations were inferior, by nature, to Western capitalist populations and that they hated us while we loved them; so we went to war with them in order to prove our love, to give them the gift of democracy. But it all went very badly … and since that time a myriad of official stories, sanctioned by the powers that be, seemed to be nothing more than a joke. It is quite true, then, that the winter was not over.

My dear reader, you might expect me to say, at this point, that there is nothing left to be done. That this deconstruction offers us a definitive narrative of how things have really happened. But this is not the case. It is true that the seasons, as we remember them from childhood, no longer exist. It is amazing, however, that behind this transformation of nature we still find a humanity which recognizes itself in the exploitation to which it has been submitted and in the resulting misery, and which, accordingly, is filled with indignation … Or even more: a humanity which, free of memories and of nostalgia, still reacts and inhabits spaces where it is possible to develop not only new life projects, but also a nearly unconscious passion for freedom and justice which replicates the experiences of a forgotten past, as they emerge from the unconscious, from the realm of desire. All that I can do now is to wish all my readers the joy of this renewal of spirit.

— *Antonio Negri, Christmas 2012*

A New Public

1. For twenty years things had been going as they needed to go. At least from the time of the crisis of 1971-1974, when, after having absorbed the struggles of the Sixties and the Vietnam defeat, multi-national capital had re-launched its development project in terms of post-industrial modernization and of liberal politics. Neoliberalism had asserted itself during these years: opaque years, even when, as in France, they were enlightened by several offensive worker struggles (like the one in 1986) and by the follow up of the student explosions—the first demonstrations of the immaterial labor revolt—around which social protest sought in vain to organize itself. December 1995 in France signals the first *split of the masses* in the political/economic/ideological regime of the liberal era.

Why do the struggles of December 1995 reveal such a force of rupture? Why can we consider them to be the beginning of the end of the counterrevolution of the 20th century?

Various answers to this question are beginning to be offered—in great part, correct answers. In particular, it is evident that several things were overturned in the formative process of the struggle and its radicalization: the awareness of the intolerability of the processes of globalization and of the European construction within the specific realm of French acceleration, the sense of betrayal of the "republican promise" on the part of the new Presidency, as well as the body of contradictions determined by the new organization of social labor—mobility, flexibility, rupture of the labor market, exclusion—and of the crisis of Welfare. Above all, what seems important to me is the definition of the new context in which individual claims are established: a "biopolitical" context, in the sense that the struggle clashes with the body of those rules that discipline or control the totality of the conditions of the reproduction of the proletariat. In sum, the struggle assumes its universal sense, becomes a struggle "of general interest," according to the measure in which it refutes the diktat "liberalism or barbarism"; and it indicates a new threshold of possibility, in the domain of protest and of the desire for a new world.

And yet, having said this, we could never succeed in understanding the radical nature and the epochal rupture of this struggle if we were not to put in place a new query: *who is its actor?* What is the subject that has been hegemonic in this struggle? What is the social tier that has succeeded, in such a very short time, in transforming a struggle for demands into a political struggle against the globalized capitalist regime? And why? What are the material connections that have ordered the expansion of the struggle and its political future?

2. The first answer is easy: this subject is called "the public service worker." It was s/he who initiated and guided the struggle in rail and subway transportation, in telecommunications, in the postal system, in the hospitals, in the schools, in the energy sector, etc.; it was s/he who ignited and led the struggle and gave a general sense of direction to the demands of various sectors. But the answer would end up being banal if we were not to give our attention to

that which, today, these sectors represent, in a new way, within the political and productive apparatus of mature capitalism. What I mean to say is that on other occasions in the history of workers' struggles, the capacity for blocking the circulation of goods was fundamental in unleashing political clashes (the rail worker strikes, in particular, have studded the insurrectional firmament of labor history): today, nonetheless, within the organization of mature capital, the capacity to invest the system of production with determined political force becomes decisive and exclusive; the capacity to do so is invested in the workers who provide public services and transportation, communications systems, training programs, health and energy services. Thatcher and Reagan, those brawny initiators of liberal strategy, knew this very well when, in order to launch their restructuring of things, they took on as their exemplary adversaries the workers in the field of energy or those who dispatched airline communications. But why?

A not so banal answer comes to life only when we recognize that within the structure of mature capitalism the totality of the means of transportation, communications, training, energy, that is to say, of the grand scheme of public services, no longer represents only one moment of the circulation of goods or one element of the reproduction of wealth; rather, it constitutes the *structural container* of the production itself. We were told a thousand times that production had become circulation, that we had to work "just-in-time" that the worker had to become a link in the social chain. Well, the public service workers on strike have shown that by touching one link of the circulation they touch the entire productive chain; that, by acting upon the container, all of the contents had to react. And since we are speaking here not only of the structures of production, but of the *subjective forces* that define themselves within these structures, it seems clear why the struggle of the public service workers has, from the beginning, "represented" the totality of the workers and why, in the strategic place which they occupy, their struggle has immediately overtaken the global nature of the system of production and its new social and political dimensions.

From the standpoint of the objective analysis of the process of production which is so dear to those who define this struggle as "reactionary" and "conservative," we must immediately rebut that these struggles and their principal actors are central and decisive to the new mode of production; they, the actors, have elevated the struggle to the highest level of capitalist "reform" and for this very reason they have temporarily brought it to a halt.

3. But it is not simply the laborers, and in general the public service workers, who have been the actors in the struggle: it has been equally the millions of women and men in Paris and in all the cities of France who, in order to reach their place of work or simply in order to move around from place to place, submitted themselves to war-time conditions, truly pitiful conditions. The media have illustrated this struggle with lyrical tones—first in order to try to organize the revolt of the "users" of mass transit, then—once this project had been defeated on a big scale—in order to exalt the civility and conviviality of their behavior, at any rate in sympathy for the effects of the strike. But hadn't industrial sociology, neoliberal ideology and all the writings of the State recounted for us, for years, how, in the post-industrial era, the users themselves are the producers of service? How could these producers of ideology now blatantly deny what they had said, attempting to place the users against the service workers or even seeking to identify them as a separate community?

In fact, the "users" are "co-producers" of public services. They are such according to differentiated figures (that range from a maximum of passive consumption and a minimum of interactivity to a minimum of passive consumption and a maximum of interactivity: in the first instance, the users of the energy services will serve as an example; and in the second case, the users of telecommunications, of training and of health services). Now, within the struggle, this "co-production" has shown its own self awareness. The "users" have recognized the struggle of the workers who, together with them, produce the services, as being in their own interest. If these services are a co-production, then their essence is public. One does not deny that there can be contrasts and that contradictions can arise between the supply and demand of service: we want only to emphasize that even these contradictions place themselves inside the public dimension. Thus, when the service workers have turned their struggle into a recognition, a defense and an affirmation of the public character of their production, the "users" are totally recognized as "co-producers" *of this struggle.*

Thus, the marching in the snow, hitchhiking a ride, standing in line, the endless waiting, become episodes of the struggle. The strike, in its efficacy, was made manifest not only by the loud union marches, but above all by the festive marches every morning and every evening. It was not a "strike by proxy"; rather, it was a widespread strike that extended to the social realm, a part of daily life. In the vocabulary of strikes invented by the proletariat in struggle (the union strike, the general strike, the "*grève-bouchon*," the wild strike, etc.) a new term has been added: *the metropolitan strike.*

Let us be careful, however: when we emphasize this metropolitan "co-production" of the struggle we also identify a concept of the "public" that has a revolutionary value. In the co-responsibility that the "users" feel with respect to the practice as well as to the services strike, one cannot avoid recognizing a true act of "reappropriation of the administration." A direct and subversive act. From the awareness of the nature of this act, our reflection cannot avoid leading us back to its preconditions: to the identification of public service, and thus of its management and of its most general productive functions, as being something in common. Common, as are all the products of the cooperation: from language to democratic administration. This is a definition of "public" which no longer has anything to do with its "state-related" definition.

4. The State discovers its own capitalist character when it seeks to privatize public services. On the other hand, the struggles reveal a subversive character which goes beyond the realm of the State and of its function as the guardian of capital—even when some of the actors of these struggles maintain "French style public service." In fact, I believe that very few people consider it plausible to defend that trace of the Third Republic which, having been renewed in the Fordist compromise between popular forces of the Resistance and Gaullist technocracy, has survived until this day, in an anachronistic way. The struggles tell us that if a "public service in the French style" resists, it will be expressed in completely new terms: as the first experience of a reconstruction of public service within a democratic dynamic of reappropriation of the administration, of the democratic co-production of service. Here, in fact, by means of these struggles, new problems open up: *constituent* problems. It's a matter of understanding the meaning of the public aspect of the services, an aspect that, by removing itself from the privatization and rules of the world market, removes itself also from the ideological mystifications that conceal the globalizing and directly capitalist function

of the national State. The awareness of these problems is implicit in the struggles. It represents their subversive potential. Moreover, if it is true today that the services constitute the shell of every form of productivity, state or private, if it is true that these services demonstrate, in a central and exemplary way, the role of cooperation within the totality of production and circulation, then this new concept of *public* will constitute the paradigm of every new experience of socialized production.

Therefore, the public seen as the totality of the custodial activities of the State aimed at permitting the reproduction of the capitalist system and private accumulation, has now ceased to exist. We find ourselves in the presence of a *new concept* of public; that is, a form of production organized upon interactivity, a concept in which development of wealth and development of democracy become indistinguishable, as are the widening of the social bond and the reappropriation of the administration on the part of the productive subjects. Here the elimination of exploitation becomes visible not as a myth, but as a concrete possibility.

5. But this new subjective dimension of the public is not something which touches only the "social workers," the workers, that is, in social services. It is also something that encompasses, as we have seen, the co-producers of the services, and therefore all the citizens who work. The "Everyone together" theme of the slogans of the struggles, presented, then, a new community, a productive social community, that demands recognition. This recognition is twofold. It is, in fact, on the one hand, the dynamics of re-composition that runs through the movement; it is the *community of struggle* which all workers are reminded of by those workers who, because of their position, give shape to the essential plot of productive cooperation.

On the other hand, the recognition sought is that which consists of the *reappropriation* of service, be it on the part of the community in struggle, or on the part of those who, while working, utilize the services in order to produce wealth.

In this way, the struggle functions as a foreshadowing of the goal towards which it aims; the method—or the being together in order to win—is the foreshadowing of the finality—or the being together in order to construct wealth, outside of and against capital.

What is interesting to emphasize here is that, within the struggle that we have lived out, and above all where public services were in question, the concept of *community* was enriched by essential articulations. The concept of community has often been attacked, even, and above all, in subversive thought, as something which mystified the concrete articulations of exploitation, flattening them into a figure in which the associative collectivity of the subjects was given by the unity of the function rather than in the contradictory articulation of the associative and productive process. In the course of the struggle we are analyzing, there appears for the first time an extremely articulate community, a *Gemeinschaft* that contains within itself all of the characteristics of multiplicity—and that, as a social and productive totality, opposes itself to power.

Reflection on this movement leads us then to pose the problem of the *transition* to a superior level of productive organization, where the public might be considered as a unity of social functions that, by richly articulating themselves, do not demand the separation of levels of production and of levels of power. On the contrary, the reappropriation of power within the productive function and the construction of the social bond become a *continuum*. The problem of the transition towards an autonomous social community, towards communism, will no longer consist only in the definition of the forms of struggle against the State; on the contrary, it will reside essentially within the definition of the times and the forms in which the reappropriation of productive functions on the part of the community will be possible.

"Everyone together" is a plan of transition to communism. These struggles allow us to begin to call again by name the real movement of the transformation of the present state. And if the work to be done in order to recompose, within the imaginary, the real movement and development of history is immense, that does not prevent us—at an extremely high level of possibility (or rather, there, where capitalism constructs extremely high forms of cooperation)—from beginning to fill the utopia of the movement with words that capture its desire.

6. The slogan "Everyone together" was launched and embraced by the movement, in contingent form, as an invitation to the workers in private businesses to enter the struggle. We have seen how the slogan has since been transformed. But it is true that its original meaning, its original invitation, has fallen into the void. Why? Why did the workers of the "juridically" private sector of the economy not enter into the struggle?

The explanations that have been given as to why the workers of the private sector did not enter into the struggle are very realistic: they range from justifications having to do with wage structure (wage individualized according to measures of implication, thus subject to the immediate repression of the owner, as far as strikes were concerned) to justifications having to do with the crises of trade unionism in the private sectors of industry and of services. These explanations, even though realistic, lose sight nonetheless of a structural element of private enterprise, and that is the fact that in private enterprise the tendency of the transformation from productive structure into public structure of service has not yet been rendered evident; and there is also the fact that this tendency is hidden, on one side, from the strong permanence of *manufacturing industries*, and on the other, from the infamous prevalence of the rules of private profit according to *financial models*. Perhaps the moment has arrived for saying that the productive functions bound to manufacturing production are, for multiple reasons, bound for extinction. And that, as a consequence, the layers of workers bound to the manufacturing functions are the most susceptible to blackmail and threats of unemployment, and thus *the weakest*. Precisely for this reason, they are less capable of conducting struggles of attack. They are closed, by now, within a paradox: in the moment in which they struggle, they will be constrained to do so in order to destroy even the places of production from which they receive a wage today. They are a bit like the peasants in the French Revolution of yore: they will fight in order to enable victory not for the system of production in which they are implicated, but for another system of production in which they will be trounced.

But this interpretation touches not only the workers of the private manufacturing sector. By now, in the private sector the service firms are present in ever increasing importance. The big manufacturing companies have "eliminated" functions directly and indirectly productive, in ever increasing breadth, reducing them to commercial services and inserting them within the context of social production. And it is in the private sector of services that the rediscovery of the public, and hence the recomposition of the new proletariat, is possible. It is possible where the forms of labor, in the private sector, assume temporal flexibility and spatial mobility as fundamental characteristics—there, where profit takes form, just as in the sectors of public services, above all upon the *exploitation of social cooperation.*

In the December struggle there was delay and confusion in singling out the form of the invitation given to the private sectors to participate in the struggle. This invitation had its traditional form in the appeal to the workers of the private manufacturing sector. In the course of the struggle it was to be, instead, the workers and the operators of public services, and also of private services, who would need to recognize themselves within the new concept of public—and thus within the cooperative reappropriation of the production of wealth and a construction of the democratic administration of the productive society.

7. We can return now to identifying the subject of the December struggle. On a superficial level this subject is represented as the worker in "public services"; in another instance, it appears as a "social worker," or as the producer of social relations and the producer of wealth by means of these relations; in a third instance, this identification is reinforced by the fact that the clients for these services, that is, the citizens in general, have co-produced the struggle; in a fourth instance, it appears evident that the public nature of the service is the strategic locus of the exploitation and thus of the new contradictions upon which the struggles of attack can develop; and in yet a fifth instance, it is clear that even the operators of services in the private sector, that is to say the majority of the workers of the private sector that has been restructured within the services, will be attracted to this cycle of struggles.

But *the social workers are immaterial workers.* They are such because they are highly educated, because their work and their effort are essentially intellectual, because their activity is cooperative. A production made up of linguistic activities is by now at the center of society and of its system of power. Thus, the social workers are immaterial in as much as they participate in the new intellectual nature of labor.

But this new intellectual nature of labor is "*bios*," the entire life of generations and of singularities. The subject of the December struggle has shown, by way of the struggle and its objectives, the entire complex dimension of life as production of subjectivity—and thus, as the rejection of the subservience of social intellectual cooperation to the development of capital.

In any event, the workers in struggle were saying to the governing authorities that if you do not want to acknowledge the freedom in this collective intellectual nature of associated labor, you will be forced to acknowledge its centrality, its power—to put up with the impossibility of discussion of wage, of social reproduction and of economic-political constitution, without taking this reality entirely into account.

Telecommunications and education represent the most significant sectors of class, from the point of view of immateriality, of an interactive public, of "*bios*"—here the *General Intellect* which Marx had foreseen as the fundamental agent of production in mature capitalism reveals itself as "*bios.*" In the processes of *education*, the labor force is constructed and reconstructed, continuously, along the entire path of life and of generations, in full interactivity, not only between active singularities, but between these singularities and the world, the *Umwelt* which surrounds them and which is continuously constructed and reconstructed by human activity. *Telecommunications* represents, in the near future, the totality of the circulation of productive signs, of cooperative languages—thus, these active singularities constitute the external figure of that constant capital of which human brains have taken possession again. And it is by means of education and telecommunications that the processes of production of subjectivity are confronted by the processes of subservience of the productive subjectivities and construction of surplus-labor-profit.

Thus, it is upon these junctures that the struggle focuses on the form of appropriation—because education and telecommunications represent the highest point, and the most explicit structure, of production as public service.

8. The December struggles present a formidable challenge to revolutionary theory. In these struggles it is the workers themselves who are the hegemonic actors: the workers in the sectors of material and immaterial services; that is to say, the social workers in the fullness of their productive attributes. Consequently, these struggles place themselves at the level of mature capital or, as one might say, postmodern and/or postindustrial capital. The service workers give us a close up of social productivity and they show the contradictions that are revealed as this productivity develops. The problems of the emancipation from capitalist demand and of the liberation from the mode of capitalist production are posed now in a new dimension. The manufacturing industry and its workers lose definitively the central role which they had had in the unleashing and direction of the class struggle, while the service workers, including, and above all, those who provide services within the private sectors of mature economies, are strongly called upon to enter into the game of the revolutionary struggle.

Theory, then, must now confront this new reality. It must work in general on the relationship between "general intellect" (that is to say, immaterial and intellectual hegemonic labor) and "*bios*" (that is to say, the dimension in which intellectual labor, in the form of constant re-appropriated capital, opposes capitalistic demand which by now has become completely parasitic). But above all, it must work around the nexus that pulls together *social interactivity* and its *political* forms, production and politics, productive power and constituent power. Lenin had already posed the problem of the relationship between economic appropriation on the part of the proletariat and political forms of this appropriation. In his time, and within the productive relationships that he was considering, realism led him to consider the term "dictatorship" to be a decisive term. Our utopia of liberation, without smearing Lenin, who was the first to understand the necessity of having revolution and enterprise march together, detaches itself radically, nonetheless, from his point of view. It can do so, realistically, because today production is a world of interactive relationships that only "democracy" can constitute and underpin. Democracy, a potent democracy of producers, stands today at the center of our investigative interest.

To construct a public that is set against the State, to think of the democracy of the producers as something set against the parasitism of capital, to single out the forms in which the interactivity of production (revealed by the development of services) can be articulated by the (renewed) forms of political democracy, in order to discover the material fabric of the *political coproduction of the social*: these are the new tasks of theory. These new tasks are urgent and as extremely alive as were the struggles that introduced them.

Let us be careful: many theorists of social reproduction in the postmodern era are already examining analogous problems. All of the "community-minded individuals," that is to say, all of the social scientists who have not accepted liberalism as the only philosophy, especially in the country which is the prince of capitalism, the USA, are working on the problem of bringing to light the relationship between growing social cooperation and production of democracy.

But the December struggles go far beyond these main themes: because they pose the problem not only as possibility, but as necessity, because they anticipate a solution, showing that democracy of the multitude is a revolutionary fact. Here, then, is another theme, certainly not secondary: what does it mean to revolutionize social cooperation, re-appropriating the administration democratically, in order to manage the totality of the production and reproduction of society.

9. With the December struggles we have entered into a new phase of political practice.

The first problem is evidently that of re-opening the struggle, after its suspension. It is, consequently, that of widening and sustaining the front of the social worker, in public services and above all in the private sector. It will also be a problem of expressing in the broadest and most powerful form the contributions of the subjects of education (school, University, etc.) and of telecommunications to the new perspective of the construction of the revolutionary movement, and of co-producing these struggles together with the citizen workers.

But here there emerges the second, and fundamental, problem: that of defining a form for the struggle and for the *organization*, a form that needs to be coherent with the new concept of the public that we have been reading as the expression of the December struggles. It is worth saying that we seek a form of organization that can allow, more and more, for connecting the categorical claims to those general claims of *biopolitical wage*, of the extension of *public service*, of the *reappropriation of administration*.

It is evident that the capacity, revealed by the workers in the process of struggle, to *reorganize upon the territory*, thus breaking the traditional professional division of French unionism, is a capacity that will be able to be accepted as a paradigm of the unifying recomposition of the objectives of the struggle and of the general form of the management of the struggle. In fact, these forms of organization prefigure new political instances (no longer merely pertaining to unionism), both mass and grass-roots in nature. They reveal, by paradoxically binding themselves to the origins of the organization of the worker movement, a central element of the organization of post-Fordist production: its social diffusion. This *unitary localization* seems really to be the base for a generalization of worker interest in wage and in the struggle over the conditions of social reproduction; but, at the same time, it is the unique base for the possibility of movement from that initiative of reappropriation of the administration and of public services that, alone, can allow for the opening of a horizon of struggles heading towards democracy.

PART ONE

INQUIRY WORKSHOP

By Means of the Network of Social Production,
for the Organization of the New Subjects
of Living Labor

1

New Social Movements
and Political Realignments

One thing that is for sure is that, in and of itself, neither the proletariat nor the feminist movement, nor the ecological movement, can pretend to represent, within the coming years, the hegemonic subjects of the struggles of transformation: one understands that what we mean here is each movement for itself, isolated. Neither the exploitation of labor, nor the hierarchy and division of the sexes, nor the catastrophic scenario of the destruction of the planet, is, in and of itself, capable of providing a logical plan of collective action, a unified concept of antagonism and thus of constituting a base, even a minimal yet communal base, for recovering the mass movement. After the defeat, in the field, at the end of the Seventies, this truth was thrust upon us by the exhausting of the residual energy of the movements during the Eighties. "What now?" Somberly, this question was asked by a militant of that extreme French left that, sophisticated as it is, is no less radical or intelligent: "Farewell to the proletariat, farewell to feminism, farewell to ecology ... And then?" There was neither nostalgia nor resentment in his words; rather, there was a certain impatience, and the awareness that those movements, each independently, for itself, had arrived at fundamental results but had run its course; there was a sense of annoyance for all those attempts at reconstruction (and representation) that reduce themselves to the sum, to the amalgam, to repetition—as if, by drawing together footage of experiences already lived, it would be possible to discover a new force, that surplus of invention that, alone, would allow the movement to resume its path.

Only in this way will we be able, on the other hand, to confront the problem that, as 1992 approaches, is posed in an ever more urgent manner: "Which left, for which Europe?" We must recognize immediately that the political world, the official one, of the parties of the historical left and of the organizations of the labor movement, offers a quite insufficient response to these problems. Every attempt at constructing a leftist force on the European level has always demonstrated an inertial drift to the right—a drift that has become frightening in the only case of effective success, the case of Eurocommunism. No new data indicate that those grand electoral machines of which we are speaking would be better suited to place themselves into a radical process of transformation. So, then, what to do? Perhaps we should admit that if Mohammed does not go to the mountain, it will be the mountain that will go to Mohammed.

Let us begin with the statement of fact that there are social struggles, even if they are insufficient—and there are many of them—on our continent. They are, as has been said, insufficient in terms of constituting, in and of themselves, in their uniqueness, a hegemonic plan of collective action: nonetheless, we think that the multiplication and extension of social movements can do nothing other than reopen a political process. If this is true, and we shall try in what follows to prove it, we shall be able to pose two more questions for ourselves, questions which are perhaps not irrelevant: if these movements impose realignments of political forces, even traditional ones, in what form does this occur? And what is, consequently, the element of innovation, the new strategic content, that characterizes this passage forward?

Take Germany, for example. This is the European country where movements (environmental, pacifist, anti-nuclear, for civil rights, for housing, etc.) have assumed greater breadth, continuity and depth. This had to do with movements that essentially proliferated from the bottom, from the civil society of small groups that were developing local initiatives and that were often succeeding, through a pragmatic approach, in spreading their own initiatives across the entire society. "Sticking together," "doing something with one's own means": these were the initial passwords, very elementary, but often capable of giving flight to grass roots associationism and of leading this associationism towards the independent programming of national campaigns. In this way, the problem of political representation was not overestimated; rather, it was thought to be a false problem. Those same "*Grünen*" moved along a terrain that did not claim to be the terrain of the representation of the movements: they were simply a "service" of these movements. In Germany, then, the movements, by developing themselves from the bottom, and by self-monitoring the political processes being advanced, have conquered, in an independent manner, a national dimension; they have autonomously broken through traditional political territory without becoming slaves to that territory.

The pressure upon the political has been, from the start, the transformation of this political territory. No political force in Germany can exclude the fact that the movements of struggle have an immediate and direct institutional impact: and recent struggles have demonstrated this definitively, above all those very violent housing riots in Hamburg. It is upon these foundations that a certain realignment of political forces, even traditional ones, is in action: but, more about this later.

A second example concerns the struggles that, in Italy, have by now been developing in every sector of public administration and above all in those related to transportation and education. These struggles are directed by the "Cobas," committees formed outside of the unions, according to grass roots organizing models. It is not an exaggeration to say that the "Cobas" have reconstructed social conflicts, after the "decade of lead" from 1975–1985.[1] They are now gaining effective power. For more than a year now, the "Cobas" of the railroad workers and of the teachers, to speak only of the strongest and most active of the "Cobas," are succeeding in blocking, when necessary, the entire sector in which they operate. The fundamental effort is not that of putting oneself in contact with them and with other social groups in struggle. The themes and objectives upon which the "Cobas" were organized have had to do mostly with wage; but recently, and ever more often, protest and demands have been articulated as the proposition of transformation, and political discourse has arrived at the center of the debate.

In fact, education and transportation are a very delicate point within the ideological and productive system of late capitalism; and they are one of the junctures upon which the problems defined by the restructuring in progress rise up most acutely: the comprehension of that centrality, and the willingness to weigh, in an antagonistic manner, upon the decisions that have to do with the future of these social activities, promote an extremely powerful tension within the "Cobas." As in Germany, also in Italy, then, the movement is in

---

1. Translators' Note: This is the period of extremely violent protests and terrorist activity culminating in the assassination of Aldo Moro, the Christian Democrat leader.

search of wider political space. Differently, however, from what happens in Germany, in Italy the existing political forces, be they green or red, even while attempting to recognize the specificity of these dynamics, are also placed in difficulty by the radical nature of new grass roots movements and by their inability to be integrated into the tradition of political representation. Having said that, we can still add that also in Italy a political realignment is in progress, one which involves—beyond the greens—the left of the social democracy and of the Italian Communist Party, and—*last but not least*—important sectors of the Catholic world.

If we now turn to the third among the great countries of continental Europe, to France, we find ourselves in the presence of analogous processes. Certainly, here, according to an old tradition, "movements are seen only when they explode," and thus it was, in fact, for the student movement at the end of 1986; thus it was also for the successive emersions of the antiracist movement to the point of the hegemony of *SOS Racisme* in 1986. But this does not mean that the movements are not weaving their daily fabric, that they are not continuously charting paths from civil society to political society; and it does not mean that one cannot, when wanting to, grasp and describe these movements in terms of what they become. In fact, precisely because of this discontinuity of theirs, the French movements are those which are most exposed to an institutional integration. Characteristic, apropos, is the trajectory of *SOS Racisme* which, having recently subordinated the theme of liberation to that of racial integration, now plays an ambiguous role at the institutional level. But who can claim that this ambiguity can have only a negative role? Especially in a country as centralized as France, where all social communication is forced to move along the constraining path of the political. In these weeks, the "Juquin constellation" that was formed by gathering the forces of the communist left and the "*rénovateurs*" who recently left the French Communist Party, in the course of the presidential electoral campaign, shows that even at this level of institutional complexity it is possible to make known the innovative contribution of social movements.

We can now begin to respond to the questions initially placed before us. It seems clear, in the first place, that the social struggles, in continental Europe, are not only amply diffuse today, but they have put in motion a mechanism of multiplication, opening up a new cycle, no longer defensive, but offensive. A cycle characterized by a broad opening towards the political, always in a unique manner (and differently in Germany, Italy and France), but not, for that reason, any less effective. And thus we respond to the second question, and that is to the question as to whether or not a form of hegemonic organization is recognizable in these movements. Even in this regard the answer is positive: the form of organization consists of a passage towards the political which does not cross institutions of representation and does not accept delegated functions or separate headquarters. But with this, the political is not negated, as in the Seventies: one expects, instead, reappropriation to the community in struggle, to the movement, rather than claiming the negation of the political, rather than expressing the radical refusal of it. But this process is not only organizational—it is also programmatic.

Let us begin, with the above understanding, to respond to the third question which we had posed for ourselves: what is the element of innovation, of strategic proposition that crosses this phase of the movement? Is it the development of a program of social struggles of reappropriation and of an alternative project? Is it a real and true "constituent power," that which continues, slowly but surely, to construct itself? Here the thematics of the proletarian movement, of feminism, and of the ecologists can very well live together; in fact, they can articulate themselves not only within a transverse organizing process that permits maximum communication among the struggles, but within the demands (against the enemy) and the construction (within themselves) of a power capable of recognizing the new determinations of social productivity of which all the citizens are equally participants. It is upon this terrain that new unifying objectives are defined, objectives that constitute a terrain of confrontation and of communal struggle: a guaranteed income for all workers, men and women, students and the unemployed, etc.; massive reductions in work hours; a higher and higher educational system that is constantly being renewed, and the possibility for all the citizen workers to access the highest level of science; the realization of freedom of expression, against the monopolies of information; etc., etc. That is what the French call the "reinvention of the social." In this moment, when the deafening brutality of the conservative offense is finally wearing itself out, there is a rebirth of a demand for power, or better yet, of reappropriation, of radical transformation of society and of the State.

This process of political redefinition of social forces is by now completely evident. And there is a behavior, in the dominant political class, that is particularly striking: a behavior of disarmament, of impotence, of a kind of neutrality, even on the part of those forces that in the Seventies were violently opposed to the new developments. It seems as though they consider the appearance of the new social and political world to be inevitable. The political realignments at this point are inevitable, difficult but necessary. In France we see the beginnings of big maneuvers (on one hand, the "Juquin constellation," and on the other, the notable unrest in the left of the socialist party); in Italy the transversality of the new thematics touches all the forces of the left and even part of the Catholic world—and divides them; and finally, in Germany the "green" penetration no longer touches only the left of the German Socialist Party, but also important sectors of the Christian Democratic Left. The tranversality of the rallying and the radical nature of the foreseeable choices are now beginning to create the outline of irreversible deadlines. Deadlines of division? Is it perhaps necessary that a process of redefinition and of renewal of the left must pass through the division, as tradition teaches? The processes of political realignment—one could note—those processes which are timidly in progress, do not go in this direction: rather, a certain unifying spirit is perceivable. But the realignment is, for now, only the echo or the reflection of the social movements; it has not yet directly confronted those movements. When it does, when the mass of socialist forces, always subjected to the centrist drift, even after overcoming neoconservative digression, will split in order to show that a new left has arisen, beyond the restructuring: well, that seems inevitable to us.

2

Worker Restructurings in Europe

Analysis of the Cycle of Struggles in the Eighties and Nineties

A new cycle of worker and proletarian struggles probably came to light in Europe in the middle of the Eighties, after the crisis of 1983–84 and parallel to the economic recovery. The characteristics of the cycle of struggles are totally new in relation to the struggles of the preceding decade, struggles which had ended with the decisive defeat of the working class and a profound restructuring of the State and of industry. Here we pose three problems:

1. What might the characteristics of the new cycle of struggle be and how does this new cycle distinguish itself from cycles that immediately preceded it?

2. What might be the fundamental characteristics of the capitalist restructuring of the State and of industry, and their effects on the make-up of the proletariat, and how one can picture the strategic continuity of this new cycle of struggles?

3. What are the position and the role of the immigrant populations in this context of forces and movements?

1. The Characteristics of the New Cycle of Struggles

The new cycle of struggles was formed as of the onset of the social movements. This is true for France, where these movements take the form of great waves of sectorial demands that become mass demands (from the student struggles to the transportation and postal struggles, from those of the nurses to that of the Peugeot car factories). It also is true for Italy, where the movements take shape, outside of the union context, as horizontal and inter-categorical "grass roots Committees" (from the sector of education to that of rail workers to the struggle of the metal workers). Or in Spain, where the movements find their best expression in highly politicized social movements (education and the struggle against NATO). And even, on the contrary, as in Great Britain, where the movements were set in motion by forces that were placed within the sphere of the union left (transportation, nurses, railroads, schools)—or, lastly, in Belgium or in Germany, where they are developing intense demand-oriented guerrilla tactics (like that of the metal workers fighting for the 35 hour week) within the very structure of the union. In all of these situations one finds common characteristics and homogeneous behaviors in the forms of organization which the movements take on, in the forms of struggle which they assume, in their objectives, in the relationships which they establish with unions and political institutions, and finally in the general conception of politics which, together with these relationships, is beginning to take shape. What stands out most in these struggles is that which immediately distinguishes them from the struggles of the preceding cycle—it is their form. Here are some examples that illustrate these new data in France.

The Organizing of the Nurses

The horizontal organization and the method of "making decisions" in general assembly, the formation of delegations with a precise mandate, in brief, all of the inheritance of a direct democracy (not interpreted in a bigoted manner) is present in this movement. What is particularly interesting is the fact that the organizing represents an indispensible condition, one that permits the struggle to commence. After having gone through experiences of "union betrayal," which either they themselves had experienced, or about which they had been informed, the workers trust no one but themselves. In the Seventies, when we arrived at a horizontal organization of the struggles, that organization took place at the end of a long clash based on an extremist expansion of the meaning and objectives of the struggle: and this was verified not without giving evidence of the limits of the assembly method. Today, on the contrary, the organization is the form itself of the "speaking up"; it is the condition of the struggle of which we must absolutely take heed. What ensues from this, in the second place, is a form of hard, uniform, rarely violent struggle that is enormously concerned about the means of external communication and about internal involvement in the work place. Even in this case, the form of struggle is not extremist, since it is not wrested from the unions and reappropriated by its protagonists through the exasperation of its forms, as was often the case in the past. What we witnessed, then, was the paradox of identifying the enemy from within, rather than from outside the subject in struggle. Today, on the contrary, the enemy is sought out where s/he resides, where the power of decision lies, and one seeks to avoid the extension of the points of conflict and of all the lacerating acts of internalizing the difficulties of the struggle in work situations. Thus, the nurses seek alliances in all of the health related sectors, and above all they seek the support of the patients and the mutual understanding of the population, by punctually making public their own functions, their own preparation, their own responsibility. They do not single out either the hospital administrations or the medical structures as the enemy; rather, they identify the enemy in the political and administrative places responsible for important budgetary decisions—in a way in which what seems to be apparently a watering down of traditional class struggle, reveals itself to be in reality, right from the beginning, an operation of theoretical simplification and of the political rising up of the clash.

Thirdly, the determination of the objectives is characteristic. The thrust of wage concerns is undoubtedly central to all the struggles of recent years. But recognizing this thrust is not enough for grasping the nature of the objectives, even given the expectation of satisfaction from the monetary point of view—objectives that possess an intensity that is immediately perceived as something different by the actors of the conflict. This difference lies in that which rotates around the wage issue: the affirmation of the dignity of the exerted social function, the need for seeing this dignity in a new way, or, better yet, for seeing it as something irreplaceable and, consequently, worthy of compensation by virtue of its function as a social necessity. The concept of "social necessity," or of the unpredictable nature of the satisfaction of a social need, substitutes here for any reference to the mechanisms of the market. As a result, a profound egalitarianism and an elementary communism circulate within these struggles, even if the struggles are rarely expressed in ideological, polemical or extremist form. Another way of thinking about this is possible if the flexibility of the work force and its mobility and continuous formation have been asserted and imposed upon mature capitalist societies in order to allow for high levels of competition and of extraordinary mobilization of the productive forces within the frame of an ever better form of social productivity. Moreover, it must be clear that these new qualities of the work force need to be remunerated, not only for their level of knowing, of devotion to labor, of the claim of continuity (and the resulting accumulation of sacrifices, of exclusions, of risks), but also for their social potential and their collective usefulness. What results is the important effect on the way in which these workers perceive themselves and will perceive themselves, from within their work place, at the end of the struggle: since winning on the wage issue will signify being at least recognized as protagonists of the collective management of a necessary function of society.

The New Relationship with the Institutions and the So-Called "Refusal of Politics"

A fourth original element of the struggles of these new movements: their relationship with institutions. Today these institutions are considered, at all levels, as opposing parties and, at the same time, as points of communication. The refusal of all union and political manipulations is joined together with an unscrupulous utilization of union spaces and channels, of political places and figures, with the sole objective of winning the battle. One could paradoxically affirm that where the unions were at one time the bridge of communication between the political and the base, now their role is often overturned—certainly not because of their good will, nor because of any ideological excessive desire to please on their part, but because yielding before this necessity has become, by now, a condition of survival for the union apparatus in the work place. And the same is true for the politicos and for their apparatus. And this does not occur without ambiguity. This new configuration of the struggles often gives way to very severe clashes, especially within the unions, where a large part of the apparatus has been "cornered" by the new movements. But more and more it is becoming acceptable—and this is being internalized especially in the non-ideological unions— to embrace the fact that these unions consider themselves to be institutional structures (of the State, of the employers) devoted to the orientation and mediation of social conflicts, rather than as an instrument of the workers or of the direction in which they are moving in the management of the struggles.

There is a fifth and last element to be considered: the so-called "refusal of politics." This is articulated around the refusal of traditional delegation—but with its own specificities which make of it something profoundly different from the refusal exercised by the old anarchic-unionism. In reality, within these new movements we find nothing, absolutely nothing, of the anarchic-unionist tradition. We have already seen this with reference to the form of the struggles, of the organization, the objectives and the use of the union: in no instance can the struggle be considered a palingenesis, immediately liberating; and, on the other hand, direct action, and the insurrectional utopia do not seep through the individual behaviors of the great majority. In the moment in which we begin to consider the refusal of politics, this difference becomes even more important but also more singular: because in the struggles of the new movements, what is articulated more precisely are the identification of political places of decision making and the awareness that with the organization of the State of advanced capitalism everything is political, and in particular the planned-out management of services and of public expenditure. The refusal of politics that is summarized in the new movements is, then, something extremely complex: or, if one prefers, in the first place it is a sort of sly determination to avoid the much too strong obtuseness of the power of the State and the hope of being able to get around it; it is also a profound distrust, in as far as the capacity for representation by the union and by political parties is concerned; and a distrust in the responsibility of administration; it is, finally, a very bitter disillusionment with the inability of ideology to correspond to the vital necessities of our society and to the needs of the workers. On the other hand, given the way in which all the actions of the new movements are positioned upon a threshold where only politics can make decisions, the recognition of the central position of politics becomes the desire for a new definition, the need for a displacement—in brief, the new movements feel the necessity of not being simply the makers of demands and of new needs, but of being the sites of a redefinition of power.

2. Capitalist Restructuring and Its Effects on the Composition of Class

All of this needs to be explained by returning to the structural causes that allow for the identification of these new behaviors. Actually, we are witnessing a modification which, constructed within the last twenty years, has touched the actors of the struggle in an essential way. This modification has fundamentally followed two branches. One, so to speak, comes from society and moves toward the world of labor, introducing there a radical cultural modification and the irreducible prospect of grassroots political autonomy; this occurs through the experience of feminism, of ecological awareness, of youth movements, of anti-racist struggles and of social conflict in general. The other modification comes from the world of labor and moves toward society, carrying with it the awareness of the new conditions under which production is developed; this occurs through the criticism of the restructuring which the factory and labor market have undergone. In these last twenty years the factory as the center of productive labor has been destroyed;

production is now accomplished through society, entirely reabsorbing its productive force and stringently integrating its subjects. In other words: automation and information technology have transformed the organization of labor to the point of displacing the processes of exploitation from the labor class to the entire society. If it is true that this displacement has destroyed the political primacy of the labor class, it has not, however, eliminated exploitation; rather, it has broadened it, implanting within it the given conditions in the most diverse spheres of society. So, these transformations are not lived out only as an ulterior condemnation for the worker: one perceives also the possibility of gaining access to a higher level of education, of escaping a pre-established destiny, of reconstructing one's capacity for labor and one's own life expectations, above and beyond Taylorist deformation. And it is upon this new composition, at once ethnic and political for the great mass of workers, that the new movements find their nutriment and establish their hope for liberation.

What Is the Working Class Today?

In order to explain, in more precise terms, what we have considered above, let us ask: what is the working class today? Fundamentally, this can be summarized in three categories:

a) The traditional work of the laborer (professional laborer and common, unskilled, laborer) persists essentially in the large factories which have not yet been restructured, in small and medium sized businesses, often in the form of an exasperated Taylorism of informational technology. Indirect labor, labor which is not immediately productive, carried out in mechanized and computerized services, is always more able to be assimilated into the traditional work of the labor force.

b) At the extreme opposite of the structuring of the labor market, we find ourselves in the presence of important quotas of "undifferentiated labor," at the margins of productive labor (under-the-table work, temporary work, etc.), or at its interstices (domestic labor), or in the residue of preceding forms of organization of labor (in the work of the artisans, in agriculture, but also frequently in manufacturing).

The subjects we find in this multiple market of the labor force are different in style, but always, nonetheless, valued by the general productive process. In each instance they have certain directly productive functions, or certain reproductive functions, or they are utilized as a "reserve army," that is to say, as a force of pressure upon the salaried proletariat.

These marginal subjects can, however, become autonomous; they can give life to alternative projects and assume also certain constituent functions in a new societal project (alternative experiences in the economy and in communities, in Federal Germany, for example).

c) At the center of the current technical composition of the working class we find *restructured labor*. It is restructured in the real sense of the word, or rather, it is endowed with a great awareness of the labor cycle, or literally computerized, that is to say, endowed with a new productive quality within the great automated industry—where the role of the technician-workers is valued more and more within the management of the process of labor and of industrial transformation. Labor is also restructured in information technology, in the fields of communication, continuing education, and in the sciences, where living labor takes on an aspect which is, yes, immaterial, but with a secure productive effect.

In the end, the restructured work of the labor class dominates inside the social factory, where it effects, primarily, the "shaping" of a new model of *productive social cooperation*. Here it can assume directly the constituent functions of a new societal project.

In this way we can understand the reasons for, and the sense of, the modification of the behaviors that we have pointed out in the new cycle of the struggles. *These struggles occur as movements* since the labor has become social, since the exploited subject circulates throughout society and tends to find her/his place politically, with the possibility of influencing the process of accumulation—within the social realm, and in relationship to the political forms of power over society.

3. The Place and Role of Immigrants: The Weak Point and Strong Point, at One and the Same Time, of the New Composition of Class

And now the last question, *last but not least*. What are the place and the role of the immigrant populations in this context of strengths and of movements?—and what is their strategic position within the new cycle of struggles? Immigrants represent, at one and the same time, the weak point and strong point of this new composition. They are the weak point since these workers are inserted in a particular manner into one or more specific markets of the work-force and they are utilized as elements of pressure, or, more explicitly, of blackmail, in relation to the other sectors of the labor class. It is pointless to ignore this fact; we well know the infamous capitalistic desire for using the immigrant work-force two times over: the first time as man-power to be exploited to the maximum as the neoliberal bosses do; and secondly, as a sector of class to be placed in opposition to the others, as the "fascist" bosses do. But the immigrants also constitute a strong point, among others, of the labor class as a whole. And this is true not only because they are necessary, and sometimes decisive, for economic development during a phase of growth like the one being prepared with the formation of the European Common Market. It is true also because the immigrant populations reunite, across lines of color and of communal exploitation, that which the political powers seek desperately to divide, across the lines of the structuring of the organization of labor. The immigrant workers are present within the three sectors which we have defined as constituting the working class—in the traditional sector, as in the marginal sector, in a massive way, and they are beginning to be present also, with the second generation, in the sector of the restructured worker. This horizontal growth of the immigrant presence within the global work force is furthermore characterized by a very strong mobility, be it industrial, or social— and this is what interests us most. The immigrants are always social individuals. Their existence, though often relegated to the lowest levels of social organization, does not remove the fact that their problem and their essential determination have a social quality. Even when they have access to the highest levels of the technical composition of class, the immigrant workers are always humiliated because of their reality of being immigrants, because of the social character of this condition. From this point of view, immigrant workers express, with immediacy and spontaneity, a class interest that, in the metropolitan sectors of the labor class, begins to structure itself through difficult mediations, and only from the political point of view. In a cycle of struggles in which wage and economic demands become displaced more and more upon the political terrain, within a historical situation in which the development of the struggles makes no sense, except to the degree in which the struggle succeeds in organizing requests for power that involve the entire society and its organization, the immigrant populations find themselves to be representing, spontaneously, the highest point of the claim of power. The result is that today it is unthinkable that a cycle of struggles, and thus a proletarian reconfiguration, will not include, from within, a red line, strongly accentuated, of the political initiatives of the immigrants. Has this movement already been created? Does this tendency already exist? One paradoxical fact often strikes us. We hold on to the idea of presenting this fact here, not as any proof, but as an example: in certain European countries, and in Great Britain in particular—where the repression of the struggles has certainly been among the most ferocious, as much in the factories as in society itself—the memory of the workers' struggles and the tradition of mass insubordination are kept alive above all by the immigrant workers. This memory, as such, is of little interest to us: what is of great interest to us is the fact that it reappears, and this is the case among the immigrants, this reappearance of the memory as the motor of a collective intelligence of the struggles, as an indication of a strategy of movement which develops as much within the factories as within society.

3

Social Struggles in a Systemic Setting

Since the middle of the Eighties a new movement of social struggle has opened up—*new* because the characteristics of these struggles are new, *movement* because these struggles are beginning to configure a multi-year cycle of experiences of breaking the social order of mature capitalism. The new characteristics lie in the radical democratic form of the struggles, in the transformation of their relationship with unions (which is becoming more and more the simple channel of transmission of the grass-roots will), in the social dimension of the objectives, in the search for social support of the struggles on the part of the old segments (above all the workers, but now also the peasants) of the class struggle, in the emergence of the female component, of the tertiary component and of the intellectual component (above all the work force in training) within the process itself. That one can speak of a new cycle of struggles is proven, then, by the fact that these struggles are amply differentiated from those of the Seventies (except for the foreshadowing they had had in Italy and in Germany); these struggles break with their defensive character against the restructuring, assuming, instead, that the restructuring is a context of the struggle; they bring to life mass objectives and behaviors that are bound to the new contradictions of the restructuring, and they begin to constitute a succession of experiences, of completely original moments of rupture and/or of contraction.

Even in this moment, in Europe and, above all in France, we find ourselves in the presence of broad movements of struggle. In France the peasants and the Renault-Cleon workers, the "perpetual movement" of the nurses, the workers in the electronics-aviation sector, the truck drivers, the medical services personnel, etc., have within the last few months profoundly attacked social peace. In what way and to what extent is it possible to consider these struggles as the base for a re-opening of political spaces and of a re-launching of objectives of communist transformation? Can the new social cycle of the struggles forge a *new political cycle* of attack against capitalist power?

Let us leave the irony of this question of ours to the apologists of "capitalism as insurmountable horizon." As far as we are concerned, we know that capitalist strategy, and that of the State, are analyzing the current movements as seriously as are we. In fact, the bosses and the functionaries of social peace are working assiduously towards the goal of sheltering the structures of power from the struggles; of breaking the movement, precisely within the cyclical and accumulative tendencies which it presents; of configuring a *new form of control* (social and political) suitable to the new characteristics of the struggles. What makes up this new form of control?

The new control presents itself in three forms. The first is that of preventive micro-control, and it has as its fundamental actors the union functionaries and scholars of social things. The difference between the old factory boss with respect to the new social *contre-maître* is still relevant, since the former attempted to control the workers within their social setting, while the latter intervenes directly upon the social setting, seeking to break every possibility of communication, of restructuring of the generalization of the struggles. The corporation is opposed to the movement. The transversal corporate unity is made to act as an element of compression and of suffocation of basic initiatives. What is happening to the struggle of the nurses, this "perpetual movement" which appears and disappears, in order to reappear enriched by ever stronger objectives, is characteristic of this form of control: there is an attempt to water down and soften the movement within the split sociality of the medical corporation, while the movement of the nurses, instead, lives and renews itself in its relationship with the entire society, in comparison with the problems of the crisis of the Welfare State, in the hope of representing the generality of the problems of life (of the reproduction of the labor force), in contrast to the values of the capitalistic administration of life.

The second form of new control consists in the requalification of its frame of reference. The movements are immersed in the systemic whole: in other words, every modification of the structure (statutory, regulatory, wage-related, etc.) of one category touches all of the others. Thus, a fluid and dynamic globality that determines the whole opposition is set against the molecular movements of the social struggles. Neoliberalism has exalted the multiplicity of the social actors; it has brought the all-social back to plurality: and now the State, in all its sovereignty and with the anxiety of the general equilibrium, intervenes in every little struggle, in every fragment of movement. Oh, how beautiful this neoliberalism is, allowing us to see the Government as the counterpart of every singularity in the process of struggle!

The third form of control consists in the increase (and in the consequent tightening) of the norms of negotiation. From society and from the relationships between workers' associations and employers' associations, to the State and to the control of the Ministry of Finance over everything that moves; all the way, all the way up to the end, to the new European rules, purely financial and monetary: a multiple blackmail, repeated upon a scanning of times that are becoming more and more tight and of spaces that are becoming more and more restricted.

The awareness and experience of this new framework of control, in its various dimensions, have by now penetrated the struggles and have adopted their protagonists. How can the new forms of systemic control of the struggles be *broken*? The question is a practical one. The question is a new one. In fact, it is totally evident that the request for generalization of the struggles cannot traverse the forms that tradition has taught to the workers: the sectorial or corporate widening, and—secondly—the general strike. In both cases, at the current level of the development of the new movements, these domains of generalization are immature, from the subjective point of view, and unsuitable, from the objective point of view, for constituting spaces in which the counter-power of the workers can democratically and autonomously organize itself. These spaces are the prey of the official representations, union and corporate, which—within the crisis of political and union representation that characterize our era—brutally alienate, or better yet, remove every illusion of democratic representation and of contractual efficacy. These spaces are organized within the systemic structure of the repression of the struggles. General and corporate strikes are typical instruments of the "reduction of complexities," understood as a technique for pacification and for a conservative restructuring of social equilibrium (or of the conditions of capitalist development).

How, then, can *the reconstruction of a general horizon of movement* position itself in an effective and politically acceptable manner? With difficulty, but no less clearly, in the course of the latest struggles the conditions of a strategic answer to the question have started to be articulated. Above all, this answer begins to seep into the behaviors seen in the struggle.

There are two characteristics to point out: on an immediate level, the struggles seek always to place in evidence the *connective* elements of social labor, to bring to light the *cooperative* social aspects of every demand. This is true whether we consider the case of the nurses, where the maturation of these behaviors has reached a high level of maturity; or the case of the peasants who are beginning to face general ecological problems; or the case of those who work in the auto industry, or in transportation, or in air traffic control where the relationship with growing automation is becoming a general social problem: in each and every one of these cases, a program of new social cooperation passes through the struggles. There is no struggle without a utopia: in all of the new struggles, after the fall of the socialist project, there reappears a new proposal, political, real, profound and articulated; a proposal of reorganization of the social universality of labor, seen from the grass-roots perspective, from the capacity of the workers to construct a democratic alternative. Productive cooperation can be managed from the ground up; the universality of the interrelations of the post-industrial economy can be socially watered down within the activities of the social subjects.

From here we can move on immediately to the second characteristic of these struggles. What we mean here is a second response to the systemic nature of state control, based upon the awareness that only a permanent activating of the social subjects can permit the re-founding of democracy. *Today*, the *"democratic" and "political" realms are constructed within and by social struggles*. The political system of mature capitalism is inert, its dynamics are parasitic, its norm is economic. Mature capitalism no longer recognizes democratic politics; it ignores the expression of the general interest, or rather, it presents this expression in the form of bureaucratic generalization, of necessary and absolute globalism. The struggles, on the other hand, in their far-flung proliferation, indicate a rebirth of the political-as-constituent-power, as the synthesis between the activities of the subjects and new social objectives.

To consider the social struggles within their systemic milieu means, then, to conquer the capacity for living out entirely the paradox for which the political is indicated within the structure of the State, of control, of pacification, wherein the political no longer exists and, above all, there is no democracy. Where confusion, instead, is signaled and the irreducible complexity of the social struggles is denounced, therein lie the seeds of a democratic conception and of innovative power. The current struggles are beginning to weave the base of this new territory of the political and of democracy; it is only by pursuing these struggles, by studying them and practicing them that we will be able to wonder about the tools of a new democracy within the framework of a cooperative organization of labor that invests all of society.

But in order for this to happen and to become clear to everyone, we will need—let us not convey hope here, but let us express something that we feel in the air of the times—to see other social sectors enter into the struggle, especially those that express an extremely wide spectrum of socialization (*like the students*, like the proletariat of the outskirts of the cities, like other sectors of the female work force). The goal is to create a mass movement, to fully politicize, within the massification, those experiences of planning and of democratic reconstruction which the current individual and minor struggles put forward.

4

Peugeot: Restructured Factory and Production of Subjectivity

Recently a book and a film about a factory were released in Paris; or rather, I should say, a book and a film about the whole network of Peugeot factories which has undergone, in recent years, a restructuring and, last year, an important workers' struggle. The book, *Les Caprices du Flux, Les mutations technologiques du point de vue de ceux qui les vivent*, was published by Editions Matrice (Collection Points d'appui. MIRE). The film, *Voyages au Pays de la Peuge*, was produced by Im'Media.

It is worth it to discuss these two inquiries, so different from each other under certain aspects and yet convergent in their scientific and political conclusions.

The research conducted by Y. Clot, Y. Rochex and Y. Schwartz on the automation of the Peugeot factories is interesting for many reasons. Above all, it is interesting because it does not examine the modifications of the organization of labor from the point of view of economic rationality, but from the point of view of "those who live it"; which is to say, from the point of view of the worker. In our current predicament, displacing the theoretical point of view is an ethical choice that opens up a new theoretical space. Secondly, the method used (multidisciplinary and centered upon the psychopathology of the worker) allows us to span the economic and sociological categories without being subjected to the institutional obligations which descend from them, in fact permitting us to place at the center of investigation the subjectivity of labor. As a third consideration, we must see how the researchers utilize Marxist categories and how they demonstrate, at the same time, with reference to these categories, the space of efficacy and the limits of the interpretation of the new organization of labor. In brief, this study can be considered as an analysis of displacement at the level of the social organization of production and its becoming automated, of the Marxist contradiction between process of labor and process of valorization. This contradiction, which Marx enclosed within the necessity of the means of production, had been redefined by the critical Marxism of the Sixties as a form of antagonism between cooperation and hierarchy (in "*Socialisme ou Barbarie*"); it was also redefined, in the Italian labor movement, as undisguised opposition between labor autonomy and power, between self-valorization and discipline. But we will return to the definition of this antagonism later—for now, let us consider the constitution of living labor in the transformations of the "Japanese factory" which constitutes the most interesting object of investigation.

The core fact that can be derived from this is the following: labor identifies completely with subjectivity and with the social conditions of productive cooperation. If labor, by now, is only labor of "regulation," of production, "the part of labor prescribed for each individual act diminishes, to the advantage of the part of choice and of decision that every productive act always contains, but which gains the upper hand here." There is, then, a displacement of the content of labor upwards, from execution to the responsibility of decision making. Responsibility that is necessary for the management of what is unpredictable in the automated factory and for the continuous improvement of the quality of the product. The authors recall, very usefully, that the new methods of organization of labor represent, simultaneously, an overtaking and a continuity of Taylorism. Indeed, without the daily practice by the mass-worker of decoding and upsetting the prescriptions of the "method agencies," no car would ever have come out of the factory. But now "the old prescribed finalities given to the mass-workers have become the automatic operations of the machines themselves. The informal goals of regulation by means of which the mass-workers had anticipated the technical system are now prescribed to the new all-purpose workers." The polyvalence, then, is nothing other than the formalization and development of other steps of that which is known to have been the real work of the mass-workers. From this point of view, the overcoming of Taylorism—which was founded on the separation between execution and regulation, but which in reality functioned on the "*savoir faire*" of the mass-workers—is the recognition of the centrality of living labor within the organization of production. But it is, above all, the professional workers who can help us to grasp the new quality of labor. The "conductors of automated installations" illustrate perfectly, by their activity, the change of course. The intervention upon automated devices necessitates new competencies, but above all, it necessitates a new relationship between the worker and her/himself. "Suddenly, activity is no longer standardized, divisible, comparable. As this activity becomes more and more interior and non-apparent, it becomes more and more difficult to measure it. The activity is founded upon decisions to be made, and thus it is more difficult to prescribe it. Because the subjects must imply their judgments, this activity is hard to calculate." The most important characteristic of the modification of the organization of labor is, then, the return to subjectivity of the worker. As in every systemic organization, also in the factory it is a "metalinguistic" effort that is requested of the workers. Acting upon an activity (or: the capacity for intervening on the conditions of the activity) must draw its energy from the entire personality of the person. "The Taylorist norm and the systemic obligation are distinguished, one from the other, by the direction of the action: the latter addresses essentially the psychic behavior of the subject. It has no other objective than that of finality of the second degree. It considers a relative activity in and of itself and not as referred to an object." What is evidenced here is the heuristic intensity of another Marxist theme: the most general abstraction of labor (or the activity which reflects upon itself) produces the most intense individualization. Labor can now delve into that which is most individual and most specific in the subject. Here the entire life of the individual is invested.

It is significant that, in order to grasp the new quality of labor, the researchers are obligated to have recourse to the categories proper to the conceptualization of labor in communication. These are concepts such as "interface," the function and management of "interface," the active combination of different and abstract elements, which characterize the description of labor. The labor of planning, of execution, and the information and education processes are all blurred within a single flux. From this point of view, labor which is internal to the factory is no longer specific in nature. On the contrary, it is part of a general tendency towards the constitution of immaterial labor which is defined by the implication of subjectivity, and therefore of the entire symbolic dimension of the subject.

But the originality of this research consists not only in the fact of demonstrating that, even at the internal level of the factory, fundamental production is the production of subjectivity. In a certain sense, also the sociology and the economy of labor, contrasted with the "Japanese mode of production," arrive at these conclusions. The originality of the research that we read consists also of the fact of illustrating the radical alternatives that open up in the process of restructuring. The abstraction of labor does not solve the contradiction between the labor process and the process of valorization; rather, it exasperates it. The alternatives at the internal level of the factory diverge, the more they play on the problem of the "sense of labor." If "the soul must descend into the factory," it does so according to its own rules, and these are the rules of a subjectivity "whose knowledge and sociability are no longer the fortuitous result or the potential secondary benefit of a life at work; rather, it is a subjectivity that is the source of all global productivity." The alternatives are produced by the fact that production remains a "capitalist" production, which implies "expropriation," "exploitation," "reappropriation," and thus, conflict. This comes with ethical consequences, and even more so with economic and political consequences. The process of labor is subjugated to the laws of production of value, as always. The criteria for economic management of productive time are imposed from the outside, be it for the individual worker or for collective labor. This instigates the total implication of the individual, but the "psychological" potential is employed in a derisive manner. The codes of business are imposed in a disciplinary manner upon the request for free participation in labor. The quality of labor that one blathers about is valid only in the measure to which it is functional in relation to quantity. "It is perhaps here that we find the origin of a feeling felt widely among the workers: that of being invaded by an economic and financial process that intrudes upon the life of every individual. And this is so, the more one has to do with an invisible chain and with the challenges which one's personal life presents in terms of an abstract and strictly bookkeeping approach to the general productivity of business." The "great economy," the "affairs of capital" are always there, with their specific exigencies. Hence the strange paradox: "one feels that wings are sprouting, but that they are soon chopped off." The sensible alternative is not to be found as simply an alternative of management (which at other times was the claim of self-management); rather, it passes through the consciousness of every worker as a contradiction between the motivations and the goals of her/his activity. "In fact, the prescription of the goals is in no way weakened. On the contrary, it is optimized, around the optimal functioning of the technical system (zero defects, zero obstructions, zero stock, etc.), this system itself being controlled by the global norm of cars/per/day: 1,100, 1,200. It is a bit as though we had passed from a Taylorist prescription of operations to a 'just in time' prescription of subjectivity." It is essential, finally, to note that upon the basis of this analysis production becomes social, because the mode of production, exactly like the mode of control and perhaps even of that of insubordination, all of these modes are concentrated, by now, upon subjectivity and upon communication. The old factory that once served as a model of "disciplining" society is now evolving towards a social model of "control." This evolution, at the moment, concerns certain parts of the factory more than others, but it already has, evidently, assumed a driving force and a strategic form.

If, upon this basis, we go on now to look at the film *Voyages au pays de la Peuge*, what we see before us is nothing other than a series of confirmations of this process. The film documents the modification of the mode of labor at Peugeot, from the point of view of those who have lived it. A formidable gallery of characters illustrates for us what happened in reality: a series of mass workers, white and of color, but also professional workers and those "*interimaires*" (young short-term workers, making up between 10 and 30 per cent of the work force at different times). The social rapport of the worker is very strong, the cultural homogeneity (especially among the professionals and the "*interimaires*") is an essential element of the picture. But, beyond the visual analysis of the transformation of the factory, the film sets forth also the chronicle of the Autumn of 1989 struggle—a struggle that collided with the most advanced departments of the Peugeot factories in Sochaux and Mulhouse. It is like the litmus test of the analyses we have conducted to this point. A mass struggle, born from the request for higher wages, made by those miserable people who, despite the subjectification of labor, continue to be paid by the boss. And yet, this struggle is not absolutely one of the old wage struggles, let us understand, which we got to know (and which Peugeot has known: the film provides us with the documentation of this) in the Sixties and in the Seventies. It is, instead, a struggle which, in its forms (the union is by now reduced to a "chain of communication" of the will of the base) and in its motives (the recognition of the new nature of labor and its payment), highlights very new problems, which lie within the new labor condition: why and how to work? And this question is imme-diately articulated on a social level: how should we live and what should we live for? Antagonism is presented as an alternative which, placing itself within labor itself, opens itself immediately to social alternatives. The refusal of labor is not diminished by the new productive placement of the worker in the automatic mode of production; nor is it attenuated by the subjectivization of her/his productive participation. This refusal shows itself, on the contrary, as a request for power—the equivalent of that potential which, in the process of production, for each individual, in her/his own individuality, one seeks to activate; the equivalent of that social process which, for every individual, lies at the base of that productive capacity.

We had read in the sacred texts that communism was the synthesis of the maximum of the social potential of labor, united to the wealth of individuals and to their singular capacity for enjoyment: now we see it in the articulation of productive potential and of the refusal of the system of social control that every one of the workers in struggle "*chez Peugeot*" expresses. The production of subjectivity, typical of the restructured factory, also produces antagonism.

5

Toyotaism: The Japanese Model
and the Social Worker

At the beginning of the Seventies one began to speak of the "social worker." By this was meant the tendency towards a new configuration of the productive subject in the period which saw the escape of the industrial system from "Fordism," the exhaustion of the centrality of the "mass worker" and the first apparition of an integrated system of industrial automation and of the computerization of the social, as a renewed base of capitalist production. In the Seventies the hypothesis of the "social worker" was essentially political. The notion of "social worker" was intended to indicate the new labor force which (expelled or already beyond the limits of the Fordist system) was beginning to display new expressions of antagonism, planted in new places of productivity, as in the tertiary infrastructure, in the educational and academic infrastructure, in diffused social labor, in the world of communications and in all of the sectors of immaterial labor. The political representation of this new subject was, on one hand, polemical, since it concerned the institutional labor movement, from which it called for the recognition of the irreducible potential newness of the social situation, thus calling for the movement's departure from the corporate defense of the mass worker. But this representation was also constructive where it conveyed the proposal of a politics that anticipated, with the autonomy of the new productive and social figure, the period of capitalist restructuring, the passage—that is—from the Fordist phase to the "total production" phase. As we know, the hypothesis of the "social worker" clashed with and was repressed by the official labor movement, with an argument that proposed deceitfully, to the mass workers and to their organizations, that they manage (together with capital and in linear forms) the process of restructuring. This politics of the labor movement was ridiculed in the Eighties by capitalist initiative: capital showed itself to be self-sufficient in the restructuring and it swept away every alternative.

The defeat of the political hypothesis of the "social worker" does not overthrow the heuristic value of the notion. Rather, the twenty years that followed the early Seventies brought many elements of proof to the definition of the new subject and filled with material contents that conceptual essence, which at first was potential and prospective. In any event, the concept of "social worker" is today, after and through the restructuring, the center of the scientific and political consideration of capital and of the State. Whether it will become the center also of the official labor movement is a question that touches upon the problem (yet unresolved) of the survival of this movement. What is interesting here is not the destiny of the labor movement, but rather, once again, the problem of the definition of the concept itself, after twenty years of critical, sociological and political work on this problem.

Benjamin Coriat publishes a book: *Penser à l'envers: Travail et organisation dans l'entreprise japonaise* (Paris: Bourgois, 1991). This book can allow us to approach some of the results of the research that has been done in the last twenty years on the concept of the "social worker." Coriat is well known in Italy, where he has published *La fabbrica e il cronometro* [*The Factory and the Timekeeper*], in the labor series "Materiali Marxisti" (Milano: Feltrinelli, 1979). He is part of that "school of regulation" that has translated in France some of the fundamental concepts of "Italian workerism" of the Sixties and Seventies, along the lines of a specifically economic terrain and with undisputed institutional efficacy (his group regularly interferes with the definition of social politics of the French socialist government). In 1990, with the same publisher, Coriat had published another volume, *L'Atelier et le Robot*, in which he had studied the movement from Fordism to mass production in the electronic age. In *Penser à l'envers* the anlaysis of the mode of post-Fordist production is grounded upon the analysis of subjective categories that define themselves within that shift.

The scene is Japan. It is worth saying that Coriat's book is fundamentally dedicated to the contrast between American methods of production (Taylorism and Fordism) and what can well be called, by now, the "Japanese mode" of production. Coriat places himself within the analysis of the new subjective configurations of production by means of a study of the thought and organizational practice of T. Ohno, the head engineer and later the director of Toyota, the inventor of the Kan Ban method. As is well known, this non-technological, purely organizational method provides for production at stock-zero by way of the multi-skilled responsibility of the workers and of the groups into which they are inserted in their workshops of production, and the independence of each group from the other sectors of production. Thus a new functional division of labor is put into action, and this division provides for the "automation" and self-activation of the worker, on one hand; on the other, it provides for the application of a "just-in-time" method, that is, a linear integration of the departments of production (inside or outside of the factory) within the process of parallel work flows: the real flow of production that goes from the mountain to the valley, and inversely from the flow of information. The worker, de-specialized and rendered multi-skilled, is activated in the productive process in an autonomous, entrepreneurial manner. This holds true with regard to the functional division of labor from within the firm; but it also holds true with regard to the relationships between the individual departments, and it constitutes the protocols that regulate the relationships between firms on the social terrain. This terrain is defined, then, at different levels of organization and of abstraction, as the true and proper circulatory domain of information and, consequently, of production.

I do not intend, in what follows, to summarize the wealth of the analyses and of the elaborate phenomenologies of Coriat. It is sufficient to remember two additional elements. The first consists of the resolute apology of the Japanese mode of production in contrast to "American" techniques of the organization of labor, even when these techniques develop and over-determine, in an electronic and automatic manner, the classical Taylorist pattern. Coriat strongly emphasizes, on the other hand, the specific historical conditions of the two models of organization of labor: the American model asserts itself, at the beginning of the post-war period, against the considerable power of the professional workers over the times and rhythms of manufacturing; the Japanese model is born of a series of compromises (fixed within the second phase of the post-war period) between a capitalist management coming out of the military defeat and a working class that presented itself then as the only force capable of national reconstruction. The first model is based upon a defeat, the second upon a compromise. The second political consideration introduced by Coriat consists of retaining the Japanese mode of production as being resolutely modernizing, not only in the sense of economic efficacy, but above all in the sense of the definition of democracy within labor relations. The productive individualization of the subject, here determined, permits, according to Coriat, the movement from the "incited implication" of the worker to her/his "negotiated implication"; it permits, that is, the breaking of the traditional despotic pattern, in order to substitute in its place contractual devices and compromising norms. Strictly speaking, Coriat's thesis is more radical: he holds that, if we want to avoid a "two-speed" society, one in which the corporatization of labor is opposed to the marginalization of social labor potential (this is the necessary effect of neo-Taylorism), the only path to be taken is the one which involves the application, in the democratic sense, within the universality of implied social relations, of the Japanese model of recognizing the individualization of the productive subjects and of their cooperation. The substance of socialization, individualization and contractualization of labor relations is proposed for the reformist activity of the workers' movement: the institutional movement, since Coriat knows no others.

Keeping in mind what is maintained by Coriat, if we now return to the "social worker" theme, we can develop some observations. First of all, we must strongly underscore the insistence on the individual and social elements of the new figure of productive labor. By now it seems, in fact, impossible to define productive labor from outside of the juncture between the individual multiskilled (almost entrepreneurial) ability of the laborer and the complexity of the social relations (formative, scientific, cultural, mercantile, etc.) that constitute, more and more, the new figure of productive labor. The Japanese mode of working reveals and interprets, in its own way, that rupture of Taylorist alienation of labor and of the despotism of the factory which the workers' struggles, starting from the Seventies, had indicated as the privileged object of worker hatred. At the same time, the Japanese mode of labor seeks to organize the product of the refusal of "that" labor, exalting the individual search for a complex productivity and the social determinations which, genetically and functionally, are contained in that refusal. From this point of view, the notion of the "social worker" undergoes a substantial enrichment. The concept of social productivity is individually carried out and socially articulated.

But in the same moment in which the Japanese mode of production interprets and organizes the new figure of labor, it mystifies the subject of it. It is evident how inadequate Coriat's reformist political conclusions are to the contents of his analysis. Caught up in the institutional drift which in the Eighties invested the entire "school of regulation," he accepts at face value that mystification of "participation" which Japanese capital uses for its own ends of accumulation and social order. The mystification consists essentially of the fact that, in the Japanese mode of production, the individuality of the creative performance of labor and the sociability of the formative processes of productivity are bound to heteronomy and determined within the impossibility of nailing down a linear and fundamental nexus of communal political expression. The social genesis of productive labor splits away from capitalist command; its expression is interrupted by the organizational function of management. To propose, as Coriat does, that we substitute for organizational intermediation of the large firm (including "its" unions) which defines, Japanese-style, "codetermination," with a vague project of codetermination in the "German or Swedish style" is to end up in a situation in which nothing changes substantially: in any event, the continuity of individual creative labor and of social labor ends up splitting; the social condition of production ends up suspended by the insertion of capitalist command—the only command authorized to legitimize and to organize productive society, not to mention extracting profit from it.

It's a question of true *"penser à l'envers."* Not beginning with those Toyota engineers whose intelligence cannot be limited to the horizon of industrial organization, but with those new subjects who, in the factory and in society, stand out in the communal nature of labor and of its articulations. Industrial organization is not the matrix, but is rather the consequence of this communal social substance of productive labor. Before having been translated into Italian by Fiat, the Japanese mode of production was, for example, invented here by us, by the thousands and thousands of workers in the tertiary sector of labor and in scattered industry, who, in the Seventies, escaping from the factory, based their capacity for resistance and reproduction upon the sociability of productive labor. It is a question, then, of beginning, once again, from these conditions of a very high form of socialization, from the social virtuality of living labor, in all of its forms (potential and actual, in development and in production, material and immaterial, intellectual and manual, tertiary and scientific, etc.) in order to identify ways to trace production back to the political arena, without accepting the infamous and overbearing (because of being useless) misery of the indetermination of a business managerial system or of a parasitic employer. Yellow or black, green or red, whichever it may be.

Coriat's essay on the Japanese mode of production is useful, then, within the limits it defines (and that is, beyond his political ignorance and his predisposition to a confused reformism), for allowing us to advance our definition of the "social worker." This is a concept that, after a long absence, must reappear in the debate of the Italian left if we want to find a link between the analysis of the social and of the productive figures that constitute the social and— on the other hand—the theme of the political. It is an essential concept, if we do not want the radical modification of the labor class and the transformation of the modes of extraction of surplus value, from the factory to the network of the social fabric, to take away also (together with the hegemony of the traditional figure of the worker) the antagonistic dimensions of the productive process. It is a concept that, while solidifying and actualizing itself, makes communism reappear as a condition of every movement.

6

Productive Networks and Territories:
The Case of the Italian Northeast

My experience is not that of a sociologist, but rather that of a militant politician in Italy of the Seventies, an experience—I believe—that was rather important because it unfolded from within a profound mutation of the productive structures. This mutation affected political activity through the forms and contents of reflection and intervention.

The book which I am discussing here, *Benetton et Sentier: Des enterprises pas comme les autres* (Paris: Publisud, 1993) is the result of two research projects produced for MIRE (Ministry of Labor) and for the Ministry of Public Facilities and Urban Planning. These research projects have to do with the development of small and medium sized firms in the northeast of Italy and they describe the process that has bound the diffusion of productive industrial labor in that territory to the construction of a great multinational industrial power, Benetton. In these projects there is also a comparison between the models elaborated upon the small and medium sized Italian firms and the important Parisian (and French) experience of *Sentier*—that is, of the "fashion" industry, decentralized in the productive processes and concentrated in the economic processes.

My interest in the small and medium sized industries and in the industrialization of the Northeast presents an aspect of consideration somewhat paradoxical: this aspect is born, in fact, from within and as a consequence of a (theoretical-practical) analysis conducted for a long time and in depth upon a group of large petrochemical factories located in the Venetian mainland, in Porto Marghera. Why has my research passed from the large factory to the territorial proliferation of production?

In order to respond to this, it is necessary above all to remember that, at the end of the Sixties, approximately 30,000 workers were concentrated in Porto Marghera, organized in the Fordist manner. Around a central system of production (essentially the production of propylene and of its derivatives) a network of ten industries divided its labor force, industries that were developing the entire supply chain of petrochemical products, from explosives to fertilizers, and even to the threads of textiles and the production of light plastics. So, between the end of the Sixties and the beginning of the Seventies, in this *kombinat* there developed an extremely elevated level of worker and social struggles, with moments of conflict and repression, and with the consequent restructuring of the organization of production and closings/re-openings of the labor market. In response to the first oil industry crisis of 1973-1974, the large petrochemical firms began diminishing production, in part, and stimulating, in part, the automation of their plants: as a result, they "liberate" themselves from the work force—and above all, they liberate themselves from those political and union militants who in the preceding years had led the struggles. These people were strongly attached to the territories that extended around the factories of Porto Marghera, for 30 or 40 kilometers especially towards the north of Venice. The factories of Porto Marghera had been built in the Thirties and Forties upon the lagoons of the Adriatic, but only in the Fifties and Sixties had they been adjusted for mass production and caused a mass labor force to be placed into action. The people whom we had met in the factories, with whom we had conducted the struggles, who now found themselves fired, had entered the large factories of Porto Marghera in the previous decade. This was not, then, a young labor class; in fact, for the great majority of them, it had to do with an agricultural proletariat which had had the experience of emigration in German factories and in the industrial zones of the Rhine, and which only in the last decade had re-entered the "homeland." These workers were now fired from the factories of Porto Marghera because, after their return, they had fought in these factories—not only for a better wage, but also, and above all, for a radical transformation of society. Between 1973 and 1975, more than ten thousand workers were thrown out of the factories of Porto Marghera, in the industrial capital of Veneto.

My comrades and I, who had fought with these workers who were now fired, followed them, then, in their new adventure in life and in constructing new possibilities of work.

According to Italian law there is no national unemployment compensation, there is simply the "Cassa Integrazione" (CIG). For a certain period of time, as negotiated between the factory, the industrial association and the union, a part of the wage is paid to the workers who leave the factory for reasons of crisis, restructuring, etc. In the period which interests us, given the relationships of power that existed, nearly 95 per cent of the wage was paid to workers with CIG status, and for a period that could go from five to nine years. This means, practically, that the workers were leaving the factory with almost their entire wage. This was because of their political strength. But the workers (whether fired or not) could also show this political strength of theirs on the territory where, in previous years, interpreting the Fordist bond between the factory and what surrounded it, they had established some points of strength, often veritable associative counterpowers, formal and/or informal. It is upon this base, starting from these positions of strength, that some of the autonomous entrepreneurial projects are set up—financed in part by CIG, but above all by having politically effective recourse to the support of the local communities, parishes, savings banks. The workers who had been placed into the world of unemployment—the same ones who had conducted the struggles and whom we were now following in their new experience—were thus entering into that which in Italy is called the "political market" and it is in that market that they had the possibility of organizing the financing of new firms.

We must now remember that in this same period one witnesses in Italy, and above all in the highly industrialized areas of the North, the first phase of decentralization of industrial activities on the part of the employers, the "placing outside of the factory" of many activities and services, all the way to the subdivision of segments of production. This initiative of the capitalist entrepreneur of proliferating in the North those activities previously organized from within the factory corresponds—at the beginning of the Seventies—to the density of the factory struggles and to the impossibility of controlling them. These operations of decentralization are accomplished by means of the creation of business firms where the operations are composed (in complex forms) of factory bosses and/or old style workers, factory bosses and also engineers or academics. Often the firm that decentralizes is in some way a contender in the game itself.

This process of decentralization is extremely broad. It configures a central aspect of that which, after a few years, will come to be called the passage from Fordism to post-Fordism. It is still necessary to emphasize that this first process of territorial proliferation of production has at least two paths of entrance. The first is the decentralization of some industrial activities on the part of the entrepreneur, with the goal of destroying the rigidity which antagonistic behavior brought about in the factory; the other (which can never be underestimated) is the one brought about by the entrepreneurial activity of new social subjects who often come from the factory (from which they were thrown out), who always construct the financing of the new activity within the local political market, and who, finally, organize productive cooperation on the territory.

This observation seems very important to me. In fact, it is a matter of how to avoid, when one speaks of the passage from Fordism to post-Fordism, falling into purely economic logic. What I mean to say is that, in my experience, the Taylorist organization of labor and the wage based organization of Fordism crumble before resistance and specific alternative initiatives, historically experienced, and politically relevant. The labor force is not only the object of this transition, but also its subject. The capitalist initiative that starts at the beginning of the Seventies, by experiencing automation in the factory and decentralization (by means of information flow in the surrounding territory) outside of the factory, does not take place within a power void, but within a situation characterized by profound conflicts, by a dialectic of forces that touch equally upon political relations and technological relations and developments.

We should add, in particular, that the dissolution of the old labor class of the factory, and the first processes of the new segmentation of the labor market (and with these, of a new labor force, autonomous in its behavior, often entrepreneurial, more and more immaterial) do not correspond only to the interest of the employers: they are often also products of the struggle against salaried labor and the sedimentation of the collective will to overcome it.

However, I am speaking here about the Seventies in the region of Veneto. What I have described so far occurs principally, in the beginning, in two areas: first, north of the province of Venice and around Treviso; second, upon the central axis which goes from Venice through Padua, Vicenza and Verona, towards Lombardy. It is in these areas that the junction of industrial decentralization and subdivision and, on the other hand, entrepreneurship "from below" becomes the engine of territorial transformation and the creator of a new industrial landscape, already in the second half of the Seventies. The small and medium sized firms multiply, often with the highest forms of technology. In a very brief period of time these firms experience forms of collaboration in the services and forms of cooperation in the management of the territory (the formation of the labor force, the creation of infrastructures, foreign commerce, a presence in the political market, etc.). Up until the end of the Seventies, it would be improper to speak of productive networks in the technical sense, but it is evident that all of the conditions for allowing the networks to take form are already present. With regard to this matter, we must insist upon the fact that the network is not simply a technological production; it does not depend exclusively on the fact that some technologies allow for its existence; rather, we must focus on the fact that certain productive energies are organized within cooperative social communal forms. The territorial embedding of the workers who now, inside the territories, present themselves as new entrepreneurs is from this point of view a central element of the development we are analyzing.

Nonetheless, if there certainly are some important local traditions from the productive point of view, we need not exaggerate the weight of tradition in the territorial embedding of proliferation of production. In the "scientific" literature that, in Italy and in France, has followed the genesis of these new productive forms, we often find ourselves in the presence of a sort of historical epic: "Behold the intelligent workers who come from the *Rinascenza*, who have always had great professional competence, an immemorial tradition …" All of this is perhaps poetic (for those who love the pathetic), but certainly hardly true. For me, at first, these apologies of tradition have always seemed purely ideological, profoundly reactionary—and I see it as no accident that those ideologies of the "Third Italy" and of the "Renaissance districts" have today become an integral part of the political discourse of the parafascist Northern Leagues. However, this is not the place for political judgments: it is the place for judgment of the truth. And so, we can immediately say that, from the most elementary historical point of view, the anthropological continuities of the subjects of the small and medium sized firms,[1] territorially spread out with respect to the history of the territories of the North, are completely imaginary. In the Turinese North, just as in the Milanese North, the entrepreneurs of the new expanded industry are essentially immigrant workers from the South, during the last thirty years, or Sicilian-Lombardian or Neapolitan-Turinese "Beurs"—to give just a few examples. They did not acquire their capacity for work and for undertakings from the Renaissance tradition, but from their hard Fordist work in the Volkswagen and Fiat factories: that is where the metamorphosis took place, in the Fordist period and in the struggles of the mass

---

1. Translators' Note: Piccola e Media Impresa: P.M.I.

workers. As far as Veneto is concerned, there was no immigration there, not even from the South of Italy: there was only a century of emigration, towards Borinage and towards Lorraine, to Switzerland and along the Rhine—it is from this hard work, from this hardly Renaissance tradition, that the desire is born to do away with salaried labor; it is from this collective experience that the force for imposing the mutation and living it collectively is born. So then, let us try to be serious and let us leave aside the charming Renaissance readings of the great evolution of industrial labor in the North of Italy. These readings have often been interesting when they showed us productive integration, functional complementariness that characterizes certain productive spaces: but the theory of the districts is ridiculous, simply ridiculous, when it claims to give a historical explanation of this process.

In fact, what we see is not an old, but a new figure of the entrepreneur which imposes itself here. We call this figure: the "political Entrepreneur." This entrepreneur operates within the assemblage of all the institutional factors that pre-constitute industrial activity, that permit its reproduction, that form the labor force, that organize social cooperation. The political entrepreneur is the autonomous agent of social labor that is more and more cooperative in the territories of production. But we will come back to this concept.

Let us turn, instead, to the theme of tradition. Certainly some continuities exist, not of long historical duration, but of brief economic duration. In the area of Padua, for example, there is an old tradition of special foundries: but it is only in the Seventies, in response to the decentralization of the production of radiators (first by Fiat, and then by Volkswagen), that we find an increase from a few hundred workers in this production to ten thousand of them. In the area of Pordenone, in Conegliano Veneto, etc., there had always been an old tradition of labor in the manufacturing of industrial enamel, a tradition reorganized by the large appliance industries between the Fifties and the Sixties (like Rex/Zanussi): but it is only in the Seventies, in the moment of industrial decentralization, that the reorganization of the production of replacement parts for appliances occurs on the territory. And we could go on at length with examples, in order to show how the only true continuity and tradition that crosses through this transformation is the one that is imposed by the mutations of the labor class, by the development of the entrepreneurial forces at its center, and by the new relations of strength that the struggles and cultural and political maturation have succeeded in imposing upon all the other subjects of industrial and territorial politics.

Let us go back to the core of our argument, where we had left off. We had said: it is in industrial decentralization that the new entrepreneurial initiatives install themselves, often in complex forms, often in subordinate respect for the industry that decentralizes. Why do these new industrial initiatives become independent and develop autonomously in such a short period of time? Above all, there are economic reasons for this. By working in small scattered units throughout the territory, by lowering the cost of production in a substantial and even cruel manner (it is the families and the children who, in the beginning, are often put to work), the new entrepreneurs beat all competition. Every ground floor of the houses that the workers had built, with their savings from their emigration or from the good times of guaranteed wage, becomes a laboratory. But the capacity for being competitive derives not only from the lowering of production costs. These are people who, beyond knowing how to organize labor, have no difficulty in getting into a car or a train in order to go in search of new markets, so as to liberate themselves from the protection of the old bosses, in order to broaden the volume of production, etc. This is why the new small and medium sized firms, even though they were born of decentralization, become autonomous. All of this occurs in a very brief period of time. And simultaneously with their independence, these entrepreneurs develop forms of cooperation with other entrepreneurs, associations, and every other instrument necessary for developing entrepreneurial activity and for consolidating it.

Alongside these initiatives, there are other processes of entrepreneurial constitution that, although being profoundly similar, differentiate themselves, nonetheless, from those Venetian processes that we have described, because they are developed in different local political situations. Let us consider, for example, the Emilian experience. In Emilia, in the years about which we are speaking, the intervention of the public powers (of Regions, Provinces, Municipalities) was fundamental in the support given to a type of development analogous to the development seen in Veneto, where the local political powers intervened only *post festum*, after phases of contradictory fumbling: in Emilia, on the other hand, public intervention was contemporaneous, cooperative in the determination of the process of development of the small and medium sized firms spread out within the territory. Local public power in Emilia is—as we know—very homogeneous: this has permitted its initiative of regulation of the scattered process of production in the territory. This intervention was not original in terms of the goal which it proposed; it was original, however, in terms of the administrative instruments that were utilized. And it was thus praiseworthy because it avoided a certain overload of exploitation and of suffering in the process of the transformation of the mode of production.

The Emilian experience is also important from another point of view. By placing in evidence the direct relationship between administration and production, it reveals that this relationship is unavoidable. And, in fact, that is what we verified in Veneto (and what could easily be verified in the other regions of Northern and Central Italy, in which analogous industrial developments have occurred). When the local administration does not follow the innovative activity of the new entrepreneur, it is the entrepreneur her/himself who develops the activity, directly, in the first person. Thus, in Veneto, in the same moment in which the small entrepreneur invents her/his firm, s/he is obligated to take on the burden of a series of directly political functions in order to obtain infrastructures, and some services, in order to mobilize productive energies within the territory, and to organize these energies in an effective manner. So we find ourselves once again in the presence of that original figure of the entrepreneur which I have called the "political entrepreneur."

I did a little study on the use of time and on the comprehensive functions carried out by these small entrepreneurs. Now, in my little study, I was able to verify that as soon as the firm exceeds the limits of familial management, the small entrepreneur is occupied less and less with production and with the commercialization of the products itself: on the other hand, s/he becomes more and more occupied with the general conditions (more or less political) of the development of the firm—from the question of taxes to the problems of services and infrastructures, to the problems of the training of specialized personnel, etc. This happens in Veneto, certainly, and in the other regions that we have always considered analogous. We can ask ourselves if this is true also for Emilia. And we must respond that the situation, even in its diversity, presents many elements of analogy: because, if it is true the initiative of local powers replaces and integrates the functions of the "small entrepreneur," it is true, on the other hand, that small and medium entrepreneurs have become, more and more, participants and, often, leaders of local administrations.

I must now conclude my argument. In order to do so, I wish first of all to emphasize strongly that I have not tried here to make an apology for the new type of scattered small and medium sized industries; nor have I tried to describe the paradise of the genesis of firms. We are now far away from that experience: it was an exceptional experience, but it lasted, more or less, for five or six years. Already at the beginning of the Eighties, and certainly starting from 1983-1985, we find ourselves in the presence of a recession of this experience and of a difficult regulation of it. The small and medium sized industries are, then, constrained either to build an original cage of productive activities (the collective cage, in the Benetton style, which sees itself as a multination of the informal organization of scattered production), or to renew some relationships with the large firms which now present themselves, on the market, as the loaners of tertiary services to the industries (from invoice factoring to banking services, from supporting, to exporting, to consulting, etc.). This is the moment of generalized computerization of services at the firms. It is by means of this computerization that the large firm (Olivetti, Fiat, etc.)—having already been expelled from the territory in the moment of innovation—is re-entering in a decisive manner. However, in an initial period, the relationship remains balanced—it is only after 1983 that the presence of big industry within the territory becomes decisive again, capable of re-shaping the tensions and directions of the development. Since 1983 the political parties of government have been doing everything possible to help the large firm to take control of the territory again. Looking back again upon that period (and having before our eyes, at the same time, the essential characteristics of the current crises in the Republic of Italy), one is forced to note that the response given to that crisis by the frustration and desire of the small entrepreneurs was terrible—creating absolutely reactionary instances in the years following 1985. In any event, a large group of small and medium sized businesses is able to maintain its own independence in the face of the recovery of control of the territory on the part of big industry. We are speaking about the small and medium sized businesses that succeed in directly connecting to the international market. The most powerful driving force in the resistance-to and breaking-away-from the political system of territorial control on the part of big industry was organized around these small and medium sized businesses.

The manner itself in which I have presented this picture to you, seeking to historicize it and to singularize it, instead of abstracting and showcasing it, indicates that I do not maintain that the specificity of the Italian small and medium sized businesses, which are organized upon productive territorial networks, can be considered exportable merchandise. The scattered Italian small and medium sized businesses are not an economic model: they are a large, singular and perhaps unique experience that is realized as much within the terrain of industrial development as within the terrain of class struggle and of the transformation of the working class. When I was working at the Parisian *Sentier* I met some researchers who were seeking to come up with a model of the Italian small and medium sized businesses, and they were trying to find in the *Sentier* some analogous elements. I permitted myself, then, to repeat that such an endeavor was one of absurd analogies. Now, if we want to insist upon the characteristics of the uniqueness of the Italian experience of the small and medium sized businesses scattered upon the territory, we must add, paradoxically, that we can identify in this activity a certain equality in the treatment of labor subjects. All of them exploited in the same way! All of them implicated in the ferocious rhythms of labor! But all of them together, during, before and after work time! The situation experienced in the Seventies and in the first years of the Eighties, before the ethnic market of the labor force gained strength even in Italy, is certainly not a Southeast Asian situation. The elements of community prevailed over the elements of separation and still do, in these Italian areas; despite the resumption of the ventures of large and extremely large industries, the labor market remains fundamentally unitary, not dual, and social development moves on with one speed, not two.

But what is most important to observe is the irreversibility, even during and after the period of crisis that struck this first moment of transformation of the mode of production, of the symbiosis of political and social, economic and cultural elements in the activity of the entrepreneur.

What I have recounted here is perhaps a useful fable for understanding, in concrete terms, how we can pass from Fordism to post-Fordism not only on the basis of the will of the boss to widen the exploitation of the factory to the surrounding territory, but also on the basis of an attempt at liberating the proletarians, the workers who have worn themselves out working like animals, in an idiotic manner, in the Fordist factories. Certainly, the conquest of autonomy, the ability to organize social labor and to form productive networks, and the strength to impose a new model of production are not sufficient if their impact is not felt at more general and effective political levels. I have the vague impression that these forces of the Italian small and medium sized businesses are working actively on this problem. The mistakes, and certain monstrous implications that we see coming to pass before our eyes need not take away our interest in analyzing these unrepeatable but certainly tendentious phenomena.

PART TWO

THE DECLINE OF "WEAK THOUGHT"

Philosophical and Cultural Statements

What Has the Intellectual Become?

A "new" French "philosophy" has retraced—to the joy of its citizens and that of the people who watch State T.V. (I was once among these)—the history of the concept of the "intellectual" in France. From the Dreyfus Affair to the First World War, from the Twenties to the Popular Front, from the Resistance to the Algerian war, from 1968 to the great crises of the Eighties, the figure of the intellectual as witness and critic of her/his times was photographed in broad daylight. Intellectual—witness, intellectual—"committed," intellectual—"*maître à penser*": the history and the materials offered were interesting. On the other hand, the "new philosophers," by way of the reconstruction of the history of the committed intellectual, "Parisian style," were playing their own game: that is, they were showing that intellectuals were almost always mistaken in their objectives (whether on the right, like Benda, or on the left, like Sartre); but they were showing that, even while mistaking their objectives, they had constructed a precious instrument of critical orientation based upon the transcendence of ethical intervention and upon the authority of the testimony of truth. It is a question, then, of separating the critical organ from the uses that had been generated by it. Under these conditions, the "new philosophers" were laying claim to the inheritance of this critical device, critical for themselves and for their peers.

As far as I am concerned, the "new philosophers" about whom we are speaking produce reactions of disgust. They always have their mouths full of grand principles; universality is their food and the absolute is their drink: nonetheless, when they speak of the "rights of man," you get the feeling that they are white and male; when they exalt the free market, you know that this means capitalist and boss-driven; when they sing world order, their music is military and American. What could be more odious? And yet, this time, listening to the "new philosophers" as they speak about intellectuals and their function, about the critical organ that their history has constructed and about how they and their accomplices intend to use this organ, I did not take offence, nor did I feel insulted. I felt stunned, and I asked myself why I felt this way. In response, a voice inside me whispered: "Let the dead bury the dead." What meaning could this lugubrious entreaty have? Why did the consciousness and the mute reflection so provoke me? Why was I not offended by the usurpation of the "*maître à penser*" device, and the appropriation of a function that for me, in other times, was loaded with a certain sacredness?

In one of those same evenings, jumping from canal to canal, I had come upon a debate concerning the Gulf War, a debate in which another "new philosopher" was in disagreement with an old and wise thinker of things political. In his bellicose inspiration, the "new philosopher" was accusing the "old" one of expressing an erroneous judgment on the war, by refusing to assume a universal point of view and claiming, instead, to be working within the subjectivity of the refusal of war and of the propaganda of desertion: refusal and desertion that, in this case, had no rational or political horizons upon which to stand. I asked myself if the old, honest thinker of things political were not correct, by refusing to present himself as "*maître*" and to hide himself within the testimony of the universal. Insisting on continuing to analyze the question, I interrogated myself thus: Can the universal, today, be anything other than the illusion of unattained knowledge and, for that reason, the inevitable prey of the manipulation of power? Is it possible to proclaim it, with no possibility of living it? What in the world could "*maître à penser*" be today if not the parrot of universality, knowing nothing of difference and antagonism?

These considerations brought me, little by little, to the center of the problem, which is that of recognizing the position of intellectual labor, today, in our society. So then, the universal intellectual, "*maître à penser*," is truly and definitively dead in our society. That type of intellectual was presented in one of two ways. The first way was that of the proposition of truth from the external realm of the world, as a criticism of existence; the second way was that of the proposition of truth from the internal realm of the world, as a transformation of existence. We had inherited the first position from the criticism of the "Ancien régime," from Enlightenment optimism; and the second position had been lived by us as an overturned product of the "disciplinary society," as an ethical commitment and an act of revolt from within the society. But of what use can these two models be today? What they have in common is the diversity and separateness of the intellectual, her/his privilege with regard to the masses, the superiority of intellectual labor to manual labor. Even in the most exasperated forms of theories on intellectual commitment you will always find the declaration of the difference of intellectual labor, and the apology for its superior dignity. And perhaps that was true, even in those times. But today, isn't this presumption simply ridiculous? Can it still be recognized as an independent function of the intellectual with respect to society? Can one still even imagine a separate position for the intellectual within the division of labor and of its organization? No, absolutely not. The only response we can give to these questions is purely and simply: no. And it is for this reason that the pretense of the "new philosopher" as someone who still represents the "*maître à penser*" device stinks of death.

The fact is that in the society of communication in which we live intellectual labor has become labor like any other. The intellectual is no longer separated from existence, but is inserted into it in the most intimate and profound manner. Her/his work is what constitutes reality; one needs to be an intellectual in order to produce, to communicate, to live. By now, our hands serve only for maneuvering the computer, the head serves for doing everything else. Our bodies are invested with our capacity for thinking, as much as labor is transformed by the capacity for computerized planning. Of what use is a "new" or "old" philosopher in this situation? In any event, the "old philosopher" serves more than the "new" one by virtue of the fact that the "new philosopher" needs, in order to exist, to renew intellectual mystification, while the "old philosopher" can congratulate her/himself for having become a "soft" planner of information technology.

At last. For the first time, finally, we intellectuals are able to begin to speak as members of the proletariat. Finally, the separation from labor is finished, a separation that made us feel strange and in some ways as though we were participating in the exploitation of the workers. Now we know that the work we do with our heads is nothing to be envied on the part of anyone else. On the contrary, our work alone is truly productive, and we intellectuals, as a community, are the ones who invent and configure the materiality of the world. And setting aside that small share of modesty that remains in us (and which never causes evil) we can also add: we intellectuals are, as a group, the exploited and the salt of the earth.

The different, separated, knowing intellectual—the animal that alone was able to create a long and dolorous historical situation of the exploitation of manual labor—is done for. Today the intellectual can speak as a common individual. The opposition to exploitation is something that is born today from the heart of the intellectual as a common individual. The intellectual is the subject of material labor. Every presumption of universality is foreign and inimical to the postmodern intellectual. The intellectual is the laborer. Let the politicians draw conclusions from this.

2

Chronicle of a Transition

Le magazine littéraire opens every year with its September issue, the Parisian season. On the cover this year is Gilles Deleuze. The issue contains about fifteen essays, one unpublished (in French) by Foucault, an important interview with Deleuze, and it illustrates the entire critical and philosophical activity of this author—his work on Bergson, Spinoza, Nietzsche, on modern empiricism, on the logic of sense, contributions to cinematic aesthetics, etc., all the way up to his last beautiful work on *Leibniz and the Baroque*, without forgetting, actually strongly emphasizing, the two books dedicated, with Félix Guattari, to describing the links between "capitalism and schizophrenia": *Anti-Oedipe* and *Mille Plateaux*. A first grand homage to the "nomad philosopher" (thus reads the subtitle of the report in *Le magazine littéraire*) and also a first documentation of Deleuze's international success.

But why Deleuze? The reasons are not lacking. In the first place, Deleuze is in the bookstores with *The Fold*—a formidable study on the thinking of Leibniz—and with *Périclès et Verdi*, a lecture in memory of his very close friend Châtelet. Secondly, Deleuze retired just this year and it is customary to pay homage to the masters on this occasion. Then, perhaps, thirdly, less noble motives are at the base of the canonization of this troubling character: meaning that the Parisian publishing machine needs to consume its idols with a certain order—so, Deleuze is the last of the great philosophers and essayists of the post-war generation, those who developed their careers between the time of the Resistance, the Algerian war and the experience of 1968—after this generation, and only after having exhausted its publishing value, another one will be discovered. But not even this seems like a sufficient reason. In fact, only two years ago, a similar operation would have seemed completely inconceivable.

Not a century ago—two years ago: Deleuze was a marginal figure in French philosophical culture. Since isolating him was, however, impossible, no more than one annoying citation was owed to him. They were the years of the inexhaustible babbling of the *nouveaux philosophes*: only now do we know that they were the last. Deleuze was among the very few who resisted, observing ironically that one could continue to be a communist who, like himself, had never been a Marxist and that in any event he did not understand how the criticism of Marx could mysteriously cause every analysis of capitalism to disappear. So then, behind this issue of *Le magazine littéraire* (which, beyond everything, is very close to the publisher Grasset, who is the godfather of the *nouveaux philosophes*), there is really something else—the sign of something new, the allusion to a transformation in progress. Certainly, it is not an earthquake, and not even deceptive summer thunder—as fragile as it is, the world of cultural news can be a symptom of more profound occurrences.

This is the case, then. We were so inundated in the Eighties by such an incredible mass of what was "new" that it didn't seem possible for us to raise our heads above water. New philosophers and new economists, and then industrialists, merchants, politicians, priests, doctors, jurists … all "new." Nothing wrong with this, if it were not that some very concrete effects accompanied those evanescent qualifications: the deregulation of the labor market, the weakening of the Welfare State, wild privatization, primal anti-Sovietism, support for imperialism in Israel, in Nicaragua, in South Africa, the monetary strangulation of the developing nations, and so on, all the way to the construction of paradoxical scenarios for regional slaughter, in the Gulf and in Afghanistan. This permanent counter-revolution was flavored with psalmody on the rights of man, set to music in concert-exhibits, sanctified by the televised fundraiser. One last, nearly unnoticed and not pleasing effect: "new" poor people and "new" exploited people.

When we were not suffocated by all of this (and many were) we were, however, surprised and dazed. This is how we can explain the silence with which we welcomed all the "new" things. But there was something else: the taste for self-criticism and a bad conscience held hands, insinuating doubt, even where there was no reason for doubt, bringing our hearts, if not our intelligence, to the brink of repentance and of desperation. We looked around us and discovered that in our best friends exhaustion had become an incurable disease and that for so much love with regard to others, hatred took over with regard to ourselves. And even more: though we had not conceded our hope to the crisis, we still found ourselves so alone that a simple reflex of opportunity could convince us of the irrationality of our condition. By confessing these moods, which were those of a generation, I do not intend to claim here that self-criticism and repentance, exhaustion and loneliness have nothing to do with the "new" things—to the contrary, those moods were interwoven with the "new" things, and it is difficult (and not very interesting) to find anyone who is without sin. But even in admitting all of this, the only conclusion that one can draw is perhaps known but not useless to repeat: for one generation only the revolution was too heavy to bear. The crisis followed this revelation.

And it was difficult to escape from the crisis. No, indignation and anger in the face of too many unbearable spectacles were no longer enough; no longer enough for our daily meal of injustices and iniquities which the information offers us. Those driven to the revolution by simple generosity, then, just to open their eyes again upon the political sphere, required a counter-assurance, a surplus of rational conviction. Nonetheless, these spectacles were not lacking. At the end of the Eighties, in spite of the neo-liberal boastings and the provocations of post-industrial culture, the Welfare State had held out. In spite of the insanity of our anti-Sovietism and all the provocations, the political picture of the Russian empire began to be modified and prospects for peace were being confirmed everywhere. In spite of the ferocity of repression, the neo-colonial system, in Israel, in South Africa, was up against a wall. To whom did we owe all of this? Once again, and always, to the revolt of the exploited. To the resistance of the labor class, to the struggles of the proletariat, to the movements of the damned of the earth: they are the young people dancing, carrying the caskets of their murdered brothers and sisters in the face of the brutality of the Afrikaners; they are the David-like young people of Gaza and of Jordan.

Back to Deleuze. To people who, like him, have never renounced the hope-principle. Here then is a first meaning to give to this if not unthinkable, certainly unexpected re-apparition of Deleuze at the center of the Parisian philosophic scene: the sign of a profound and solid continuity emerging from the disaster of an ephemeral cultural counter-revolution in the Eighties.

The success of the last campaign organized by the *nouveaux philosophes* against the Heideggerism in contemporary French philosophy was unique. This campaign, after Sartre and Marxist Hegelianism had been eliminated, was supposed to unleash its terror against Foucault, against Derrida (and, marginally, against Deleuze). The campaign had a triumphal beginning, with extraordinary support from the "media," with the absolute legitimizing of causing the accusation of Nazism to rain down upon anyone who had flirted with Heidegger. And yet it ended disastrously for those who had wanted it, because the political conditions of the debate, within the conditions of world history, were radically modified; and if Nazism remained indecently filthy, still, the ones to bear responsibility for it today were not so much the pensive Heideggerian philosophers, but rather the most irate accusers, the "new philosophers," neo-liberals, neo-colonialists, deregulators. Bernard-Henry Lévy, with acute opportunistic sense, took to the world of poetry.

But it is not enough to consider Deleuze as the continuity of a past time. He is also the discoverer of a new sense of knowledge. Together with Foucault, to whom he dedicated one of his most impassioned writings, he is the philosopher of the postmodern: he does not simply put up with it, but he assumes it as the universal base from which to promote a thinking of transformation. Nothing, he tells us, will remain equal to the past in this reconciliation of ours with a period of great social struggles and of constituent projects. What we are comparing ourselves with is not a new philosophy, but a new nature. In these years of repression, the seed sown by the events of 1968 has borne fruit: its flower has been disseminated, as though from a wild plant. The transformation of that which exists lies within the new accumulation—from the antifascist resistance to the desire for communism, from 1968 to the present, the rediscovery of the parents in the children and of the children in the parents, the real maturation of a radical desire for transformation and for justice. If the revolution is too much for one generation, it is not so for the unity of several generations.

Deleuze, then, is not the only sign of a transition that has taken place; he is also the active reader of the dynamics that organize this transition and the producer of symbols for a new, and most radical, movement. This issue of *Le magazine littéraire* is, then, a huge slip of the powerful Parisian publishing industry, and it reveals how much ground has been accomplished, secretly, productively, by the desire for communism. Finally, a well deserved celebration of the twentieth anniversary of 1968.

3

"Come Back, Sweet Terrible Ghost": Nietzsche Today

Better never to have been born than to be born then! The second half of the 19th century was, in fact, what Nietzsche described: the place of the undoing of values, the beginning of an infamous age in which modernity wears itself out and Europe begins its irresistible decline, the dawn of death. Nietzsche cast a critical Apollonian eye upon this catastrophic horizon—upon a catastrophe which his gaze anticipated for the future century destined, beyond the chronological period of the 19th century, to take delight in the apocalypse of the two wars of the 20th century, with all their deadly devices accoutrements.

There is in the work of Nietzsche a brief fragment dated "Lenzer Heide, 10 June 1887" which seems to me the culminating point of his meditation. In it he formulates briefly some of the truths that run through his later writings. Europe, Nietzsche explains, governed itself upon the hypothesis of Christian morality which conferred upon man absolute value in the flux of becoming, because it also recognized the sense of evil in the world.

But in the development of modernity another value was being nourished and was expressing itself: the value of truth, or, perhaps better to call it the will of truth. So, this force, which at first was the prisoner of morality, liberated itself in Nietzsche's century, unmasking the acceptance of evil to show it as hypocrisy, and then showing theology to be a pack of lies; this force destroyed morality and acted as a stimulant on the road to nihilism. This crisis is still dominated, Nietzsche adds, in Europe of the 19th century by the disciplinary means that control the critical potency of truth. But the breakdown of this theological discipline can already be seen, the death of God is imminent. Will other hypotheses, as absolute as those of the Christian God, enter the scene in order to make man accept the evil in history? Of course, but truth will not be able to stand it—and only through nihilism will the possibility of truth and the dignity of man be established.

Nietzsche lived this situation desperately; he announced this death and—as much as he could—he testified the truth. He died in doing so. He lived like a terrorist of the truth and he exploded himself upon the bomb he had dropped. In the last century.

If Nietzsche were alive today, on the brink of the 21st century, what would he have to say about the new era? Looking around himself, he would recognize the realization of his prophecy, multiplied a thousand times by every kind of cruelty and exploitation, by the disaster of every form of resistance, by the triumph of vulgarity. He would see the petty bourgeois villain in command everywhere, throughout the Empire, in States and in societies, in armies, in industry and in banks. He would see the moral "*tartufferie*" (which was once the exclusive domain of the churches) which has become our communal food, diffused upon Hertzian waves; and the egotism, the narrow-mindedness of the spirit and the resentment which have become the currency of our great institutions and civil "mores." You should still be alive now, dear Friedrich, and living among us!

Why? Above all, in order to remind us of what you were already saying then, and that is, that culture alone (or to be more precise, that freedom of the spirit which is born from the critical mind, joyously tireless in questioning everything) can respond to the repression of *Zivilisation* and of the State. That nihilism alone, which is the destruction of every dimension of evil by seeing it as a necessity of being and of history, can allow us to live out our finite existence heroically and to construct our history.

Secondly, herein lies the principle of being Nietzschean today, rather than in the previous century. The livid dawn of mature capitalism deprived Nietzsche of the possibility of reacting materially, while it provided him with his critical lucidity of conscience. It is within this ontological impossibility that we find Nietzsche's criticism, a stigmata of death. The terrorist act of criticism ended up in madness. Today everything is different. The great Churches, national and/or socialist, have been smeared with infamy and dishonor, from Red Square to the Berlin Wall, from Tiananmen Square to the ghettos of Los Angeles. The great international institutions have taken their place, exasperating their hypocrisy and cruelty, as if in a parody.

What would Zarathustra say about the IMF or about the World Bank? What would he say about the UN or about the N(orthern) G(overnmental) A(ssociations)? And what would Nietzsche have to say about the king who has no clothes?

In this new Dionysian dawn which, after 1968, with great difficulty, has risen upon our horizons, we live and work today in Nietzschean fashion. Can nihilism, being the one and only consciousness of value, the only constituent force of being, do its job concretely? Is it possible, consequently, for the terrorism of criticism to find new life, for Dionysius to inaugurate a new dawn open to the desire to destroy every form of repression, every lie, every State?

And just as Hamlet called out to his father at night in the castle, so do we call upon old Nietzsche, in this new dawn, crying out: "Come back, sweet terrible ghost …"

4

More Marx?

More Marx? What a bore ... but we were expecting this. Now that we are experiencing—so immediately evident and so scary that they keep us up at night—market slumps and crises, misery and poverty, it was inevitable that some beautiful soul would express nostalgia for Marx. On Wall Street, the capital of all markets, it is said that everyone is claiming to be a Marxist. In Paris, the capital of fashion, you can even find a *"nouveau philosophe"* (who just a few years ago in Afghanistan, with the Islamists, was cutting off the noses of Marxists) who says to you: "and yet Marx was not entirely wrong ... a new Middle Age is looming on the horizon, the free market needs correcting!" Thus, hypocrisy reigns while privatization and the dismantling of the Welfare State continue (at an ever more breathless pace, it is true). We must distrust this reappearance of Marx!

But we also distrust those nostalgic Marxists, those incurable comrades who, while winking an eye, repeat their orthodox prayers by which a hidden complacency with regard to the memory of past Eastern European regimes is accompanied by resentment, by a whiny loyalty to tradition, by a historicism that justifies everything, by a radical inability to understand the power of the desires that give structure to the "new man" of the present crisis. In this case,

Marx's appeal hides the historical catastrophe of a loyalty that was betrayal. Because Marx is a thinker devoted to freedom.

More Marx, then? Yes, but on one fundamental condition: that is, that we consider him not as the interpreter of the XIX and XX centuries, but as the philosopher of the liberation of the future. Gilles Deleuze, while preparing to publish a new book entitled *La grandeur de Marx*, admonishes: Marx is the author of the XXI century. Why? Because Marx carries the criticism of capitalism and of "really-existing socialism" (which is an absolute derivation of the original) beyond the limits of their crisis. Now, the Marx of the XXI century points out three central problems: communication, globalization and the empire, the new form of labor and the use of machines. It is on this terrain that some important voices are heard, be they old or new, however unexpected and rebellious. This is the Marx that must live again.

Within the critique of communication, understood as a critique of the present-day form of alienation, Jacques Derrida came out with his recent *Spectres de Marx*. The Marxist analysis of the fetishism of goods, he tells us, is fundamental to exposing the regressive contents of post-modern culture and of the function of communication as a present day form of exploitation: from Goebbels to the Gulf War, as present in daily life as it is in spiritual life. On the topic of globalization, our old friend Noam Chomsky tells us that, "in addition to Marx," once again Tiberius and Caligula are building an empire where rights and freedom are useless terms and the exploitation of man spreads ferociously, tomorrow even more than yesterday, inside our cities, as well as along every dimension of the known world. Deleuze, finally, shows how the wealth of the new forms of life, created through work and the use of machines, has produced a "new man." We need not wait for him, but we must express him. By means of machines, he adjusts his single desire to the collective desire and he perceives the possibility of founding a new democratic political regime, one that is pluralistic and creative: communism.

Here we are at the crux. It is not possible to separate Marx's name from that of revolution and communism. Take it or leave it. Outside of any hypocrisy, outside of any nostalgia, there stands Marx who theorizes, for the future, the nature of the new communist man. Marx: a name that will always evoke more and more affection, but will also always evoke great hatred.

5

Compassion, Terror and General Intellect

One strong point in the attack waged by Hannah Arendt against the French Revolution in her *On Revolution*, consists of the identification of "compassion" as a matrix of Jacobinism. The revolutionary yields to the social, listening to its lament, impersonating its misery, allowing itself to be dragged into the regurgitation of its irrationality and desperation. But in this suffocating contact, the revolutionary loses the ability to reflect on the conditions of the political, as the only transcendental possibility for creating ways of articulating social conflict and the functions of representing society. In that subordination of the political lies the root of "terrorism," which is the veritable "political representation" of the compassion of the social realm: this gives rise to an optimism of the will that clashes with both the finiteness of singularity and the irreducible multiplicity of "freedom." The revolutionary Jacobean word denies freedom by speaking of "liberation": but its plan is compromised by its exclusive adherence not to the cause, but to the effects of the lack of freedom. The negativity of compassion cannot produce liberation; it produces only a radical operation of reducing the real.

The Jacobean temptation is ever-present. It renews itself every time that compassion emerges in the guise of pathos in any given era. How can one not "suffer with" the youth of the Intifada, massacred by the oppressor's clay pigeon shooting? Or with the civilian Iraqis butchered by the most sanitized of technologies? How can we not recognize in terrorism the only form of resistance to a suffocating, systematic order, centralized in international power? Why not declare this way to be universal?

Hannah Arendt's criticism, in its haughty intellectualism, is not up to dissuading one from living the transition from compassion to terrorism. The alternative model to compassion that Arendt puts forth consists of indicating the possibility of a social organization, a "constitutional" one, within which the limit to the proposal of freedom is recognized as a structural condition of the constitution of freedoms and where, through "political representation," freedom presents itself as the progressive expansion of the law. "American liberty" versus "Jacobean liberty." Arendt creatively alludes to this transition: the constitutional revolution is a plucky young lad who appears to renew the world with his pure spontaneous power and not via demeaning emotions. All of a sudden, the myth of Virgil's Fourth Eclogue and that of the Tocquevillian notion of American individualism wake up under the same blanket. But this waking up inside a constructive myth demands that one has crossed through realism and through the hard knowledge of limit as necessity. Nor is this "cynicism" a vice: rather it is a virtue that opens up political thought to constitutionalism, to "parliamentarianism," to the rules of international law and upon this horizon it verifies a form of representation suited to the finiteness of the existent and to the multiplicity of freedoms. Here, then, in contrast to the political space characterized by the emotion-terrorism paradigm, is a new political space: cynicism-parliamentarianism, American constitution of freedom.

If irony and disdain were not enough (which, in the current situation of world history bring to mind American liberty and various King Kongs who enforce the rules), other arguments would be available for rejecting Arendt's liberal-constitutional masquerade. Actually, the measure of the impotence of freedom in the face of the instrumental rationality of power, and the excess of parliamentarianism in the face of cynical insurgence have been described by Max Weber, once and for all, and abundantly whined about afterwards, by all those brilliant souls who went adventuring in the wide territories of Atlantic freedoms. The fact is that the connection realism-parliamentarianism can be as mystifying as the connection emotion-terrorism can be destructive. Parliamentarianism, and in general every form of representative constitutionalism, by definition, negates the autonomy of the normative action; it removes and distorts the recognition of the intolerable and it does not know how to conceive of real temporality as anything other than the result of pre-established rules and measures. A sophism dominates them: the new and the living must be eliminated in order to regulate innovation and life. The constituent moment cannot be defined, or named, except within the established order. In this manner one of the most fetishistic celebrations of power is carried out. And King Kong goes wild.

Therefore, we ask again, how can terrorism be avoided if the path of parliamentarianism is not viable? The search for an alternative is guided by first recognizing this: both terrorism and parliamentarianism are the products of one machine, the machine which represents the "disciplinary society." Hannah Arendt and her pseudo-innovative pedophilia have never gone beyond this limit, nor have the thousands upon thousands of insurrections of pathetic volunteerism ever reached beyond this historical boundary.

Now, in the disciplinary society, the children, or the subjects, are always swaddled in their individuality, and consequently disguised within representative mutilations, or alternatively, paraded to elicit compassion, like bloody mannequins. In the disciplinary society the dogma of political representation reigns uncontested, equivalent to the hierarchy of the workplace, and this situates Arendt closer to the young Saint Just than to the emotion or cynicism which might separate them. Since representation is expropriation, it is the rupture and violation of the communal substance of productive labor, of the "communal ego," of humanity itself, and the disciplinary society bases its development on this condition.

But we are no longer within such an ontological situation: this is the second recognition of an alternative search. The disciplinary society of the genesis and development of capitalism has expired. Its socialist redundancy is happily extinct. And if the external figures of political society and of the international order are only superficially altered, if they react with a breathless attempt at controlling the underlying ontological transformation (and displaying all the more the anguished monstrosity of discipline)—that is because what is truly being altered is the general perception of the self, as well as the forms of self-expression. Communication is the sole base for temporal existence and the communal self is the sole form of its expression, of its work, of its imagination. How can one profess to represent the communicative subject, the social worker? How to surpass and transcend (because this is what representation means) the "general intellect" which is the communal substance of the social worker? These questions lead to no disciplinary response, but only to autonomous development.

I am an ordinary man. Our intellectuality is ordinary. It is the form of labor and of productive communication, thus it is the source of the social and the plot of the political. The behavior of this new perception of the productive being demands no representation, neither from the individual nor from the realm of compassion. It is both presence and a sense of ordinary duty. In the society of the *Ancien régime*, the intellectual was searching for truth from outside of the world and presenting it as a critique of existence; in the disciplinary society, the intellectual, in a dialectic relationship to the world, was offering her/his *engagement* to the process of transformation; in the society of communication the search for truth, and involvement in the world take place on a horizon that can be traced back entirely to the productive self-determination of the collective intellectual subject. As a collective *agencement*, as an "agency" of the revolutionary subject. As a "constituent power." We are both the social and the political. There is no little boy who will entertain us. The intelligence which we express is not a predatory and avant-garde gazing upon the other: it is the communication and the work which form us. From us originates that living work which shapes the world, its time and the social and political relations of its every innovation. Here is where revolution is planted; and communism, installed within the real, nervously waits for the constituent power to organize itself within the empirical consciousness of the ordinary self. We are returning from the exodus; and in this return we discover a third constituent pairing: "communism" versus "constituent power." And it is only the definition of this political space that keeps us from following the path of terrorism.

Because, in effect, the realm of compassion remains. Hannah Arendt heightened only the miserable side of terrorism. The other side, its pathos, remains alive. The "general intellect" is capable of pathos. The pathos of a highly radical yet quotidian communism, which takes delight in living labor, but whose violence is triggered by the cruel survival of imperialism, by the distressing repetition of disciplinary control, and by the expression (as empty as it is senseless), of superfluous, useless and extravagant capitalist power. A pathos that situates the cause for the lack of freedom, which is the existence itself of power, within a sphere of irreducible contempt and metaphysical disgust. Rational pathos, which, through the consideration of the limits of singularities and of the multiplicity of freedoms, constructs the converging materials and the organizational progressions of both the ordinary self and the collective intelligence.

Which is to say: our compassion for the youth of the Intifada is completely present in the general intellect and it is indeed a stage in its construction. In the wavering construction of the revolutionary process, between exodus and return, between misery and wealth, between anticipation and mass movements, the synchronic moment of the new creation reinforces the diachronic nature of the events and actualizes an irreversible genealogy. The construction of the political agency of the general intellect in the direction of the production of constituent power is a process that transforms the absence of memory (which life always forces upon us) into the presence of the entire results of past and present battles. Living labor based upon historically accumulated and ontologically fixed capital. In any case: beginning again means not turning back.

6

The Infinite Nature of Communication /
The Finite Nature of Desire

Never so much as in the current period, and ever increasingly, has the relationship between the media and spectators been so demonized. The media message has been increasingly represented as a gunshot that strikes and annihilates the spectator, the poor target of an omnipotent power. This obtuse and depressing moralism has become the habit of a "left" that is by now incapable of analyzing and proposing anything positive, still barricaded within its bastions of useless whining. Daily life dominated by the media monster is portrayed as a scene of ghosts, of zombies, doomed to a destiny of passive reception, frustrations and impotence.

Nor does this demonization circulate solely within the definition of the relationship media-public-daily life. The "science of communications" supports it well. In fact, communication is consistently debated within the realm of information, and the media are seen as linear functions which disseminate within society messages of Pavlovian efficacy. As has already happened in the linguistic sciences, today in the science of communication (better to say in the "so-called" sciences of communication) language has dried up and subjectivity has been expelled. Whatever there is of the ethical, of the political, of the poetic, of the interactive, of the not immediately conversational, in the relationship between media and public (as has already happened between subject and language), has been drained. This scientific reduction (so to speak!) is the basis of a terroristic idea of the media, of the complaints of the moralists, and above all, of a concretized and intransitive dimension of political life: there is nothing that can be done! There is no possibility of escaping from this slavery. Here power reaffirms its sacredness, within the realm of this very new modernity.

The Left can do nothing other than propose the theory of manipulation and pity those spectators who are reduced to being passive receivers. Indeed we do not want to deny the regressive effects that the current world of media brings upon its users. Indeed we are not insensitive to the deterioration in taste and collective knowledge, to the colonization of lived-in worlds. Furthermore, it seems to us abundantly evident that the media machine is not truly innocent when it brings about these effects. In the current power system, the media machine knowingly produces infected codes and epidemics, meant to block and short-circuit the mechanisms of symbolic production. A strategic and instrumental choice of informative contents, a systematic reversal of the senses and of values, extreme commercialization of information, reduction of communication to venality and futility: the list can go on and on … Once all of this is recognized, is the theory of manipulation valid, can it support itself all the same? Are the doom-saying of the latest critical school, and the calls, from the latest Frankfurt critics, for a lyrical liberation from the dominance of the commercialized media still current? No, the human being is not one dimensional, and the concepts about which we have spoken up to now, which the left, moralizing and pessimistic, claims as its own—these concepts must be categorically rejected. In the first place, because they are not true; in the second place, because they produce ethical impotence and political defeatism.

So, they are not true. This is not the place to take up again the long, yet always productive, discussions that have characterized the development of the linguistic sciences and their departure from the era of shabby and mechanical structuralism. It is enough to recall that the objectivistic and functional rift in linguistics suffered from Bakhtin to Hjelmslev, from Benjamin to Deleuze, to cite only a few key writers, has been in part repaired. If today it is possible to speak again about the science of communication, it is only so on the basis of a theory that re-introduces ontological and subjective dimensions, and poetic and creative elements into the description of the collective connections that take shape within the structure of communications and media. The collective efficiency, ethical-political, emotional and creative, which operates in the world of communication is an irreducible element, a resistance that opens up other paths: above all it, is the foundation of new constructions of subjects and of new inter-relationships that are always being actively produced. The "machine-based" entirety of media communication is a world of transformation and of composition, just like all the other "machine-based" worlds into which our lives have been inserted. Marx had taught us how capitalist accumulation would change the human being, the worker, to the point of glorifying productivity, to the point of drawing from it a productive force capable of self-recognition and thus, capable of revolution. In the accumulation of communication human beings transform their conscience and realize that they are able, collectively, to recognize the increasing possibilities of both knowledge and transformative capabilities, which can only grant them more freedom.

Here we are at the center of the matter, here where the world of communication presents itself as a place in which the great social powers of knowledge and of cooperation position themselves as the exclusive productive forces. The collective labor of humanity takes its shape from communication and the communicational paradigm identifies itself, in a manner which is by and large increasingly more evident and powerful, with the paradigm of social labor, with that of the social productivity. Communication becomes the form in which the richness of the world of life organizes itself. The new subjectivity establishes itself within this context of machines and work, of cognitive instruments and of poetic self-science, of a new environment and of new cooperation. The human labor of producing the new subjectivity places itself consistently upon the virtual horizon which the technologies of communication are forever widening. As always, with reference to Marx, it is necessary to return to the analysis and critique of labor in order to identify the reasons for exploitation and revolution. Even in this case: that is, when communication reveals itself to be the machine that dominates society, but a machine by means of which the coopera-tion of consciences and of individual practices reaches the highest level of productivity — productivity of the subject, cooperation of the subjects, production of a new horizon uniting wealth and liberation. Within the fabric of communicational labor the last resistances of a reified capitalist world, locked in its rapport with the nature and the fetishistic determination of the horizon of goods, fall short. Reality, nature, and society are led into the flow of events; the communicative action of the labor-force, of the communicating consciences, of the cooperating subjects, thus become capable of effecting the transformation, radically, beyond every limit that marks the finite nature of our desire. A finiteness that is confronted only by the infinity of the task.

We are now entering a post-media era. This knowledge is the basis for the second critique of the theories of communication that power offers us today. It is here that the line of inescapable political slavery (and of the uninterrupted exploitation of labor) is demystified. That is, when one understands that the success of the communicative paradigm and the consolidation of the media horizon, in its virtuality, in its productivity, in the universal reach of its effects, far from determining a world trapped in necessity and in reification, indeed open up battlefields for transformation and for radical democracy. It is to the center of this new space that the fight should be brought. The fight to destroy all the elements and the agents that repeat, in the new way of producing subjectivity, the old measures, the codes and the miserable paradigms of the ancient arts of domination, the fight to reclaim the media and all the articulations of communication. There are many negative actions to be found in this area: how to destroy the private and/or state system, the capitalist monopoly of communication? How to wipe out the communication professionals' actions, as well as the whole system of power codes that are being transmitted? How to dig up the earth under this center of production of ideological apparatuses? But if the negative actions are extensive and arduous, even more important and demanding are the positive actions to be carried out. It is necessary to imagine constructing a common system of public communication from which both public and private are excluded. To construct a system of public communication based on the active and cooperative inter-relationship of subjects. To connect communication/production/social lives in ever more intense forms of cooperation and proximity. This involves, thus, envisioning a radical democracy, both in society and in production, which takes shape within the conditions of the post-media horizon.

7

Understanding Being through Language

Outline of a Life, History of a System of Thought: this is the subtitle Elisabeth Roudinesco gives to her impressive *Jacques Lacan*.[1] Her book is something more than a biography, and yet, in the manner of great biography, her work has the curiosity, the structure, the information, and, that which matters most, the breathing of history. Roudinesco succeeds in a difficult undertaking: that of making the biography coincide with the central stages of the genesis, development and affirmation of the system of Lacan's thought. An exercise in genealogical hermeneutics. From this point of view, Roudinesco's claim that this is the third volume in her *History of Psychoanalysis* in France, covering one hundred years of Freudian history, seems appropriate. This volume is an essential complement to the others. Indeed it joins the other two volumes, shedding light sometimes on events already recounted, a light not only different but also completely original—a light that comes from a most unique and profound source of innovation, from a powerful and impetuous presence, from an extraordinary will to know; those things, precisely, that represent Lacan's life and work.

---

1. Translators' Note: English translation by Barbara Bray (New York: Columbia University Press, 1997).

What exactly makes up the innovation that Lacan contributes to philosophy and to analytical practices? It is known that this innovation consists of the acceptance of the central role of language. That is to say, Lacan interprets, between the Fifties and the Sixties, in France, that *tournant linguistique* which characterizes contemporary philosophy and which, in a different form, finds in Heidegger (in Germany) and in Wittgenstein (in Great Britain) its pre-eminent authors. Lacan integrates the continental linguistic revolution into the Cartesian and French tradition of "I think," which is the tradition of thought and the practice of subjectivity. We must be careful here: French culture never succeeds in *simply* taking on a foreign philosophical innovation. "Translating" in French is always something wickedly different from transferring phonemes and/or concepts from one language into another. The Lacanian "translation" of the "linguistic shift" is thus a work aware of its own challenges, and consequently, it is an act of tampering with historical meanings and literal meanings, with the goal of creating a system adequate for taking on new analytic work: that of understanding being via language. Thus, Lacan moves within the harsh depth of culture, and it is precisely upon one of its most resistant elements— language—that he applies his force.

Roudinesco shows us how the conditions of this split were ripe and how Lacan practiced them, reassembling them in his war machine. Let us consider here, briefly, two or three essential passages from the Lacanian march towards the affirmation of the linguistic shift in the analytic camp, exactly as Roudinesco narrates them. The first passage is represented by the experience of Bataille and his group, in the Thirties and Forties. Without this unique translation of Nietzscheism, without this trans-surrealist rebellion, without this destruction of the last elements of traditional humanism and rationalism, Lacan's work is unimaginable. The second passage is characterized by the reception of Heidegger's thought, in the post-war period, thus beyond and against Sartre's interpretation and tradition. An immediately anti-humanist reception, indeed, which allows for, at the same time, both the separation from any historical illusion, and the completely positive project of reconstructing ontology via linguistic analysis. The third passage is that of structuralism, that is, constructing a horizon of scientific communication that becomes hegemonic, in French culture, during the 1960s, and which allows for the exchange of philosophical experiences between psychoanalysis, linguistics, anthropology, political philosophy, etc.

Roudinesco allows us to live at the center of this story. Some formidable characters live there: Koyré, Kojève, Bataille, Beaufret, Heidegger, Sartre, Althusser, Levy-Strauss, Jakobson—and many women, beautiful and rebellious, alongside Lacan. Here a scientific revolution takes place, one which situates the demystifying power of Freud in contact with the highest level of philosophical speculation. In this way, Roudinesco concludes, Lacan succeeded in spreading the plague of analysis, critique and freedom, all normalized within society by late capitalism, where everything is language and communication.

8

The Sense of a Distinction:
The Right, the Left and Bobbio

"As is well known, the use of these two words (right and left) dates back to the French Revolution, at least with regard to internal politics. We are dealing with a most banal spatial metaphor whose origin is completely random and whose function was solely to give a name, two centuries distant from the here and now, to the persistent, persistent because essential, dichotomy-like composition of the political universe."[1] Bobbio's first affirmation consists, thus, in the recognition of the essentially and originally dichotomy-like structure of the political universe: right and left as historical specification of the polarity "friend-enemy."

Secondly, let us try to make sense of this dichotomy. Towards this goal, Bobbio formulates the idea "according to which the distinction between left and right corresponds to the difference between egalitarianism and inegalitarianism" and so "at the last minute, this difference turns into the difference between the perception and the evaluation of that which renders people equal or unequal" ("which translates practically into contrasting evaluations of that which is significant in order to justify, or not, a discrimination.")

---

1. Translators' Note: The English quotations from Bobbio's book are by the translators. Norberto Bobbio, *Destra e sinistra. Ragioni e significati di una distinzione politica* (Roma: Donzelli, 1994).

Consequently, we rule out that "the other great ideal which accompanies, like the ideal of equality, all of human history—the ideal of liberty," can be used as a criterion for distinguishing between "right" and "left." This is, rather, a significant criterion for distinguishing, as much for the right as for the left, the moderate wing from the extremist one, the first being libertarian, the second being authoritarian. Thus, freedom is not a subject for debate, nor is it a divisive question. As others have said, history is over, certainly not this history, but the history of freedom. Now then, at the center, sits moderation: "On the center-left, doctrines and movements, both egalitarian and libertarian, for which we could today use the term 'liberal-socialism'"; "at the center-right stand the movements that are both inegalitarian and liberal," the conservative parties, in this case, which accept the democratic method but refuse to extend equality beyond the formal limits established by the application of law. Opposite them are the extremists: on the extreme left, the egalitarian and authoritarian movements (from Jacobinism to Stalinism), "on the extreme right, anti-liberal and anti-egalitarian movements and doctrines." Without any margin of error it seems possible to understand that the party desired by Bobbio is centrist: preferably the socialist-liberal version; yet equally compatible with his scheme could be a conservative, democratic party, one that governs by adjusting the formal conformity of interpreting the laws to meet social necessities.

Yet something is not working here. Bobbio promised us, from the start, to keep political philosophy and the science of politics together, evaluation and description. But here we cannot understand where the "friend and enemy" have wound up; or, to put it better, they have been erased from the picture which defines the right and the left, and have been projected onto the extremist marginality, while previously it was thought that the dichotomy of politics would present itself as both essential and persistent. In effect, Bobbio's defining machine is pulled insistently toward the moderate synthesis of freedom and equality, as though towards a point where the oppositions melt away. Neither the alternatives, with respect to this ideal point, nor its articulations, seem fundamental to Bobbio; only the concise unity is fundamental. Thus, the first result of the conceptual separation winds up being the unification of the right and left, which at least is a good step forward in the political distinction ...

But let us pretend that the distinction proposed by Bobbio, instead of melting with the first ray of the sun, resists instead. Can we, in this case, put it to use with positive results in order to distinguish political positions?

For example, assuming the validity of the equivalence "left-equality" ("not in Utopian terms but in practical ones," as Bobbio explicitly requests), was the liberal Piedmont monarchy or the fascist monarchy closer to the left during post-Risorgimento Italy? And which was more to the right? And during the Resistance, who was on the left: The G.L. (Giustizia e Libertà) or, rather, the cominterns who landed in Salerno? And is the "progressive" liberalism of the Nineties more or less to the left of the bipartisan governments of the Seventies and Eighties? And, looking around further: what is the difference between the right and left in Russia, today? The "persistent and essential dichotomy," based upon the "principle of justice," does pirouettes here, to speak euphemistically: egalitarianism presents itself on the right: the "free market" on the left ... Certainly, the situation could still change, increasing the difficulty and ambiguity ... but then why waste words like "essential and original" to define a dyad that is usually mobile and at times completely reversible? A dyad that is not only empty, but idiotic and inept at catching on to what there is that is new, and that is effectively original in the behavior of mass politics in these recent years: were the protestors of Tiananmen Square on the right or on the left? And what about those workers who fled socialist Germany by getting around the Wall and making it fall? And what about the nomads, the immigrants, the refugees, the exiled, and the fugitives who cross borders ignoring meaningless warning signs; are they on the right or on the left? And if young people reject the politics of the left or of the right, and if the unemployed …?

Therefore not only does the distinction "right-left" proposed by Bobbio fail to establish a rigorous foundation, it is also ineffective from an analytic point of view. This does not take away the possibility that it may work in the minds of some and that it almost establishes a flag in the Lilliputian world of Italian "progressive politics." Feeling nostalgic for the good old days, the parliamentary and bureaucratic rhetoric of the "left" seeks justification—and, as frequently happens in this case, it tries its best to shape itself in a naturalistic syntax. Perhaps, everything comes down to this: Bobbio lends his genius and his professional *savoir-faire* to this translation (a little grotesque, a little pathetic) of parliamentary procedure into philosophical language. He takes the equivalence left-equality to an absolute level: but not too much, because, in fact, he prefers the center. He lends a hand to a left which is politically in crisis, but without exaggerating. In that naturalistic syntax, or rather, natural-legal syntax, moderation lies at the center of reflection. In fact, the true "left" for Bobbio is found within the "mixed group" of parliamentary concepts.

This having been said, Bobbio's work is not innocuous. It may seem to be, for that which it reveals: a useless and lazy nostalgia for the past; but it is not so for that which it conceals, that is, the tedious determinations of a society dominated by the capitalist organization of labor. From this perspective, Bobbio's equality is nothing other than the ghost of the circulation of goods, or if you will, of the translation of use value into exchange value, including all the stuff of violence, hypocrisy, of domination, corruption and great principles that this involves. There is not a breath of creativity in this scenario: instead, the oppressive air of institution dominates. The ghost of political representation is put forward (equipped with a suitable topography of right and left), and it is magically tilted towards the "great value" of equality rather than towards other values. As has already happened in other sad times, *chez* don Benedetto Croce, we find a reason here why we cannot say that we are … of the left!

But why should I want equality? As is known (and Marx, who was not "of the left," explains it thoroughly), the question is meaningless. Were it not to be meaningless, it would express jealousy and envy; that is because human beings are constitutionally unequal. If I want to be equal to others, I must commit myself to an abstract (but no less dangerous) paranoia. In reality I do not want to be equal to anybody: instead, if I am a person gifted with a healthy intellect, I want all the difficulties and obstacles in the path of the development of my freedom and that of others to be removed. I want, therefore, to have the same possibilities as others have to pursue the development of my person, and to carry out freely my appetites and desires. My wish is not for equality but for the determination of all those relative inequalities that allow all people to develop their own singularity. The foundation of democracy (and, without contradiction, the foundation of communism) is not the development of equality, but the freedom of the individual, as a positive, cooperative action. For Roosevelt as for Lenin, freedom is positive action carried out to counter need, fear, falsity, and exploitation. Equality is thus simply a product of freedom, and where there is no freedom, there is no equality. We must not oppose inequality, when it can be passed through by freedom; rather, we must oppose equality when it is offered as conformity and equal rule.

Thus it is in opposition to this lethal equality that resistance liberates itself; acts of sabotage are carried out, exodus occurs. One of the most terrible deceptions from the period of the Cold War consisted of conceptually conforming socialism to equality. But communism had nothing to do with this leftist configuration of equality, with this envy of the masses for and against singularity! In reality, equality in really-existing socialism was nothing other than a long and effective projection of the capitalist dream of a product that circulates freely without hitches, without stopping, and that touches everyone alike; equality—in really-existing socialism—was the acceleration of the product's circulation speed. Bobbio celebrates this poverty of spirit in his construction of the "left."

Bobbio's work could perhaps interest "progressivists," but it is certainly not of interest to communists. Bobbio's book, in reality, seems to be the final product of an age in which words had a forced meaning, the final product of a shop in which everything was determined by a force as violent as it was dishonest: usury of the spirit. How hateful the nostalgia that dwells in this little book! Nostalgia for a world in which political distinction was completely subordinated to the apologetic language which each political side generated for its own purposes: both sides against communism—language that lies neither on the right nor on the left, but which opposes both the version of the right and the version of the left offered by capitalism; language as an exercise in freedom—against exploitation, against fear, against falsity. If we had to accept or pretend to move along the grotesque terrain of Bobbio's definitions and likewise glibly play with words, could we not then conclude that the dichotomy-like composition of politics, "essentially and originally," sees communist freedom as offering itself up in opposition to capitalist equality ...

But why bother to play this game? Why upset polemically—even if we believe we are able to do so honestly—the semantic direction of the great concepts and why do so in such a way as to succumb to their appeal on the grounds of the cynical natural-legality of principles? Here lies the sin of epistemological origin, the plague of academic teaching.

We are pro-freedom—but our freedom is made of *papier-mâché*, like the statue of Tiananmen ...

9

Deleuze and Guattari:
A Philosophy for the 21st Century

Qu'est-ce que la philosophie? In this co-authored book by Gilles Deleuze and Félix Guattari we find many things. Things, or an amazing wealth of thought, as well as many levels of writing that follow each other, overlap each other and cross each other. Like other works (*L'Anti-oedipe*, *Mille Plateaux*), this is a collaborative and intense text, rhizomic and full. And again, there is the fact that this book is simple. For the first time a work of Deleuze-Guattari is animated by a solicitous and profound pedagogic vein. Here one feels an effort (successful) to construct a plan of action that crosses over the previous works (both those works written together and those produced individually by the two authors); it offers a mature interpretive grid, fixed to a systematic block of concepts and of conceptual dynamics. The *first* point, therefore: a pedagogic moment, expressly declared, organized in the fixing of a conceptual fabric that separates approaches to the production of truth (philosophy, science, art) and then reunites them in the construction of the spirit: materialistically redefined by the authors as "the brain."

A *second* point jumps out at you upon your first reading of the text: the placement within the history of philosophy. The history of philosophy is always a pedagogy organized upon key concepts of a truth that unfolds historically. Here, this concept of history of philosophy is denied *a priori*: the history of philosophy, in its entirety or as the individual traditions of which it is composed, does not form a totality, however qualified; rather, it forms a composite of individualities. The eruption of thought in this area will take place in the form of individual comparisons, and its exposition will have the shape of the *Exempla*. We are dealing here with a methodological proposal of history of philosophy carried out in the tradition of Spinoza's *Scolia*: the history of philosophy is broken up into a series of problems, reduced to a discontinuity of singularity.

Not a *Geschichte* but a *Geschehen*, not a *historia* but the same *res cogitatae*. This does not remove the possibility of a separate and horizontal reading of these *Exempla*: this offers us the guiding thread of a new reading of the philosophical tradition, an "other" history, intermittent, founded not on the historical extension of a generic concept, but on the intensity of the construction of philosophical terms that reveal new things to the human brain. Every philosophical discovery is "ill timed" and "outdated." Between Nietzsche and Foucault the new history of philosophy, which Deleuze and Guattari pedagogically exemplify, is founded.

It is upon this foundation, simultaneously pedagogy and critique, that the work of Deleuze and Guattari takes off toward its first substantial goal: to define philosophy with respect to other forms of knowledge production, science and art, not in an encyclopedia of the spirit but in a hermeneutics of singularity. Herein lies the *third* plan of reading of *Qu'est-ce que la philosophie?* And this is the central point, where the definition comes from the ability to confront difference. Therefore, what is philosophy? "Philosophy is the art of forming, inventing, and fabricating concepts" (*What Is Philosophy?*, p.2). And what is the concept?

The concept is defined by the inseparability of a finite number of heterogeneous components traversed by a point of absolute survey at infinite speed (ibid., p.21). [...] The philosophical concept does not refer to the lived, by way of compensation, but consists, through its own creation, in setting up an event that surveys the whole of the lived no less than every state of affairs. Every concept shapes and reshapes the event in its own way. The greatness of a philosophy is measured by the nature of the events to which its concepts summon us or that it enables us to release in concepts. So the unique, exclusive bond between concepts and philosophy as a creative discipline must be tested in its finest details (ibid., pp. 33–34).[1]

The concept is the singularity and the event of the singularity. Philosophy is not an abstract reflex, nor contemplation, nor the will to truth; rather, it is the fabrication of truth. What then is science as compared to philosophy? "The object of science is not concepts but rather functions that are presented as propositions in discursive systems. [...] A scientific notion is defined not by concepts but by foundations or propositions" (ibid., p. 117). Scientific function renounces the concept's attempt to give consistency to the infinite, and shape to the virtual: within this renunciation, scientific function nevertheless defines "a reference able to actualize the virtual" (ibid., p. 118). Science slows down infinite movement and at the center of this slowdown it creates a reflexive condition, co-extensive with infinite movement. Science is paradigmatic, ideographic, supported more by a spiritual tension than by any spatial intuition. Scientific

---

1. Translators' Note: Gilles Deleuze and Félix Guattari, *Qu'est-ce que la philosophie?* (Paris: Les Editions de Minuit, 1991). Quotations below from this book are taken from the English translation (*What Is Philosophy?*) by Hugh Tomlinson and Graham Burchell (New York: Columbia University Press, 1994).

creation doubles and individuates into "partial observers" who deploy me to the field of variables, which are constantly re-opened, in multiple ways, in as many ways as there are states of things, breaks, bifurcations, catastrophes, re-attachments which function pursues. Reference and its field are being constructed continuously; their subject is never the relativity of truth, perceived from an absolute point of view, but rather the truth of the relative constructed functionally. Contrary to the concept that becomes absolute by surveying reality, both scientific function, and the partial observers who construct this function plant themselves inside the flow of reality. As far as art is concerned (and with regard to this subject extraordinary detours open up in this book), it is sensation (*affect et percept*) that dominates here, causing aesthetic figures to rise up upon a plane of composition. Art casts us into the finite—where it strives to build, understand, and produce the infinite, the absolute in the shape of concrete expression, in the form of a monument.

Each of the three forms of the spirit, once difference has been established within the realm of perception (concepts, prospects, affects), develops, within itself, a specific ontological terrain. For concepts, this is the "plane of immanence," for functions, it is the "plane of reference," and for art, the "plane of composition." A thousand plateaus reduced to three, in the current pedagogical schematization.

> What defines thought in its three great forms—art, science, and philosophy—is always confronting chaos, laying out a plane, throwing a plane over chaos. But philosophy wants to save the infinite by giving it consistency: it lays out a plane of immanence that, through the action of conceptual personae, takes events or consistent concepts to infinity. Science, on the other hand, relinquishes the infinite in order to gain reference: it lays out a plane of simply undefined

coordinates that each time, through the action of partial observers, defines states of affairs, functions, or referential propositions. Art wants to create the finite that restores the infinite: it lays out a plane of composition that, in turn, through the action of aesthetic figures, bears monuments of composite sensations (ibid., p. 197).

Now if none of these forms has hegemony over the others, there exists a negative effect: that is, outside of these differences, within the confusion of these forms, thought does not exist; only "opinion" exists. Contemporary thought excels in this confusion, whenever it demands superior syntheses. In fact, when the singular power of the concept is reduced to the discursive form of the function, neither of the two survives, and chaos takes over again. When the power of the concept and the form of the function are subordinate to communication, then it is the relationship with being itself that is severed. The most banal, popular democratic *doxa*, the Rorty-style conversation, substitute for that philosophizing which spans an entire life and which alone renders it worthy.

Each form of perception defers to a plane of functioning. Moreover, each perceptive form defers to a figure of structural *agencement* (the conceptual characters, the partial observers, the esthetic figures). We are introduced, through the identification of these planes and the construction of these figures, to the *fourth* level of reading of Deleuze-Guattari's work, a level that we can define as "a beyond post-modern essay of philosophy."

This "beyond" is defined according to various directions of research that have only one fundamental dimension in common: the *ontological insertion*. This is the central point and the true novelty of *Qu'est-ce que la philosophie?* A profound novelty, that, in our opinion, identifies a central passage of contemporary thought and establishes in this work (as had already happened in earlier works by Deleuze and Guattari) an additional wedge in the only metaphysical system that the 20th century has produced after Heidegger; to put it better, the first system of the 21st century. Between Heidegger and Deleuze-Guattari there is, in fact, the event of 1968, or rather, the invention of the 21st century, and between them lies the defining distance of the reinvention of an open and constructive ontology by Deleuze-Guattari. The ontological insertion is immediate: that is to say that the theory of the plateaus is a theory of the transformation of perceptive forms into images of being. "Thinking and being are one and the same. Or rather, movement is not the image of thought without being also the substance of being" (ibid., p. 38). The call to Heidegger is precise. "Heidegger invokes a 'pre-ontological' understanding of Being,' a 'preconceptual' understanding that seems to imply the grasp of a substance of being in relationship with a predisposition of thought" (ibid., p. 40). But the difference from Heidegger, the essential leap forward, is equally precise:

> Prephilosophical does not mean something preexistent but rather something that does not exist outside philosophy, although philosophy presupposes it. These are its internal conditions. The non-philosophical is perhaps closer to the heart of philosophy than philosophy itself, and this means that philosophy cannot be content to be understood only philosophically or conceptually, but is addressed essentially to non-philosophers as well. [...] Philosophy is at once concept creation and instituting of the plane. The concept is the beginning of philosophy, but the plane is its instituting. The plane is clearly not a program, design, end, or means: it is a plane of immanence that constitutes the absolute ground of philosophy, its earth or deterritorialization, the

foundation on which it creates its concepts. Both the creation of concepts and the instituting of the plane are required, like two wings or fins (ibid., p. 41).

The theory of the planes is not presented here as a theory of foundation but as the ontology of constitution. This theory confronts chaos and constructs its being within chaos.

> The plane of immanence is like a section of chaos and acts like a sieve. [...] Chaos is not an inert or stationary state, nor is it a chance mixture. Chaos makes chaotic and undoes every consistency in the infinite. The problem of philosophy is to acquire a consistency without losing the infinite into which thought plunges. [...] To give consistency without losing anything of the infinite (ibid., p. 42).

One can go beyond the postmodern also in another direction, through the organizational points of being that are the intellectual personae, the partial observers, the esthetic figures. In the overview that the concept performs over the real, on the one hand territories are built, on the other, these territories become inhabited. *The ontological insertion is subjectivized.* Here, that radical constructivism which so profoundly characterized the metaphysical progress of theory, becomes singular. The concepts, the function, the affect, all become singular. In this metaphysics there is no more weakness. "Philosophers carry out a vast diversion of wisdom; they place it at the service of pure immanence. They replace genealogy with geology" (ibid., p. 44). "The role of conceptual personae is to show thought's territories, its absolute deterritorializations and reterritorializations" (ibid., p. 69). In philosophy, as in other ways in science and in art, once chaos has been traversed, the real becomes singularly reconstructed. Through this overview of the real, the concept takes on the wings of reality. The level of being which the planes of immanence reveal is different and specific: but the process, the becoming, the becoming singular of the "brain" are irresistible, in what becomes a continuous production of being.

Beyond the postmodern we eventually traverse the reconstruction of the human horizon. "From chaos to the brain." Here it is, then, the postmodern redefined in its anguished indetermination, and here philosophy exercises its vocation: the re-composition of a horizon and the building of subjects. On one hand:

> We require just a little order to protect us from chaos. Nothing is more distressing than a thought that escapes itself, than ideas that fly off, that disappear hardly formed, already eroded by forgetfulness or precipitated into others that we no longer master. These are infinite variabilities, the appearing and disappearing of which coincide. They are infinite speeds that blend into the immobility of the colorless and silent nothingness they traverse, without nature or thought. This is the instant of which we do not know whether it is too long or too short for time. We receive sudden jolts that beat like arteries (ibid., p. 201).

We search for certainties, for a few certainties, for an order of thinking which will stave off delirium and madness. But on the other hand, here we are, always, in the middle of being:

> It is as if the struggle against chaos does not take place without an affinity with the enemy, because another struggle develops and takes on more importance--the struggle against opinion, which claims to protect us from chaos itself (ibid., p. 203).

Philosophy, science, and art experience a profound attraction for chaos, and yet they fight against it. From this point of view we recognize that:

> In short, chaos has daughters, depending on the plane that cuts through it: these are the *Chaoids*—art, science, and philosophy— as forms of thought or creation. We call *Chaoids* the realities produced on the planes that cut through the chaos in different ways (ibid., p.208).

But it does not end here. There is a force which surpasses chaos, which constructs the desire for the *kosmos* out of chaos. Different forms follow one another and in this alternating movement the world manifests itself as *Kaosmos*—in James Joyce's words. It is the "brain" that navigates in this crossing which is a reconstruction, a formation— across a deed that always re-opens the infinite but yet always organizes the constructive finiteness of the singularity. "The brain is the junction—not the unity—of the three planes" (ibid, p. 208). Here it is, then, the turning point of the line of reasoning—here where the brain becomes subject, is subject. "Philosophy, art and science are not the mental objects of an objectified brain but the three aspects under which *the brain becomes subject*" (ibid., p. 210). A form in and of itself, a consistent and absolute form. "The brain is the mind itself" (ibid., p. 211). Let's go back to, and extend, the argument. Research has been done on the specificity of the fields of the expression of truth. But:

> The three planes, along with their elements, are irreducible: plane of immanence of philosophy, plane of composition or art, plane of reference or coordination of science; form of concept, force of sensation, function of knowledge; concepts and conceptual

personae, sensations and aesthetic figures, figures and partial observers (ibid., p. 216).

Now, the fact of this irreducibility does not nullify another fact, which is the interference of the planes that meet up in the brain. These interferences are complex: they can be extrinsic, as when truth is searched for in the form of perceptions; they can be intrinsic, as when the plane of immanence is formed and develops through the singular *agencements*, the processes of subjectification. With this, the order of the production of being constitutes itself and advances. But this new production of being opens up: the interferences once again become impossible to pin down because they present themselves singularly on a new plane of immanence and thus, once again, they open themselves to being. Impossible to pin down because their movement and their construction have reproduced that pre-philosophical element which is at the center of philosophy, because they have opened themselves up once again to the potential depth of being.

> Philosophy needs a nonphilosophy that comprehends it; it needs a non philosophical comprehension just as art needs nonart and science needs nonscience. They do not need the No as beginning, or as the end in which they would be called upon to disappear by being realized, but at every moment of their becoming or their development. Now, if the three *Nos* are still distinct in relation to the cerebral plane, they are no longer distinct in relation to the chaos into which the brain plunges. In this submersion it seems that there is extracted from chaos the shadow of the "people to come" in the form that art, but also philosophy and science, summon forth: mass-people, world-people, brain-people, chaos-people (ibid., p. 218).

It is through this transition that we come to the *fifth* point of reading in this book, which is that of the ethical-political perspective. In the works of Delueze-Guattari this perspective is central and even somewhat conclusive; and that is true also in this case. It is central, moreover, because the specifically political discourse is tackled right in the middle of *Qu'est-ce que la philosophie?*, right where the analysis of the plane of immanence meets up with the problems of historical events. The question of becoming clashes here with the question of the territorialization of the historic subject, and the question of historic determination clashes with the subjective production of the brain, or rather, with the singular production of the infinite, forever repeated, and the question of reterritorialization clashes with that of an ever more progressive deterritorialization. This process is the *revolutionary process*.

But to say that revolution is itself utopia of immanence is not to say that it is a dream, something that is not realized or that is only realized by betraying itself. On the contrary, it is to posit revolution as plane of immanence, infinite movement and absolute survey [...]. The word utopia therefore designates that conjunction of philosophy, or of the concept, with the present milieu—political philosophy [...]. It is not false to say that the revolution "is the fault of philosophers" (although it is not philosophers who lead it). That the two great modern revolutions, American and Soviet, have turned out so badly does not prevent the concept from pursuing its immanent path. As Kant showed, the concept of revolution exists not in the way in which revolution is undertaken in a necessarily relative social field but in the "enthusiasm" with which it is thought on an absolute plane of immanence, like a presentation of the infinite in the here and now, which includes nothing rational or even reasonable. The concept frees immanence from all the limits still imposed on it by capital (or that it imposed on itself in the form of capital appearing as something transcendent). However, it is not so much a case of a separation of the spectator from the actor in this enthusiasm as of a distinction within the action itself between historical factors and "unhistorical vapor," between a state of affairs and the event. As concept and as event, revolution is self-referential and enjoys a self-positing that enables it to be apprehended in an immanent enthusiasm without anything in states of affairs or lived experience being able to tone it down, not even the disappointments of reason. Revolution is absolute deterritorialization even to the point where this calls for a new earth, a new people (ibid., pp. 100–101).

Democracy is a tight fit for these new people. The present form of the democratic State, which wishes to present itself as the communicative *cogito* of the totality of its citizens, is weak and hypocritical. It perpetuates the capitalist stability and impedes every form of transformation. It is concept reduced to the level of opinion. The concept then sanctifies the present and empties any resistance to the present. While to resist is to create: "counter-effectuation," the reopening of pure becoming, affirmation of the event on the plane of immanence. Once again, irrelevance and untimeliness define the state of being.

Thus the political perspective gains meaning by joining itself to the ethical aperture of becoming. What then is the essence of the philosophical ethic? It lies in the creative occupying of the prephilosophical dimension, in the adherence (to an extreme) to the plane of immanence: ethics as *amor fati*, love of pure becoming.

There is a dignity of the event that has always been inseparable from philosophy as *amor fati*: being equal to the event, or becoming the offspring of one's own events—"my wound existed before me; I was born to embody it" (Joë Bousquet). I was born to embody it as event because I was able to disembody it as state of affairs or lived situation. There is no other ethic than the *amor fati* of philosophy. Philosophy is always meanwhile (ibid., p. 159).

The throw-back to Spinoza is not surprising. "Can the entire history of philosophy be presented from the viewpoint of the instituting of a plane of immanence?" (ibid., p.44). This Spinozist question is proposed as the red line of rupture in the history of philosophy, and the identification of modern choices. It is an *Exemplum* designed to fully illustrate and investigate creative choice in modernity; thus, in conclusion:

Spinoza was the philosopher who knew full well that immanence was only immanent to itself and therefore that it was a plane traversed by movements of the infinite, filled with intensive ordinates. He is therefore the prince of philosophers. [...] Will we ever be mature enough for a Spinozist inspiration? (ibid., p. 48).

Are we mature enough, then? Probably, with regard to this point, the combination of the theoretical motives that make up this picture opens itself up to more intense inspection. The ethic intersects ontology in order to make itself into political philosophy, political experience, or rather, philosophy and revolutionary experience. Singularity, by thrusting itself beyond the limits of theory, intersects each collective *agencement* presented by history, and takes possession of it through the overview of the concept, and at the same time singularity takes possession of the event, creating thus a new reality without removing this reality from the infinite. Ethics lives in the realm of the mutation of concept becoming event and it produces a new collective reality within singularity. The political appears here as a veritable entrepreneurship of being, as the social factory of the collective being, the construction of freedom by means of its mass expression. To add (or not) "communism" to this ontological qualification is only a question of terminology. The throw-back to Spinoza in the cultural phase of post-Marxism reveals itself here to be loaded with all the *enjeux* which the Marxist perspective left open. Will we be mature enough, then, in our practice of being, for a communist inspiration?

In book reviews, it is customary to indicate the *weak points* of the reasoning of the work under consideration. In this case, there seem to be two weak points. The first regards a possibly insufficient consideration of the scientific function and the absence of an analysis of its relationship with the structural technique in which it translates itself into an effective continuity. The partial observers present themselves here as engineers, and this transformation implies a specific relationship, a new relationship, between science and history, between science and event, between science and capitalism, which is neglected here, or at the very least, relegated to the background (in any case never achieving a clarity of the criticism of political institutions). What is not questioned is that *doxa* which operates within the scientific knowledge which renders it defenseless to the politics of armament, that knowledge which can offer its conquests to the destruction of the world. The second weak point regards those aspects of *geophilosophie*, or rather, the analysis of the creative territorializing of philosophy where a correct point of view—about the stratigraphic order of the course of history, about the grandiose moments of coexistence between different mental orders—seems to yield to the neutrality of a Braudelian development and to forget (or at least push aside) the antagonistic dimensions, the resistances, and the counter-implementations that lie at the origin of the dynamism of historicity (and also of the accumulation of its ontological residue—always reasonable, always tendential). The analysis of the characteristics of "national philosophies" ends up being particularly out of focus. The complete picture contradicts the ethical premises as well as the same methodology put into action in the building of the *Exempla*. Singularity, here as in the Braudelian School, seems at times flattened—antagonistic determination becomes suffocated by this singularity. The long-term suffocates the short-term, and history suffocates the event. If the perception of the historic cumulous (ontological) of the counter-effectuations is true, then, nonetheless, in this there must be evidence of a genealogy of antagonism, of plurality, of the revolution that fractures the geology of the present, yet expresses the irreducibility of becoming.

But this emphasizing of weak points bears little critical weight. They are points to be developed within a fully and substantially consistent metaphysical framework, weak points that continue to be important points of reference. This philosophy is in reality the strongest example of a "common philosophy" which presents itself, in modern times, as an alternative to modern capitalism. In its rigorous materialism it presents itself as common philosophy; in its search for absolute immanence it liquidates the postmodern. Now, this common philosophy must be compared to the new problems that it offers and reveals; it must counter-effectuate itself, its own self, in the face of the new social and political reality of the 21st century. It is the task of this philosophy to become a mime that counter-effectuates the new reality:

Such a mime neither reproduces the state of affairs nor imitates the lived; it does not give an image but constructs the concept. It does not look for the function of what happens but extracts the event from it, or that part that does not let itself be actualized, the reality of the concept. Not willing what happens, with that false will that complains, defends itself and loses itself in gesticulations, but taking the complaint and range to the point that they are turned against what happens so as to set up the event, to isolate it, to extract it in the living concept. Philosophy's sole aim is to become worthy of the event, and it is precisely the conceptual persona who counter-effectuates the event. Mime is an ambiguous name. It is he or she, the conceptual persona carrying out the infinite movement. Willing war against past and future wars, the pangs of death against all deaths, and the wound against all scars, in the name of becoming and not of the eternal: it is only in this sense that the concept gathers together (ibid., p. 159).

What then does it mean to mime the 21st century world? Deleuze and Guatttari leave this question hanging. Better yet, after having told us that the horizon is that of the revolution, after having demonstrated to us the outcomes of the ethical insurgence and having indicated to us the urgency of being and becoming, after having denounced the Rule of Law and the society of communication as current forms of despotism, and of imbecility, they pass on the baton. Who is the mime, the conceptual character who, in labor and in the collective imagination, in the 21st century, will proceed in a revolutionary direction? We believe this mime to be the *general intellect* of Marxian memory. In all probability, Deleuze and Guattari would agree.

10

Kaosmos

I am holding in my hands the latest book by Gilles Deleuze and Félix Guattari, *Qu'est-ce que la philosophie?* I want to discuss it; I do not want to join the fray of the philosophers who will study it attentively and who will say how and to what extent this book (important at first glance and after a second reading certainly worthy of being considered one of the crucial texts of philosophy of our century [completing the trilogy inaugurated by these two authors with *L'anti-Oedipe* and *Mille Plateaux*]) powerfully establishes the modern conception of philosophy and of metaphysics, reclaiming their value for the present day, beyond the perversions of the so-called post-modern ... No, I do not want to discuss it for this reason; I want to discuss it in order to identify in it the symptoms, expressed strongly, and almost violently, of a perception of our time, a perception which has become, for the mass of ordinary people, as general as it is desperate. Starting from this common perception of the world, the two authors interrogate themselves over the true function of philosophy.

We live in chaos: here lies the primary, fundamental content of the common perception of our time. A destructive chaos, inside which we cannot get our bearings:

Nothing is more distressing than a thought that escapes itself, than ideas that fly off, that disappear hardly formed, already eroded by forgetfulness or precipitated into others that we no longer master. These are infinite variabilities, the appearing and disappearing of which coincide, They are infinite speeds that blend into the immobility of the colorless and silent nothingness they traverse, without nature or thought. This is the instant of which we do not know whether it is too long or too short for time. We receive sudden jolts that beat like arteries (*What Is Philosophy?*, p. 201).

This is the chaos of our lives as people immersed in a meaningless horizon of communication, in the dispersion of reflection, in the confusion of a reproduction of the tangible that can no longer find a plan for restructuring itself. This morning, I open today's newspaper: an enormous photograph shows a crowd of exiles crammed on the dock of a Mediterranean port and another photograph shows this same enormous crowd transferred into a stadium reminiscent of Pinochet's Chile. On the next page I see homes destroyed by bombs and cannons; it could be Beirut or some village tucked away in the valley of the Slavic swath of the Danube. On the other pages of senseless blah-blah-blah journalists search for a reason for these horrifying images. I turn on the television and here are the same images, and the same blah-blah-blah, overlapping each other in a flash. Tomorrow similar images and violence will return from, I don't know, the ghettoes of America, the South African ghettoes and the desolate and famine-ridden outskirts of Iraqi cities. I open the newspaper again, I leave the news section and glance, longingly, at the cultural pages: in these pages we fing the triumph of the inessential and the contradictory. Chaos is presented here as something sought after, something appetizing, something enjoyable.

The intellectuals secrete weak thought, indifference multiplied to infinity, and thought reconciled with emptiness or its overabundance. Thought should be breezy; it should occupy itself only with not thinking about those things which it should be thinking about. Our body and our intelligence, so flattened upon this chaos and absorbed by it, become projected upon a thousand incoherent dimensions. I have my little daughter here next to me. She asks me about the things which she sees, the photos in the newspaper, the images on television. What can I tell her? How can I communicate to her something that might transcend the senselessness and the craziness that she perceives spontaneously? A destructive chaos within which we cannot find our way. A continuous reproducing of chaos, happening so quickly that memory and reflection are impossible. What is reality? The continuity of my perception is continuously broken. Every attempt to register an experience and make of it a common experience, every conversation, every reflection, all consumed by the absence of any protective rule; and delirium is the only horizon upon which the hope of self-preservation extends itself. The ordinary catastrophe is viewed as natural, that is, as a necessary development in the movements of society and the world. I continue reading the newspaper. Now I find an article in which the financial efforts of the great Western countries to put an end to the scourge of drugs are documented: but isn't it exactly this absurd world, and this communication gone crazy, that push us to taking drugs? As in certain "science fiction" novels, I ask myself if drugs are not the substance which the common consciousness requires in order to survive in this pandemonium.

Thus, Deleuze and Guattari lead us through the Hell of this world, and they interpret, in rough approximation, the disorientation and derailment of the common consciousness.

But their work does not stop at this desperate perception. Before "chaos," there is the "cosmos," the desire for order. In philosophy, in art, and in science we search desperately for this order. Once again, we do not concern ourselves here with following the refined analyses that these authors' critical epistemology offers us, the effort that they exert to reconstruct a horizon of hope based upon the construction of concepts, of beautiful works and operative transformations of the real. What we want to emphasize is how this desire, this hope, is alive in the common perception of the world, and how it must be possible to escape from this Hell. This seems like an impossible effort ... yet it is precisely this impossibility that reveals to us the effectiveness of this effort. It is the extreme difficulty of the effort of liberation, the harshness of the resistance and the primordial force of survival that reveal to us the road which, *in the* chaos, sets us *against* the chaos. Certainly that cosmos to which we aspire never looks this way. The age of Utopias has passed. But if the cosmos will not become our residence, there is a place where we can and must always be constructing, drawing out new being from chaos: the *Kaosmos*.

In the common perception of the world, under close scrutiny, this sentiment of the necessity of building something different from the chaos in which we are submerged exists with vigor. Certainly, the alternative lives in the realms of science, art, and philosophy; it lives on in the desire of each one of us, citizens of a common consciousness, to produce a new being, be it conceptual, artistic or scientific. But this new being is not disciplinary: it is not subject to rigid methodologies, nor is it confined to specific markets. On the contrary, creative desire brings together diverse experiences and then finds itself blended into life itself. Into the lives of individuals, but, even more to the point, into the life of the collective. Not into that of the collective as a separate entity from that of individuals, but into the individual collective of active citizens, capable of productive imagination. This common desire is an enormous force, Deuleuze and Guattari tell us. We do not need for philosophers to verify this; all we need is our common consciousness. It is the impossibility of resisting the chaos that propels the impossible search for the cosmos. It is the indecency of our current situation that pushes us in the direction of the miracle of a new kind of comfort. The common consciousness guarantees, in a calm manner, that the miracle is possible. A miracle that explodes every day, if we want it to, giving an ordered image to desire, to the urgency of leaving chaos behind.

Hope is an ordinary word. We need a kind of Franciscanism in order to enter into the 21st century. In the desperation which we inhabit, this extraordinary hope is obvious.

PART THREE

FROM THE END OF REALLY-EXISTING SOCIALISM TO THE GULF WAR

Political Statements I

1

Rereading Polybius and Machiavelli: With Regard to "Glasnost"

A few years ago, when the controversy surrounding the Soviet Union favored the use of the term "totalitarianism," it seemed that that world was more than just in a horrible state; it was immobile. We must now, I believe, strongly reprimand the users of this category "totalitarianism" (and dump on them the ill repute they had reserved for others), not so much because the Soviet world has become particularly gracious, but because the users of that term prevented us from understanding, in due time, the sense and significance of the political and social dynamics that made up the Soviet world. These days I have been reflecting upon the design of the new Soviet constitutional system: a large elective assembly made up of 2,250 people who, in turn, elect the Supreme Soviet, made up of 542 representatives and the president of this Supreme Soviet. This group then forms the Council of Ministers and its president. We are talking about a system of semi-indirect democracy, completely acceptable within the framework of Western democracies. Within this mechanism, it is also interesting to see that the 2,250 representatives of the Congress are elected, each by a third, within three large chambers: territorial districts (Soviet of the Union), social organizations and ethnic districts (Soviet of Nationalities). Representatives of the three chambers, in specified proportions, form the Supreme Soviet. I was asking myself: to what could this new form of Soviet government be compared? And right away I wondered if this were not a new expression of that "mixed government" in the tradition of Polybius, the ideal of which has run the course of the history of Western thought. In ancient times, as everyone knows, between Aristotle and Polybius, between Athens and Rome, a theory was formed that distinguished the three "good" forms of government (monarchy, aristocracy and democracy) from the three "bad" forms (tyranny, oligarchy, and demagogy or anarchy), and established two patterns of interaction between these two groups. The first pattern consisted of the cyclical and degenerative concept of development of forms of government which inevitably evolved into regimes, from monarchy to tyranny, from tyranny to aristocracy and then to oligarchy, and eventually to democracy: the final evolution was anarchy and from this the cycle started over again, in its original form of monarchy. The second pattern, as synchronic as the first outline was diachronic, considered, instead, the fortunate possibility that this cycle might be interrupted by a syncretic governmental figure, resulting from a combination of the three "good" forms of government. Imperial Rome should be the example of this perfect government, because within it, Caesar, the Senate and the popular assemblies organized their actions.

Now, asking my reader to pardon me for this long digression, it seemed I could precisely conclude that in this new Soviet Constitution there is a hint of traits of "mixed government." The monarchic power of the party and of its Secretary General combines with the democratic power resulting from the district electoral chambers, and with the aristocratic power that emanates from social organizations (corporate, scientific, and productive). The comparison could be brought further along if one considers that the analyses of the structure of class relations and bureaucratic appropriation lead us to consider the representatives of the social organizations (holders of the economic power in both business and in large administrations) as representatives of a true and real aristocracy. While, somewhat amazed, I lingered over these conclusions, another nagging question presented itself to me (but no less ironically): should this too be compared to the Polybius model? What then is the prevailing form of government in our industrial democracies? I did not think, in my answer, that I could go very far from the affirmation that, here too, a "mixed government" is the one that prevails. A democratic component, organized in universal suffrage, serves as the source of legitimization for the regime and as the instrument of the formation of elective bodies. From the democratic component another one is formed materially, which we can, without insult, describe as aristocratic, one which takes form within the big industrial and institutional administrations (including the political parties) and which increasingly expresses itself in its control over the "media." It is true that what is missing, at first glance, is the monarchic power: in fact, it is certainly not our Kings, more than constitutional, who can, even if residually, personify that capacity of leadership and of decision-making (as a last resort) which true monarchic power emblematically represents. But this formal shortcoming—we must admit to this—is more of a defect, in our regimes, and a mystification than a sign of radical democracy: many believe, in fact, even without suspecting an Orwellian "Big Brother," that among us, somewhere, there exists a fundamental and effective system of protection for the current hierarchy of political and social power: a monarchic power, therefore, be it a power that can be assimilated into the guarantee of international relationships which arms and defends the Western world, or be it a power identifiable in the rules of the economic and monetary order that support it. Then all the better to reveal it, not for the pleasure of classifying the constitutional charters more easily according to the models of Hellenic Antiquity, but to have, here at home, a little more "Glasnost." All the more so since, if we were to take seriously those theories of "totalitarianism" which we had rejected, and which we now mock (which, however, brought so much obscurity to our intelligent understanding of history), then we should absolutely label as "totalitarian" a regime that conceals the nature of its own ultimate effective guarantee.

Thus, rather than the regimes of "Perestroika," is it the Western democracies that are totalitarian? We are evidently dealing with a paradox here. Except that, remaining close to Polybius, we cannot forget the other aspect of his theory and his concerns relative to the evolving rhythm of forms of the State. Why not ask ourselves, then, if, in the Soviet Union, the transition from tyranny to democracy does not subject the constitutional and social structures of that country, and its "mixed government," to the possibility of optimism, in the sense of participation of society in government, of a *politeia*, that is, a *politeia* in which lies one of profound drives of our civilization? And why not question, on the other hand, whether the constitutional apathy on the part of Western democracies and their devolution into a non-participatory dynamics, do not reveal symptoms of a degenerative development? In this case, does the "mixed government" not represent a constitutional pattern propelled toward oligarchic, corporate and demagogic solutions within which secret shiftings and illegal interests, be they economic or power driven, take the place of democracy? But at the end of the day, this problem is not new. Already in 1512, Niccolò Machiavelli, who was writing his *Book on Republics*, came to ask himself in what manner, in corrupt cities, could one preserve a free State? He abruptly interrupted his work on this book, and wrote *The Prince*. Many interpretations of this famous little book have been offered. The most likely, and it is for this reason that I allude to the work of Machiavelli, is that he wanted to express the idea that the free city of Florence and the new Italian nation would not have been possible, had there not been a new "constituent power," a new force capable of creating a radical new foundation for civic life. Is this not possibly the situation in which we find ourselves now? As much in the countries of the East as in our own country? Where is the "Machiavellian moment" today?

2

Euro Disney and Tiananmen

On television, in the past few weeks and months, we have seen some exceptional things. Tiananmen Square, above all. A formidable spectacle made up of huge crowds of individuals shouting the word "freedom." Incredible acts of heroism, a lone man blocking a procession of tanks, pale youths on a hunger strike, standing exhausted behind microphones, speaking words of revolt and solidarity, crowds circling military trucks, keeping them from repressive action, and then bicycles, and then more bicycles, and young people running to lend their strong hands, to demonstrate the democratic power of a multitude awakened from its sleep of oppression. A liberating imagination in action. Then, after a few weeks, comes the bicentennial of the French Revolution. Here too, crowds—but how different! Here the ceremony was "royal," the spectacle carefully choreographed, the faces of the leaders of the seven super-powers of the earth seemed benevolent and compliant, in front of and within this enormous mass of subjects. There was no event to speak of, only the product of a colossal industrial machine. The spectacle was perfect, the separation between the appearance of the popular masses and the appearance of the masters of the earth all perfectly studied, almost natural, and in any case, linear and necessary. This celebration of power had the perfection of long-ago parades in Red Square; or rather, the much more sophisticated perfection of that celebration shown on television a few years ago: that of the bicentennial anniversary of the American Constitution. Let us remember that, even in that instance, the big machine produced products that were all natural, the style half-way between that of an American musical comedy from the Forties and Japanese war films: Reagan's profile always present in the shots celebrating the marine who planted the flag on top of Iwo Jima, and Mitterand playing his part in a dance reminiscent of *An American in Paris*. Such is life! Yet there is a difference, there is an enormous difference between Tiananmen and light-hearted Paris ... there is, and there must be.

The European Commission is multiplying its legislation in anticipation of the enactment of the Single European Act of 1992. No one knows anything about this. Instead, we all know that in 1990 the world cup of soccer will take place in Italy, that in 1992 the Olympics will be held in Barcelona, and that between now and 1992, a Disneyland, larger than the one in Los Angeles, will open at Marne-la-Vallée, near Paris.

Europeans are being called upon to celebrate the big due date for unity in a festive atmosphere. We can imagine, but never will we imagine it enough, what the European television stations will make of the festivities that await us. They will make up the climate of our life, we will speak of nothing else, and we will live immersed in this sea of representations. The faces of power will appear, systematically, in the continuous spectacle promised to us. Our free time will naturally be taken up in this continuous party through which the celebration of power will reproduce itself. When, already twenty years ago, Guy Debord was writing his prophetic *Society of the Spectacle*, he could not have imagined this immediate translation of the ways of spectacle into registers of power: it is the post-modern that has gifted us this novelty. It is American industry that has produced it for world use. Television, what a formidable instrument of pleasure! Television is celebration. But, is it really? I think about the notion of celebrating in the *Ancien régime*: it was saved by its own ambiguity, part religious, part barbaric, part domination and part liberation. The gentleman who announced the festivities and those members of the bourgeoisie who organized them—it was they themselves who were ridiculed and, in the course of the festi-vities, were brought down to equal ground. The celebration was one single moment of freedom—just one moment, but no less effective. But what remains now that could be called liberating in the television celebration? The possibility of liberation deriving from the celebra-tion is as small as the possibility of our direct participation in it. The television screen guides us, its journalists and actors train us: we are being duped into thinking that we are the ones enacting the scene. It doesn't matter, because there is no limit to the expansion of tele-vision pleasure. The Eastern countries ask for nothing more than to be able to hook up with the big Western channels, and even the most precious and fragile temples of our cultural tradition must be opened up to the making of television extravaganzas: thus, Pink Floyd alights in Piazza San Marco, and anyone against this idea is accused of being against modernity and against the masses having fun. No, really, this is all totally crazy ...

On the other end of the spectrum is Tiananmen. Nobody doubts that a yearning for freedom was at the bottom of what came to pass. But was there not also celebration? Certainly: and we saw it, beforehand, right alongside the tragedy. We saw it in the smiling faces of the young people who experienced this kind of event for the first time, who created it.

We witnessed it in the happy cries of the crowd which had peacefully surrounded the troops. The flags and the kites. The muted colors of everyday Chinese life were bursting with splendor. The multitude had discovered *pietas*, that sweet understanding of the individuality of others, which brings the masses to life, and which gave a brief moment of joy to life. Hope, that is what was witnessed in the square. Freedom and joy produced the celebration. And even after the tragedy exploded and repression won the day, along with horror, the image of that joy remained with us, something indestructible that still lives on in our consciousness. The knowledge that in this world, the multitudes will always seek freedom and justice.

We are now approaching a united Europe. Will victory go to State television networks, to their programming of a public space in which the participation and the joy of liberty are anesthetized and nullified? Everything leads to this conclusion. Will this Europe become merely a big market for big capital and its big finance system, a big market of images that take away the flavor of life? Everything is sliding towards this outcome. Unless … unless there is a big cultural and political awakening. This awakening will have to be based on our desire; it will have to superimpose itself upon images like those of Tiananmen. Ours is an absolute desire for freedom and for justice. Television does have one merit, an enormous merit: it raised the distinction between celebration as moment of domination and celebration as moment of liberation to a level of absoluteness. In the *Ancien régime*, these two moments could coexist. Today the separation, the contradiction, between Euro Disney and Tiananmen is absolute. This statement is tragic because nothing, absolutely nothing, proves to us that we can predict a return of the masses to political participation in freedom.

We are totally aware of this. But perhaps it is from the depth of this desperation that the untimely becomes possible. It is because of this desperation that we can, in a full and absolute manner, think back on the splendor of the event and transform our singular imagination into a narrative of a new world of freedom. A simple line of escape? Perhaps, but the contrivances, projects and strategies have used up their energy. They have imposed upon us the absolute: we must seize upon this absolute.

3

Eastern Europe between Capitalist Restoration and Constituent Power

Coming home recently from the Soviet Union, where he had been summoned by a group of constitutionalists, Robert Badinter, current president of the Constitutional Council of the Republic of France, and former Minister of Justice in various socialist governments, declared that he had been struck "by the atmosphere and by the effervescence of a constituent" reigning in Moscow. His interlocutors had shown him, he added, a state of mind that was completely open and a profound desire to form "a socialist Rule of law," to "shape public freedoms and to stake out a new space for freedom." On the other hand, liberal propaganda exhausts itself daily by repeating that socialism is dead, and that the only possibility for the people who were implicated in it is to embrace the liberal creed and practice market capitalism. These are positions which, at times, are taken up by the most radical leaders of the struggle against "really-existing socialism"— if it is true that Walesa believes that his country can rise up again only through capitalist repossession of that 90% of property that currently belongs to the State in Poland. If we compare the positions of Badinter, a man certainly above suspicion of sympathizing with the Soviet Regime, with those of Walesa, a man respected for leading the struggle, at one time, we cannot avoid being struck by the difference in their points of view. On one hand, we have a "socialist market economy," on the other, a capitalist market; on one hand, reform, on the other, restoration; on one hand, constituent power, on the other, the writing of the rules and regulations of liberal democracy.

The alterative could not be more drastic—the same for the perplexity of Western people, whatever their political alignments may be. So much so that the contrast becomes positively paradoxical when, beyond every ideological opposition, we hear Western entrepreneurs express and repeat words of caution of every sort regarding requests for economic intervention, direct or indirect, on the Eastern markets. We are dealing with a very high-risk situation—they insist—it is useless to dream of Marshall Plans until a series of problems, unsolved as of yet, are resolved. And the fundamental problem is the monetary one—the problem, that is, concerning a guarantee of balance between price and cost, integrated into the capitalist world market, capable of supporting international competition, and therefore still, at the point at which the socialist economies have arrived, a very radical industrial restructuring, a new politics of public spending and, above all, a reestablishment of the organization and the discipline of labor. In recent weeks, Jacques Delors has declared himself the authoritative spokesperson of this new position: not excluding direct help, nevertheless, he has emphasized the current problem, a problem of enormous dimensions, whose solution and whose incomparable social cost can only be decided by the people who are now liberating themselves from Stalinism. This means that the path to regaining democracy and determining whether it will be liberal or socialist, the path to reconstructing a productive and effective economy, and to deciding whether it will be private, public or mixed, cannot be defined amid querulous or violent requests for help—this path must be travelled by people who will test and complete it. And only by them. These little truths risk, nonetheless, appearing banal if they are not supported by some other consideration raised directly by the course of events, and by reflection upon the ideological struggle currently underway. Thus I wish to insist on two or three hypotheses, the clarification of which will perhaps render more credible the conjecture on the autonomous and democratic success of those countries seeking to free themselves from Stalinism. The first hypothesis is that of the theoretical inefficiency of considering the distinction between capitalism and socialism as being absolute. In reality, immediately after its acute revolutionary phase, and most often in its ideological precursors, socialism was interpreted as a means for accelerating capitalist accumulation in countries that had been excluded from it since the beginning of this civilization of ours. Socialism thus became confused with the modernization of these countries and from this modernization it gained its constituent element, particularly in times of repeated demands for innovation. I mean to say that, in all probability, on the one hand, many elements of socialism not only are not considered foreign to capitalism, but are indeed functional to capitalism; on the other hand, consequently, its impact upon a higher level of modernization cannot but reveal the irreversibility of certain thresholds of socialism. Conversely, the struggle against the intolerable levels of bureaucratic power in the name of socialism in the East is analogous to the protest, ever-growing in the West, against the equally intolerable transformation of capitalism into technocracy and financial bureaucracy—always in the name of socialism. The second hypothesis consists of considering the false logic of the opposition between totalitarianism and democracy. Unfortunately it is not so easy to consider the good and the bad as complete opposites: the childishness of the interpretative categories has banged its nose up against the explosion of vitality from societies (precisely like those of the socialist block) which the systems of power considered to have reached their capacity. In effect, the energy of the people and the correctness of their political system are not measured by metaphysical instruments or by legal forms: it is a movement of society that, even when defeated, as in Stalinist Russia, always reappears, and, through thousands of forms of resistance and refusal, makes reaching the capacity of power impossible. I ask myself whether this passion for the political, for participation, for the liberation of the constituent force of a society, is not more alive in the socialist countries which are moving away from so-called totalitarianism, than in our own democratic countries, so satisfied with their formally democratic hypocrisy. I ask myself whether this constituent power that lives in situations which were until yesterday completely unknown to us (and the responsibility of the Western "media" should not be underestimated here) is not itself an economic power that disrupts the simple facts of a naïve opposition between socialism and capitalism. Thus the hypothesis, or if you will, the conjecture, on a potential renewal soon to come—not in terms of a pitiful request for help and of the reproduction of capitalist models, but in the sense of a true and real exercise of renewal, of the effectiveness of constituent power.

My third and resulting hypothesis is that, if not in all the socialist countries, certainly in the Soviet Union and maybe in some other countries, the relationship between revolution from above and revolution from below (to put it in Gramsci's terms, between passive revolution and active revolution) is still highly problematic: in other words, the relationship between the direction of the CPSU (Communist Party of the Soviet Union) and the hierarchy of the administration on the one hand, and, on the other, the movements of civic society, is not totally closed off, but still, with all probability, strongly dialectical and functional. Can an effective constituent power define itself in this situation?

4

We Are All Berliners

"Wir sind alle Berliner." Never as much as today has John F. Kennedy's appeal rung so true. The grotesque, shameful, savage wall of Berlin has at last materially fallen. Along with this powerful symbol, an entire world collapses, the world in which we have always lived, the world of Yalta: that dazed world, which for forty years allowed power, in the West and in the East, to blackmail the people in a spectacularly inverted way, to entrap them with comparable disciplinary chains, to turn war into an element indistinguishable from peace. To Yalta we owe: the repression of the antifascist worker movement in Europe and in North America during the post-war years, and at the same time, the Stalinist destruction of nascent democracy in the Eastern countries; the tolerance for Francoism and Salazarism until the stench of their decay polluted the air everywhere, and in the East the perseverance of Mongolian regimes of repression and misery; the dreadful survival of colonialism and racism in the West, the expansion of Soviet imperialism, and the destruction of the revolution of 1968, in both the West and the East.

As the Berlin wall collapses, Yalta collapses. This upheaval of world history is produced by a revolution, the first non-archaic revolution, and non–19th century revolution; rather, this revolution is replete with all the signs of contemporary times. A mass of individuals, of informal groups, a wave of mass pacifist rebellion, a gigantic gathering of independent culture and grass roots democracy, a modern need for cooperation and communication, a new productive force. A victorious Tiananmen. In Berlin we do not confront the regressive forces of the revolution of Polish Catholics or the dialectal elements of the revolution of Hungarian business-men: legitimate revolutions, but limited in spirit and in scope, locked within an unfinished temporality. Berlin is the *tabula rasa* of the past and the opening to all the possibilities of the future. The passage from tyranny to democracy was embraced by a modern pop-ulation of highly qualified, specialized workers, of mass intellectuals, of people who experience freedom as a condition of their own work as well as of their own existence. This anthropo-logical rejection of tyranny is identified with the most meaningful symbol of the political condition of contemporary man, the Berlin Wall. By destroying it, the Berliners liberate us from a drift of his-tory which, at that point, presented itself as metaphysical; they intervene on the obscure foundation of our language, and they give back to us the ability to identify the intolerable.

The evidence of these events is offensive to many. The untimely and counter-effective nature of these events is such that they are so unexpected and unthinkable that they cause a disturbed and incredulous reaction—not only on the part of the diplomatic chancelleries and the organs of information, but also on the part of ordinary opinion. There is no passion more difficult to communi-cate than that of hope—above all for disenchanted people like ourselves, the people of 1968, the people who attempted a revolu-tion and failed. How can this incredible revolutionary process of the East continue? Up to what point will the tanks keep their distance? What is the staying power of *perestroika*? We have no answer for any of these questions. But there is one thing which we can absolutely say: a great transformation, possibly a revolution, has again arrived from the East and it has planted itself into the heart of the West. That lighthouse of Red Square, which so tragically went dark, now throws out fleeting but strong beams of intelligence. Capitalist gerontocracy is in the grip of unstoppable shock. Blinded by a monetarist and liberal ideology, it does not know how to respond to the provocation of imagination, nor to the new insurgence of a society, which, up to now, had been obliterated from the order of eventual possibilities. We ourselves, the people of 1968, do not understand that our defeats can now be sublimated on a new horizon, the horizon of the practice of freedom. But then why not modify the context of our discussion? Why, instead of repeating masochistic rhetoric, do we not ask ourselves: Is there a revolution? Is there a tiger? Who will ride it? Will Gorbachev ride the tiger? Maybe. But the Berliners are the tiger. The tiger is a constituent power. Something that rises up from nothing in order to propose a new social order. From the time when Soviet *perestroika* first began, we have all been realistically asking ourselves if it will become the restoration of capitalism, or the beginning of a constituent power that organizes a new synthesis between freedom and socialism. With Berlin, the game shifts: we ask that question not only to the Soviets but also to ourselves. With the shattering of the perverse mirror effect of Yalta, we have both the inversion and the generalization of the question. Whether Gorbachev holds on to power or not is, at this point, relatively unimportant. What is important is that the themes put forth in this phase of the dissolution of the *Ancien régime* have presented themselves in a manner that is irreversible.

It is upon the irreversibility of these new revolutionary realities, and not upon the eventual continuity in the ranks of a transitional government, that we must focus. It is imperative that East Germans hold on to the power they have gained for themselves, and that they be allowed to decide on a political regime of their choice. It is essential that all Berliners engage in dialogue and together exert both critical and constituent power. This dialogue must take place throughout Europe. None of us can claim that we never asked ourselves, even in the face of the ideological *débacle* of Stalinism and the disintegration of social ties within Eastern bloc countries, if the Western model was feasible for those countries. Certainly, things go well here from an economic point of view: but at what price? And up to what point? And, does the economic wellbeing compensate us for an ever more significant disintegration of social ties and for such an intensified crisis of thought and hope? No, we too have an equally urgent need for a jump-start of renewal. The attempt to construct a new sociality is not an undertaking to be left to the people of Eastern Europe. *Wir sind alle Berliner*. We are all, Western and Eastern, in the same boat. The demise of Yalta is a historic occasion—one of those rare occasions that occur in the political life of nations. Berlin represents an exceptional historic acceleration in the life of humanity. Suddenly, at the wrong moment, as happened in 1968, the sky has fallen into our hands. Previously concealed problems, new figures of collective subjectivity and scenarios of hope and of constitution, have appeared. Is it possible for us to avoid adding our own blow of the hammer to the destruction of the Wall?

Recently I was reading an article, published in *Literaturnaia Gazeta*, by two distinguished Soviet academics, Igor Kljamkin and Adranik Migranjan. Their argument, based upon the most respected model of American political science, consisted in demonstrating that the USSR is unable to simultaneously conduct economic reform (the creation of a market economy) and political reform (the creation of democratic institutions). In order to bring about democracy in the future, a democratic and enlightened dictatorship is necessary at present so as to save the country from chaos and catastrophe. Even George Bush and the majority of Western democrats (of this I am certain) are convinced of this. On the other hand, we, like the Berliners, believe that only freedom, only constituent power, can rebuild the Commune.

5

On the Difference between Socialism and Communism

The distinction between the concept of socialism and that of communism was trivial knowledge for old-style militants. Socialism was the economic-political regime based upon the maxim "from each according to his ability, to each according to his contribution." Communism was that system in which "from each according to his ability, to each according to his needs" held sway. Socialism and communism represented two different stages in the revolutionary journey, the first characterized by the socialization of the goods of production and by the political administration of transition; the second was characterized by the extinction of the State and by spontaneity in managing the economy and power.

If this distinction was clear to the old-style communist activists, today, on the contrary, in this period of the disintegration of "really-existing socialism," this distinction has disappeared, and communism and socialism are easily confused. This is the result of a hostile homologation which is carried out by the enemies of socialism, by means of the brutal eradication of everything socialist in the world starting from 1917, in Eastern Europe and the Third World alike. It is clear that these easily accomplished eradications are supported by favorable conditions. In the socialist Eastern bloc countries, during these last forty years, the ideological mystification, the bureaucratic fraud, and theoretical cynicism have represented the only forces legitimating power, and this process could not avoid producing radical phenomena of rejection. How could we have expected that "the radiant future" promised by Communism would not be discredited in societies which were socialist in name only, but bureaucratic in fact, societies in which utopia was consumed by the concealing of the real?

This having been said, let us return to the concepts and to their history, in order to observe that they are not reducible, with all probability, to present day polemics and to current eradications. Communism, in fact, for about a century and a half now, since the establishment of that "League of Communists" that operated with Marx as its guide in the middle of the 19th century, is without a doubt the central political ideology of modernity. Unlike the old utopias, this ideology bases itself on the real analysis and examination of the mechanism of capital accumulation from the worker's perspective. Through the scientific appropriation of the economic-social dynamic of the capitalist system, which lives and grows only by taking advantage of the work force, the party of the working class can plan the strategy and tactics of a communist perspective, with the objectives of destroying the mechanism of capitalist accumulation and of seizing political power. Up to this point it is Marx who provides an extraordinary scientific apparatus for this plan of action.

Thus the subsequent translation of the theoretical Marxian analysis on the level of concrete revolutionary mobilization within the new terms of European capitalism, at the beginning of the new century, and from a very close perspective of radical instability within the various political and social balances of power. This is the job that Lenin takes on. It leads him, at the beginning of the 20th century, to elaborate the organizing principles of a new type of party, the "Bolshevik Communist Party," the avant garde sector of the working class. This sector breaks away from purely union-based economics, from opportunistic and anarchic spontaneity and from the legal procedures of the class warfare of the parties of the Second International; it presents itself as a specific, pliable and disciplined instrument for seizing power and establishing a dictatorship of the proletariat. The dictatorship's objective is the establishment of socialism, that is, the nationalization of the goods of production and the establishment of a centralized planning system. But all this must take place within a radical democratic process of participation, a transition which simultaneously determines the conditions of economic growth for all and dissolves the central power and rights of the State, as well as of the Rule of law, bestowing riches and freedom upon the citizens.

The Leninist conception of the party and of the revolutionary transition is contested from within the left wing of the international workers' movement, both at the time of the 1905 revolution, and after the revolution of 1917, by Rosa Luxemburg. For her, the organizing principle presents itself as a process which (while permanently challenging, in the workplace, both unions and the Reformist party, with labor delegation and the growth of struggles) coincides with ever increasing levels of worker spontaneity and with the specific political institutions generated from that spontaneity, such as the "Soviets" in Russia in 1905 and in 1917, or the "labor councils" in Germany in 1918-19. Instead, Lenin holds that the tendency towards the self-organization of struggling workers cannot directly foreshadow the party, since the political revolutionary direction must dominate all levels of spontaneity, outside of individual struggles, with the fundamental goal of a dictatorship of the proletariat.

Is it, then, that the crisis of leadership of socialist power, after the success of the insurrection and the seizing of power, finds its origin in this contradiction and in this alternative between Luxemburg and Lenin, between a concept of communism as a constituent democracy of the masses in struggle, or, conversely, as a dictatorship of the proletariat? Many communists (because there are still many of them in the world) think so, and it is probable that the renewal of the subversive movement in the coming decades (because it is obvious that it will rise up again) will have to revisit those discussions.

But there are other problems which, in the current state of crisis of communist discourse and in the face of the disintegration of "really-existing socialism," may again become central to the discussion.

The events in Russia, beginning with the dilemmatic debate that followed the death of Lenin, hold, in particular, a great deal of interest here.

The Soviet political debate at the time was concentrated on the choice between the theses of "permanent revolution" and "socialism in one country only," considered in the context of their compliance to Leninism and to the significance of the October Revolution. Leon Trotsky, strenuous defender of the "permanent revolution" as a revolutionary resurrection against the process of bureaucratization of both the State and of the party, yielded in the face of the supporters of "socialism in one country only," for whom the unequal development in the capitalist countries, the uniqueness of the proletarian victory on the most delicate rung of the imperialist chain, and therefore the construction of "socialism in one country only," constituted the obligatory path. From the latter group, the figure of Stalin emerges fairly quickly as the ruthless executor of this undertaking, through the extreme centralization of the party and the omnipotence of the repressive administrative apparatus. The distance between the Marxian theory of class struggle against the capitalist system and the practice of the construction of socialism widens without limits: paradoxically, communism, defined by Marx as "the real movement which abolishes the present state of things," becomes the productive activity that creates, whatever the cost, the base materials of industrial society in competition with the rhythm of its own development and with that of capitalist countries. Socialism does not identify so much with the overcoming of the system of capital and that of salaried labor, as it does with being a socio-economic alternative to capitalism.

Can we, therefore, state here that the current crisis of "really-existing socialism" is nothing more than the crisis of socialist management of capital? That this crisis, therefore, has nothing to do with a possible crisis in communism? We could state this, if, paying heed to the lessons of a century and a half of the history of the communist revolution, we were to restate, as strongly as possible, the distinction between socialism and communism. Socialism is nothing other than one of the forms in which capital can be organized and administered—so much so that today the majority of the advanced capitalist countries have economic systems in which a socialist component is extremely strong. Communism is the form in which society can be organized after the destruction of the capitalist system, that is to say, after the destruction of class systems and exploitation, and through the eradication of the organizing role of the State, from above and throughout society. In addition, we must insist on the fact that it is absolutely not true that socialism is a phase, or an instrument, in transition towards communism: if anything, historically, the opposite has always occurred, and that is, that the most savage forms of economic and political oppression were experienced under "really-existing socialism," and that the so-called "new socialist" was nothing more than a perfected work horse. Communism, as Marx teaches, is born directly from class antagonism, from the rejection of labor and its organization, whether within the bourgeois model of labor or within the Socialist one. We can now revisit the new modalities of antagonism and rejection in Western Europe; but, above all, in Eastern Europe, we see them in the crisis of "really-existing socialism."

It is on account of this that the revolution in the Eastern bloc countries offers us such a formidable incentive for engaging in this discussion and in militant communist action. The distinction between the concepts of "socialism" and "communism" thus becomes trivial again, but in the way in which they contrast with one another, and not in the way in which they are confused with one another. This is because socialism is nothing other than one of the forms of capitalist management of the economy and of power; communism, on the other hand, is an extremely radical economic-political democracy and a search for freedom.

6

The Consequences of the "End of History"

Not much time has passed since, after the end of the "Cold War,"
Francis Fukuyama (an important collaborator of Reagan and Bush)
assured us that "History was over." The "American model" had
definitively won; History could not present alternatives to that. Just
as in 1807, when Georg Wilhelm Friedrich Hegel, from his post at
Jena, had been able to see the model of civil bourgeoisie society put
an end to History, so also at the current stage, from his post in
Washington, Fukuyama was gambling with his new de facto judgment: the "American way of life," the global imperialist order, and
the force of international law personified by the power of the multinationals make up the definitive configuration of the world. Surely
one cannot say that Hegel's prediction was proven by History: the
19th century was filled with extraordinary events, revolutionary
events that exercised their influence and cast their light at least half
way into the 20th century. Nevertheless, the Hegelian affirmation
has been far from ineffectual. The de facto judgment quickly transformed itself into a prescriptive judgment, and was used as such.
Consequently, each proposition that might have posed the problems
inherent in the transformation was immediately considered utopian,
unattainable, fanatical. If History—by chance—had not ended, it
was imperative to make it end. The Hegelian error became the base

of all the fascisms of the 19th and 20th centuries. Fukuyama, less protected from the irony of his contemporaries than Hegel had been from the irony of his, also had no more luck than Hegel— few took his de facto judgment seriously. To declare the American triumph as irreversible in the moment in which a recession is looming, in which the moral and cultural decline of the United States is ever more acutely felt, and Europe is shaping up to be a big power, the Soviet Union is modernizing, etc.—evidently that declaration was excessive. Perhaps for these same reasons the prescriptive implications of the de facto judgment expressed by Fukuyama is proving to be full of force, even insane, even more than the Hegelian predictions had ever been. Today the entire American ruling class seems to be prisoner of the conviction that "History is over" and seems aggressively willing to make that illusion come true. Every doubt, every form of resistance, every negation is immediately defined as insanity, aberration, fanaticism.

The Gulf war is growing before our eyes. We are witnessing a paradoxical *replay* of the Iranian revolution and the hopes that it raised among the Arab masses, before it was repressed by those same people who are today in charge. I will not repeat Foucault's mistake (and a mistake it was, even if it came out of a profound sense of History)—when the Iranian revolution had just begun and he supported it without reservation. This is not my problem today, and most likely it will not be my problem tomorrow. I do not wish to, nor can I, delve into Saddam Hussein's arguments because the sense of justice, which at times I do feel running through his words and actions, becomes incomprehensible and repugnant in the face of other words and actions. But this is not my problem. My problem is that of a denizen of the Western world, dumbfounded by the fact that History is not over, surprised by the fact that there is any desire to want it to end at all costs, aware of certain sufferings and certain miseries, of certain inequalities and certain injustices—and over there, in the Middle East, all these tribulations cannot be contained—all of which cannot be stopped by armed incursions or by propaganda wars. For me, at this point, it has become evident that the provisional end to the conflict between the West and the East has not shut down History and that, to the contrary, it has brought to light a new conflict, called North versus South. For how long can a territorial order inherited from colonialism challenge History? For how long can an unequal redistribution of wealth continue to favor the old rulers? For how long can History, or the "the pursuit of happiness" (to use the language of the old liberals), remain off-limits for those who have been excluded from it?

On the other hand, I am not so naive as to not believe that the goal of "putting an end to History" is armed, and that this enormous armament has a chance of winning. The revolutionary optimism of Mao and of Ho Chi Minh is by now far from our thoughts and far from our feelings. I do not believe that History is easily re-set into motion. It seems to me almost impossible that the South can win a battle against the North: actually, it seems absolutely impossible to me. Yet History marches on. They are the ones who create History, I say to myself. And they will be defeated ...

But what is this geographic merry-making of mine, this fitting the sense of History and its incredibly violent problem into a network of parallels and meridians? I find myself lost in my new profession as analyst of the points of the compass. Yet, going from being lost to being capable of reflection is just one small step. If the great masses of immigrants, who live here among us, I ask myself, were to discuss History, what would happen? And where would I stand? With them or against them? And through their experience, where would History take me? Or, where would it take me again? Maybe to a certain point on the compass? No, not really. The only point to which History always returns, and which always opens History up again, is the point of the struggle between exploiter and exploited, and the only choice which History offers is that of taking sides. If History is not over, this does not mean that we are being pushed to choose West over East, or North over South, or the reverse; rather, it means that we are being pushed to declare what side we are on within the terrain of the daily reality of our worldly experience: on the side of the exploiters or on the side of the exploited. It is not up to me alone to decide; it is up to every one of us to decide at what formidable point an event opens up to History.

Thus there is the risk that History is not over, better yet, that it will unfold again not only in the deserts of Arabia but in the heart of Western metropolises. There is the risk that History might rediscover its old taste for routine, for decisive choices, and for that sense of the intolerable that always nurtures ethics and heroism. But is it war, therefore, that reveals History? If it were, our misery would be greater than that of the last poor denizen of this miserable world. No, it is not war that reveals History: war's only goal is to put an end to History. The millions of armed men, the most refined technological products, the aircraft carriers and the "desert scuds" are not going to open up History; rather, they are destined for the horrible task of ending it. But their ultimate effect could be that of reopening History to our conscience: and then what purpose would war serve?

Other philosophers, often esteemed philosophers, reacted to the "end of History" predicted by Hegel by saying that the triumph of civil society represented only the "end of the pre-history" of humanity. Today their hope is renewed.

7

The Philosophical Consequences of the Gulf War

Reflections on a War, Which, as I Write This, Has Not Yet Begun

1. The sound of war is selective: certain voices come through, exhilarated by it, while other voices fall silent. The voices opposing the logic of the war today are inessential and distant: they are not even identifiable (pacifist? communist? ecological? feminist?); they are left to flounder at the margins where no one listens to them. The debate is non-existent; the spectacle of power is totalitarian. Opinion polls replace discussion: this has almost always been the case, but today opinion polls have lost even the veneer of offering any alternatives. Twenty years of "weak thought" are taking their toll: the instrumental rationality of the politicians, of the generals, of the opinion-makers, cuts through this thought like a knife through rotten cheese. There is no danger for the limp thinkers: they have already jumped ship; their language is strong now, determined, war-like indeed: it is necessary to defend the civilization which, until very recently, was characterized by the death of ideologies and entrusted to the flexible and airy void of post-everything.

The sound of war is pervasive. Cynicism and ecstatic Machiavellianism rejoice in apodictic and definitive affirmations. Nothing limp is left: moribund historicism rediscovers its splendors by exalting the right to go to war, by re-defining civilization's destiny, and the contrite souls who, trembling, used to search for Jehovah, today have rediscovered him as god of the armies. War fascinates, the amalgam rules: as it did in 1939 in the form of anti-fascism, as it did in the post-war period in the form of anti-communism, and as it does today in the form of anti-Islamism. Without adding that in 1939 those same characters were Petain sympathizers, and in the post-war period they were Stalinists: so, today, where does the warrior Muse come from? We believe that the free voice of philosophy must rise up against these monstrosities of propaganda and reclaim the ethical terrain of criticism. Against unanimity, against folly, against any logic of war, it is possible to resist. Now is the time for serious thinking, the time for criticism, not for war. In solitude, if necessary.

2. The facts are clear. By occupying an independent State, detestably taking civilians as hostages, and shattering the laws of diplomacy, Iraq has broken the international order. On the other hand, it is clear that Iraq's actions are founded upon economic and territorial claims that are, to a large extent, legitimate; that its action reveals the scandal of a colonial order based on the legitimization of medieval traditions, determined by the interests of the oil multinationals; that its call for equal treatment under international law is unanswered as compared to the situation of other territorial crises in the same geographic region. It is also clear that the Iraqi internal political order is perversely dictatorial: not unlike the internal political order of its neighboring countries. We could continue to speak at length about comparing the equal (and opposing) injustices across the region. But to what end? The raw facts explain nothing; they fall within an utterly evil infinity and constitute an inextricable sophism. Obscure facts alone explain the raw facts and critically resolve the impotence of sophisms. Everyone is aware of this: the

Arab masses who, immediately and "naively" siding with Saddam, entrust the obscure fact of their freedom to the force of anti-colonial provocation. Just like subtle diplomats all over the world, who can only focus on the obscure fact of a new international order deriving from the end of the cold war; like the strategists of terrorism on both sides, be they hidden within the western media conglomerates, or at work in the cellars of conspiracy, who evaluate the expansion of modern war on the planet, a new obscure union of the survival and destruction of the human race; and even like ourselves, if we try to understand how peace might possibly be reborn today as a condition and a path to liberation within the obscure constraints of an international order capable only of repression. We are living the beginning of a new era—only by focusing our eyes on the obscurity of the future can we possibly shed light on the present. That is to say, before the present, and the future along with it, are consumed by the fires of war.

3. Beyond the cold war, as public opinion and common sense indicate, maintaining peace is no longer entrusted to the politics of reciprocal containment and dissuasion, but to the multipolar cooperation in the "communal home" that we call planet earth. In fact, the harmony of this picture is disturbed by a number of dissonances. The first dissonance is revealed in the fact that the international order is predominantly supported by a hegemonic diarchy, USA-USSR, the only two continental powers virtually capable of making a unilateral decision to annihilate an adversary. The second dissonance is revealed in the fact that this dual hegemony is imperfect, which is to say that a functional inequality between the two protagonists is made manifest in the structural determination of their cooperation.

If both of the super-powers are in crisis, one of them has turned inward, focusing on the re-composition of internal consensus and on economic-social reform; the other, the USA, is at this moment witnessing the emergence of two new super political-economic poles (Europe and Japan) and is playing its card for definitively consecrating its imperialist destiny and maintaining its hegemony. A third dissonance is defined by the organic inadequacy on the part of the United Nations to serve as a clearing house between the parties of the imperfect diarchy that hold the fate of the world in their hands, and by the functional contradictions inherent in the current process of multipolar re-organization. In this context, the Kuwaiti crisis reveals all the contradictions of the process of reassembling the international order, as seen from the point of view of the hegemonic powers. It is very much in the interest of the United States to accelerate the process of crisis because therein it finds a formidable opportunity for reaffirming its function as an international police force—even more so vis-à-vis the new poles (European and Japanese), than vis-à-vis the specific issue of oil supplies (this problem could be solved differently since none of the implicated Arab States is driven by an authentic anti-capitalist revolutionary force). The USSR is a co-conspirator in accepting the American game because, today, an imperfect dual hegemony is for them more advantageous than a perfect cooperative order on the global level. Europe and Japan are forced to follow the rules of the imperfect dual hegemony because they are currently incapable of representing themselves as a united front on a terrain of full sovereignty: they accept the war because they are incapable of deciding for war or for peace. This is the reason why all reservations raised against American aggression are leveled so weakly; hence the cowardliness seen in refocusing the strategic discussion on the North-South collaboration which is vital for the construction of a unified Europe. Never as much as today have the European ruling classes demonstrated their inability to assume a hegemonic role. Never as much as in the case at hand have the secular or Christian social democracies that rule Europe better demonstrated that their roots are planted in the repression of revolutionary potential and that their future will unfold in compliance with the overarching international order of capital—no longer just within the internal conflict between social classes, but also in the mortal struggle that the poor populations wage against global exploitation.

4. The American policeman is modern, super-modern, post-modern. He is an entrepreneur. Like all contemporary entrepreneurs he trades his stocks in the Stock Market and expects to be able to cash them in. His business is the maintenance of world "peace." The Stock Market is the United Nations. The entrepreneur sends his soldiers to Arabia and the international community of shareholders pays the expenses. There are blue-chip stocks, such as those issued by the USSR, which yield no profits but gain value just by not entering the competition; there are supremely expensive stocks, like those that the sheiks are forced to purchase, in order to maintain nominal ownership for certain other stocks; there are trust stocks— at zero value—and they are the ones that poor countries pay for as a guarantee for future loans from the International Monetary Fund or from the World Bank. The Europeans and the Japanese vacillate between direct payment and military collaboration, preferring the former over the latter, unless, in some small way, they are still deceiving themselves about representing entrepreneurial alternatives. This fact, more than sad, is shameful. It is obvious that in economic and philosophical theory, after this crisis and this eventual

war, there cannot be any more delay in defining the new figure of the "political entrepreneur"—basically what the Nazis and the Emperor of Japan attempted to do during the 1930s and the 1940s, to become entrepreneurs of war. Today the Americans have succeeded at doing this. Clausewitz is finally listed on the Stock Exchange: it is a fraudulent market, but it is a market.

5. War is pervasive and global. The enemy is a criminal. The three types of war crimes normally defined within international criminal law (crimes against peace and against international law, war crimes in the strict sense of the word, and crimes against humanity) are rapidly being defined upon a horizon that is no longer judicial, but moral: if in fact an international order founded upon cooperation is proven to exist based on unanimous consensus from the United Nations, what difference is there any longer between law and morality? If the United Nations alone can practice *jus ad bellum*, can declare a "just war," which legal parameters (precisely those of *jus in bello*) will persist for the reprobates? But if the goal of the powers that organized the response to Iraq's illegal provocation is not to expel the invader from the occupied lands, but rather to annihilate the invader, to permanently destroy his potential for making war, to make of Iraq that which Germany was in 1945, can this war still be called "just"? Saddam is a Hitler, Bush proclaims—Bush, usually so sparing with his words. What an enormity of philosophical and ethical problems is raised by these words! In its ethical totality, in reality, everything is permissible. And it is not by chance, then, that the two subjects in conflict (The United Nations and the USA on one side, Iraq on the other) are being dragged into a game of monstrous mirroring, into a progression of equal and opposing threats. One side's atomic bomb is answered by the other side's

chemical bomb, one's systemic strategies by the other's terrorist strategies, and "global war" by "holy war." The maximum modernization strategy on one side, along with its ethical foundation, finds a worthy response in the renewal of the worst ethnic and religious archaisms on the part of the other side.

6. Critics should be allowed to take a stand. Resisting war is, in fact, always the result of philosophical criticism. Resisting war is thus the first and fundamental ethical responsibility. That being said, we cannot fail to mention that the critical genealogy of resistance is today, in the West, equivocal: so it is, and it cannot help but be that way. Equivocal in the ontological sense and thus tied to a determination of being that is not rooted in necessity. If we do not resort to dredging up old political mythologies, it is possible to identify only some moral imperatives that can be reclaimed, such as the elementary and fundamental facts of existence, but never the direction in which a movement should be organized, never with ontologically sound anchorage. And yet it is precisely within this void of purity of ethical claims and within the conflict which this purity causes with the totality of disconnected reality—it is within this boundary of incomprehensibility and violent condemnation of the intolerable, that every hope of reconstruction is placed. It is inside this empty space that an unequivocal genealogy of resistance can be rebuilt. But how? Here lies the philosophical problem. Nor can we succeed, at this moment, in resolving it. Nevertheless, we are witness to an essential condition for thinking the problem through. And the fact is that the obscure elements underlying the Gulf crisis (the conflict between North and South, between exploiters and exploited, between rich and poor, as well as the search for an international order of true cooperation) can also be found in the daily

reality of our existence—and in the "happiness" of our political system. If we do not succeed at rendering these dimensions unambiguous, the claim of resistance, no matter how irrepressible, will remain equivocal—and conversely, weak thought, insatiably limp, will be able to produce an apology for war. If we are not able to see the class warfare and the warfare of the radical perspectives of renewal in the North, ontologically, here among us, as the materiality and the necessity of our individual and collective bodies, peace will continue to be defined by the Stock Market, by the perversion of the "media" and by the initiative of the "political entrepreneur": for us, in effect, this means only abject compassion. And when the nuclear bombs start to fall, on the threshold of death, we will look each other in the eye with a dumbfounded look.

8

War, Communication and Democracy

"America," a friend says to me, "has never won a war since 1945. America has never won another war," he claims, "because it is a democratic society and because, since 1945, democratic societies are societies of democratic communication. It is the American people who forced those crazed generals who wanted to drop the atomic bomb on Korea towards peace; it is the American people who forced their government to surrender in Vietnam: a people organized by information and scandalized by the horrors of war. Furthermore," adds Paul Virilio, "this idea still holds today."

After the 1950s and the 1960s, communication has taken giant steps: today war is shown to us in "real time," the televised spectacle turns us into participants of the tragedy. A democratic society cannot accept this sort of participation, which involves co-responsibility for its effects and a proxy for its causes, immediacy of participation in the disaster and spectacular irresponsibility. "Real time" shakes up the mechanisms of democratic representation, showing that what we need to decide to do has already been done, dumping upon the citizens the responsibility for the monstrosities that war brings, monstrosities which they did not reflect upon in time. The problem seems to be clear to America's rulers. A few days before the start of the war, Neil Postman, professor of "media ecology" at New York

University, asked: "Will the imaginary, the exclusive off-spring of tele-vision, be able to latch onto the uncouth and harsh reality of real war without causing minds and nerves to explode?" "What will the moment be like when the 'coming attractions' end and we begin to fight for real, we begin to die for real?" We have begun to answer these questions. Some have maintained that only a sudden and brief antic-ipation of war, a rapid and successful raid, an "Israeli war," could have guaranteed that the democratic mechanisms of participation and rep-resentation would not be injured by the bellicose decision and the totality of its consequences. In this case, danger could have been avoided, and communication bypassed by the brevity and velocity of the event, as well as justified by the immediate success: one happy international police operation. But this was not the choice of the American government. Others thought that the solution was to show "a different" war, a technological war, a war resembling space explo-ration. This route seems to have been taken in the first weeks of the war by television networks all over the world: a "Protestant" solution, a bit hypocritical but substantially correct in the first weeks of the war. In this case danger was again avoided, and communication sterilized, presented and neutralized at the same time. But then what? Can this shortcut still work when the war becomes what everyone expects, a mass war with infantry disseminated in the trenches, each soldier with a high school diploma, in constant contact with family at home, a family that knows everything and sees everything? Will this be able to continue when images of the cormorants drenched in oil become constant, and natural disaster is heaped upon human disaster? Once again, that fundamental problem appears: the problem of the com-patibility of democracy with the management of a modern war, a total, technological and mass war. There is a choice: that of blocking information, of turning communication into propaganda. It would seem that the military hierarchies of all countries are headed in this direction, driven by an "instrumental rationality" which holds in relative, even minimal, regard the reasons for truth and democracy. But, counter to this approach, it is not difficult to foresee—and indeed this is already being proven true—a powerful resistance coming less from the sources of communication and more from the democratic citizenry in all its components. In fact, the obstruction of information violates the same principles of democracy, and reveals the necessity for war as being counter to democracy. How will it be possible to justify the claim of reaffirming law and democracy in the realm where the instruments for reaching this goal negate law and democracy?

Stated in these terms, the problem opens itself up to unfathomable questions: can a modern democracy, founded on communication, undertake and win a war without ever resorting to methods which dishonor it? Can a modern democracy, conversely, have to give in to the opinion of citizens revolted by the horror and the truth of war and convinced that the end does not justify the means? It is not easy, and indeed it seems somewhat unrealistic, to answer these questions. This does not deny the possibility of formulating some indications for the answer. The first indication lies in insisting on the fact that war is less and less an acceptable solution for the conflicts that afflict the world, and this holds true between nations and within nations. The visual solidarity that modern means of communication offer to the citizens of the world displays an actual closeness among the citizens of the world. The indiscriminate killing of citizens of the world caused by modern warfare (total, technological, mass warfare) and the destruction or the defiling of natural resources necessarily brought about by war, are, at this point, in and of themselves, repugnant. The normal conscience of modern man, molded by communication, rejects war as a continuation of politics. Does this mean that it is impossible to react to illegal acts that certain nations commit? No, certainly not. In fact, there exist—and this is the second indication—acts of "non-war" that can be effective, and possibly instrumental, in reaffirming international law. Communication creates and keeps alive isolation, blockades, sanctions, and ostracism from the international community, all of which can be effective instruments in the restoration of international law. This can only happen, however—and this is the third indication—when international law is equal for all its citizens, since, in international law, there can be no privileged or hegemonic figures who lay claim to a predetermined sense of right and wrong. We can now return to our first observations in this essay, and now consider how positive is the fact that the United States has not won any wars after 1945. This observation is equivalent to the observation that democratic public opinion, developed by modern communication, has always prevailed against its governments, against concepts of world order that have nothing to do with the restoration of law and with the foundation of democracy. Thus our wish is that even in the war that we view on our television screens today, the war that touches our consciences so profoundly, democracy will win, communication will not be blocked, and equality before the law will be affirmed upon the international arena. It is not too late to impose democracy's rules against the rules of war. And it is urgent that we do this, again, continually, without stopping. A friend of mine, watching television, recently remarked: "Why is it so hard to define the enemy, why is a single phrase not enough (as in the days when we used to talk about defending freedom and democracy) to describe what is happening in the Gulf?" The answer is simple: before explaining what an enemy is, within the democracy of communication, we must first explain what a friend is. A friend is democracy, and whatever goes against that friend, including the instruments and the propaganda of modern war, is an enemy.

9

For a Europe from the Atlantic to the Ural Mountains

A Europe that stretches from the Atlantic to the Ural Mountains, a Europe of autonomies, a Europe that maintains and extends its Welfare State, a Europe that is open to migration waves from the South and that positions itself in fertile interaction with the Mediterranean and with Latin America: is this an impossible dream?

A politician on the French left, or rather, on the little that survives of the European left, was saying a while back: "However things go, in Europe, we are screwed: if we create a 'little Europe' as the British would have it, we remain hitched to the Atlantic wagon; if we create a 'big Europe' as the French would like, we will be prisoners of a powerful and reorganized European capitalism, which is no better than the American version." This disenchanted observation does not seem right. It underestimates the possible innovative force of launching the process of a "great Europe" within the context of the world stage, as an alternative to Bush's "new world order" and as an answer to the expectations of the countries from the former socialist block. On the other hand, it overestimates the likelihood that Europeans will agree on a basic program, on a program that is void of ideal power and constituent spirit and oblivious to the reasons for the current crisis.

Let us dwell on this last point. Basically, Europeans do not really agree on anything. With the consolidation of a common market, three main problems appear on the agenda—common currency, unified army, democratic organization of powers—the level of disagreement on these issues is at its highest not only among the French, Germans and British, but also with the Italians, the Spanish and the Dutch who have, as of late, begun fishing in murky waters. The Germans want to be heard on the subject of common currency, the French on the idea of a unified army and no strong national executive branch wants to hear about a truly representative European parliament. If this "whispering" is not interrupted, no perspective is possible. Miseries accumulate atop other miseries, traditions upon traditions and it all becomes regressive. The crisis in Yugoslavia and the repetition of obsolete and perverted behaviors is the last straw in this regressive tendency in the behavior of European powers caught up in their singularity.

Now, the only thing that can put an end to this regressive tendency is the definition of a great plan, the opportunity to envision a new homeland, that is to say, a vast territory where means are commensurate with potential, where wealth and productive force are the basis of a new way of life rooted in the freedom of everyone, in broad autonomies, in the possibility of integrating vast waves of immigrants; therefore, in a wide-ranging and articulated redistribution of wealth and common intelligence.

Is it possible to imagine a new homeland? It is, if we take into account the data of the new situation that has come to be between the Eighties and Nineties from the Atlantic to the Urals.

Gorbachev's revolution and the liberation of Eastern Europe have shifted the axis of democratic culture from the Atlantic to Central Europe. We cannot keep outside that which has already entered our home with such force that it has unhinged every door. The fall of the Berlin Wall and end to the Soviet *putsch* concern us Europeans directly. The issue at stake is the understanding, the recognition that the new central mean time no longer passes though Greenwich and opens onto the Atlantic; rather, it goes through the wall that has fallen in Berlin and it opens onto Eastern Europe. What is at stake is understanding that the history of the Soviet Union and of really-existing socialism, of its victories and defeats, is our own history—European history. This is why it is wrong to object, as have a few survivors of the traditional left on our home turf, that reorganized European capitalism would not be a better outcome than that of remaining under the influence of the Atlantic market and being subordinated to the "new world order." The revolution in the East has opened up what will be an unsolvable tragedy within the internal space of the European East and of the Russian Empire, if Europe does not intervene directly, in order to reconfigure the historical process that was interrupted by Stalinism, lending to the transformation of the East its profusion of models capable of organizing labor and cultural "inbreeding," together with scientific and intellectual potential. And all this, provided that this transformation is not the integration of the East into the European West. The October Revolution was a great attempt to move the central axis of modernity, interpreted from a socialist perspective, toward Russia. The defeat of really-existing socialism has crossed over the isolation of this experience, over the cutting of the umbilical cord of a premature fetus. We Europeans, having created the hope of the Russian Revolution and the experience of a monster through the struggles of an entire century, the 20th, must now go back to considering our connection with the European East as the only chance for our European success—we are forced to do so in order to avoid defeat.

This is the first step. But secondly, and no less important, is the fact that American dominance, tolerated while defending us from Soviet expansionism, has become anachronistic in a liberated world and in light of the American crisis. Bush's "new world order" isolates Europe within a situation of economic and political subjection which is unacceptable in the long run, hysterical in the medium range and hypocritical in the short run. A desirable democracy in Europe cannot be held hostage to the obligations of a market predicated upon "cold war" logic and reconfigured today by an international division of labor to which Americans have no right of leadership.

Hence the necessity of a wide ranging plan. Hence the urgency to recognize a new homeland which stretches from the Atlantic to the Urals. Hence the novelty of the establishment of a truly new European constituent power within these spatial dimensions, within this historical framework and with this guiding critical viewpoint.

Any other alternative will lead to a catastrophe, or rather, to the irresolvable unfolding of dramatic problems. Do we want a "little Europe"? We will then become vassals to the Americans, forced every month to give money to pay for our debt to that country, and for the internal balance of a liberal devastation beyond repair, instead of paying for the pensions and guaranteed wages of our workforce. Do we want a "little Europe"? We will then spend our time dealing with squabbles between Bonn and London about central discount rates, squabbles between Paris and Rome about European transportation networks, squabbles between Madrid and Brussels over the price of tomatoes, and so forth. These are all worthy causes, but they do not account for the fact that the Berlin Wall has fallen. As far as Great Britain is concerned, it is currently in a feudal relationship to Washington; those who have been fervid supporters of that "perfidious Albion" which heroically resisted the V2 rockets of Von Braun and of European fascism, cannot accept that such a paladin of European freedom is mistaken today for a reactionary supporter of maintaining Atlantic privileges.

The European left (let us suppose for the moment that there actually is such a left and that it can regroup over these issues), having been freed from the blackmail caused by the existence of Stalinism or really-existing socialism, should be capable of this great plan. The reorganization of big European capital based on the size of a big Europe is predictable; but to what degree will it be conditioned, heavily conditioned, by the necessity of building a new process of legitimization of the State, if the process of constituting a "new homeland" is put into place? There is risk involved here, but it is a game that we can play. A constituent process based on the size of a big Europe must take into account the levels of Welfare achieved by Western countries, with the understanding that the Eastern countries are not planning on surrendering. Such a constituent process, within the wide spaces of a new Europe, will integrate a migratory thrust from the South.

A Europe extending from the Atlantic to the Ural Mountains is thus not an impossible dream. Rather, it is a historical necessity, a product of the "long fluctuations" of European history. It is a political necessity if we want to maintain the levels of Welfare that we have achieved. really-existing socialism must be reabsorbed into a European movement; its crisis is a sign of the deep and uninterrupted relation that binds into one single "homeland" the destinies of Eastern and Western Europe.

10

Nations, Racisms and New Universality

1. Let us begin with Etienne Balibar's statement that today's national principle seems to be, within the generality of the situation in which it emerges or reemerges, the sign of a "weak identity" or of political recourse to maintaining a "social network" where the collapse of strong ideological identities and of the revolutionary foundation of political communities has been most significant. This definition is acceptable in as much as it provides an interpretation of the extraordinary force of dissemination of a national principle within the crisis of the Soviet empire and of the disintegration of the political forms of really-existing socialism. But is this definition acceptable when it is measured against a different set of significant phenomena within the appearance of a national principle? A national principle wherein, for instance, we resort to themes of ethnic and cultural safeguards within social groups which partake in the growth of capitalism but are subordinated and exploited by it? This is harder to admit. In this case, in fact, the national principle, and also simply that of an ethnic entity, rather than being a substitute element in the definition of political and state associations, has a strong, offensive value, filtered through social utopia and through transformative practices. Within this perspective, let us reflect on the unique effectiveness and wide breadth of resonance that the concept of nation

has assumed, not just in terms of identity but, above all, as a tool in the struggle and in the social and political renewal of the "people without a land"—the Palestinians—or of those "people in another land"—the African Americans. It seems, therefore, that the concept of nation presents itself in at least two extreme forms. Between these two extremes we find multiple varieties. In any case, the interesting element which we must immediately emphasize is that the diversity of forms assumed by the concept of nation is determined by its *relation to something other* than the concept of nation. What is this *other?* It is the form of universality that, singularly, confronts national uniqueness. The concept of nation will be different in the case of the fall of really-existing socialism, where it confronts a void in universality; or in the case of the system of capitalism (in the examples we have recalled) where it confronts, in an adversarial manner, the fullness of universality. Historiography and romantic and post-romantic theories of nationalism are perfectly aware of this *relation to something other*. From a liberal perspective, Friedrich Meinecke illustrated, in his outdated but not useless *Cosmopolitanism and National State*, the consistent flux (from the 18th to the 19th century) of the concept of nation, the centrality of the clash between wishing for (national) individuality and the demands of universality (Enlightened cosmopolitanism).

In this *reference to other* which establishes the flux of the concept of nation, it seems pointless to dwell on how much this relation, in addition to moving toward identity, moves, above all, toward reversible, interchangeable, versatile idiosyncrasies. The relation to various universes has an impact on the concept of nation. It is enough to recall, among many others, two exemplary instances of this impact: the shift in the concept of a Jewish State when, at the time of the Six Days War, the Zionist leadership modified its international alliances and, by extension, those of the entire State, moving from a position of self defense and socialism to one of aggression and capitalism; or the shift toward internationalism in the Cuban national identity when, confronted with the hard line of the United States, the revolutionary leadership moved from radical populism to socialism. To go back to Balibar's argument, the issue is not to insist, with regards to the concept of nation, on the function of identity, but rather on its *ambiguity*, on the versatility that identity expresses and on the historical function that it plays. This said, I do not intend to reduce the concept of nation to one of accidental identity, one that can be interpreted only by means of statistical criteria and abstract typologies (as was the case with H. Kohn's sociological historiography); but it is certain that nationality taken by itself (a little bit like family, a little bit like old phenomena of proximity) is a featureless beast. In fact, for the singular principle of nation to reach the level of *ambiguous identity* is already an *extraordinary achievement*. If we use Weber's terminology, the variants of traditional and charismatic legitimacy which, alone, are capable of adjusting to the immediacy of the concept of nationhood, can be positively translated if and when they approximate superior levels of rational legitimacy.

2. What can we add at this point? Balibar's theory illustrates for us an identity which is based on fragile connection to universality, a particularity which is always put into question by its opposite. But Balibar's logic, as well as the points we have made up till now, analyzes the genesis of the situation. Are these points still applicable to the *immediate future* which the course of history is reserving for us with such violence and intensity? How should we tackle, within this new perspective, the issue of nationality? In this new perspective it

seems useless to review the points made in the history of the concept, such as, for instance, the one made about the discontinuity (which Tocqueville had not at all understood) between the territorial State of the *Ancien régime* and national revolutionary sentiment; or the one in the *Communist Manifesto* that links the genesis of capitalism to the making of a national bourgeoisie. It is also pointless to go back to the themes which were developed with singular consonance between the Second and Third International (competing only in the haste with which flags would be lifted from the mud into which they had been cast)—themes concerning the possibility of connecting national movements to socialist universality: a possibility which was happily exhausted by its opposite, that is, by its integration into the capitalist world market, with all its relative tribulations. What we should instead establish is whether, beyond the fullness of capitalist universality and the emptiness of socialist universality, we can sill identify *new models* of universal constitution. These new models ought to oppose capitalist universality and should be capable of organizing a new replenishment of the national sociological fact, that is, of unraveling the ambiguity of the concept or, at least, allowing again for its ambiguous fluctuations.

If we look for clues in the contemporary reality of the former socialist States, we do not seem to find any. The concept of nation, in the crisis of the Union, seems to connect to three fundamental phenomena. For some countries, national rebirth connects to a long "roll-back" strategy enacted by the capitalist States during the siege of the Soviet Union—and thus it is, properly speaking, an old style national rebirth as redefinition of the local bourgeoisie. For others, national rebirth (or birth) connects to phenomena of bureaucratic re-feudalization, that is, to the internal crisis of Stalinist bureaucracies and to the identification of new elements of the legitimacy of local governments. For everyone, finally, the rebirth of the concept of nation and the singularization of the effects of such rediscovery are confronted today by a particular form of capitalist universality; that is to say, by the process whereby the market has become world-wide. Essentially, this rebirth and singularization make up a ferocious attempt to find a place (individually and while paying the highest price) within the realm of the new international division of labor.

Are there any alternatives to these processes? Is there a new form of universality which opposes the globalization of the capitalism of the national dialectic?

At the current stage of definition in this process, it does not seem that there are any alternatives. The tragedy of the concept of nation today does not appear to consist in the fact that once ambiguous identity is achieved, it is no longer possible for this identity to ambiguously play on alternatives other than its placement within the world-wide market of capital. The ambiguous essence of nationality seems to become *useless to its own self.* Lacking any other points of reference, the *relation to other* that currently defines the idea of nation is internalized in the abstract—it degenerates concretely, oblivious to any universal reference, gingerly sliding into chauvinism and racism. It can, on the other hand, become an aggressive attitude, one of singularity versus singularity, against the flat horizon of the struggle for the parceling out of the advantages relative to a world market. On the current scene, *universal Balkanization* is the fate of the concept of nation. The dialectical form of the definition of the concept of nation, while lacking any alternatives to the universality of capitalism, gains strength only in the ferociousness of opposition to one's neighbor. The strong representations of nationhood which were constructed in other ages by the reference to revolutionary universality now appear as the pathetic residue of the past and of utopias which have degenerated into nostalgia; in the case of the Palestinians, for instance, regimented to the Jordan delegation in the next round of Middle East peace talks; in the case of African Americans, within the "national drug market" of *Boyz n the Hood*.

3. With universal Balkanization the concept of nation becomes barbaric. This concept has just sprung up again. It does not lose its dialectical character but translates it into a kind of universal aggression in which the principle of alterity is involved in a regressive dialectic which tends toward absolute indifference and destruction. While emphasizing this process, a powerful thinker, Slavoj Žižek, originally Slovenian but internationalist by vocation, would ask himself: *with what results?* The result is that, within a brief period of time, societies become realms in which everyone becomes a wolf toward any "other wolf," with the likely result of a generalized authoritarianism within individual countries and an ever more advanced "right to interfere" on the international sphere. But what are the results within a medium-range sphere? Here we are forced to guess. But let us try. And let us ask ourselves if, on this not-at-all-empty horizon of universality characterized by the most absolute aggression of one person against another, the paradox of a *recreation of universality* cannot reveal itself. In what sense is this true? In the sense that this universality is engendered by the very constitution of a world market, by its everyday practices, by the mobility which is intended, requested and imposed upon its subjects. Productive cooperation widens, exchanges among networks intensify and extend, and a material and mobile universality appears on the horizon. A universality which is not solicited

by old ideal fetishes but determined by this new situation, by this falling-apart of the social fabric, by the confusion necessarily created by a principle of nationality unhinged from any universal validation. *New communal tendencies* are engendered, kept together not by traditional proximity but rather by a contiguity of mobile, nomadic trajectories, by the undefined dynamics of a "desiring machine," in the relation between a forced de-territorialization and a new longed-for territory. Is it not possible now to begin to imagine a reconstruction of the world, a universality, which avoids traditional proximities (family, ethnicity, nation) and finds in the necessity of mobility, of flexible production, of a novel and widened form of cooperation, a way to create groups, associations, contiguity, novel communicating, and a productive, liberating politics?

The thought of a great Italian philosopher, Giacomo Leopardi, comes to our aid. The concept of nation was a privileged object of his analysis. He moves from a reflection on a vague and heroic perception of nation resulting from the demise of Enlightenment universalism to a just critique of the explosion of that concept through its entrance into the initial development of capitalism, into the triumph of "statistics." But this passage, he adds, must establish an alternative—a radical and endogenous alternative, a powerful alternative provided by a community of true, communicating, cooperating human beings, an alternative that is enacted in reality by the construction of a national market and that, in his poetic masterpiece, *La ginestra*, Leopardi identifies as being active in the ravines of the tragedy of nature and of History. Leopardi's perception is today all the more understandable in a future intelligence and within an ethical dimension. Because his perception is real, it is true in reality before it even becomes a concept. It is in the realm of reality, in fact, that the unification of the world market creates an unstoppable flux of migratory mobility and awesome processes of de-territorialization/re-territorialization. "Statistics" looks coldly at these processes, nations look at them regressively. On the other hand, in the real world, every day, human beings of various ethnic backgrounds and colors construct unholy *mélanges*, linguistic and cultural hybridizations, different races and *multicolored Orpheuses*. The generalized increase in productivity is due to this formidable historical process of the progressive symbiosis of nations. Neither Schengen's agreements nor other repressive measures can block these processes. In the very moment when, in our horizonless societies, these processes lead some of us to the fiercest forms of racism, and many of us to repression, they simultaneously display the *concept of nation* reduced to stupid, no longer dialectical narrow-mindedness, to *inarticulate language* in its precarious reference to an identity lacking a universal. In this way the real empties out the ideal. In this way the logic of internationalization becomes detached from the statistical rigidity of the processes of globalization, to then become recomposed in our bodies, in the necessary "diaspora," in the assimilation of all-with-all, in the ever present "cross-breeding" of new physical and cultural phenomena. In this way a new universal is shaped, a concrete universal in which the contiguity of different bodies becomes a new identity. And these new bodies will no longer need a concept of nation—verifying, nonetheless, paradoxically, possibly by overcoming the need, those powerful revolutionary characteristics that made manifest *the event of utopia* in another epoch, among a "people without a land," like the Palestinians, among a "people in another land," like the African Americans.

4. In conclusion: a) The idea of a nation has been the idea of an identity dialectically defined in relation to a universality or to alternative universalities. Balibar is correct about this; b) But if today there is no other universality than that of omnipresent and all-powerful global capitalism, the principle of difference among social groups will not be able, because of a crisis in identifying the "other," to positively constitute a national principle; c) Two results derive from this situation. The first is the possible over-determination of this chaotic lack of universality on the part of irrational and fascistic power systems; d) The second is a tension in identifying new parameters of identity, in building new dimensions of subjectivity, passing through an exacerbated and extreme definition of the crisis; e) A new concrete universality is determined by the real process of constituting a new humanity through the uncontrollable vitality of the processes of migration within the global market; f) Paradoxically, but no less truthfully, the process of internationalization and of full mobility is today sought after by human beings who desire community.

11

John Paul II's Fifth International

John Paul II's Encyclical, *Centesimus Annus*, on the occasion of the centennial of *Rerum Novarum* is not, in spite of its appeal to tradition, a social message; it is a political document in the strict sense of the word, that is to say, a manifesto, an excitement of the public spirit, a program. For this reason it is interesting to comment on it, for what it says and for what it reveals. And for the reflections that it can inspire in us.

First of all, throughout the encyclical, John Paul II expresses his deep emotions over the 1989 revolution in the Eastern bloc countries. Although he did so much to cause this revolution, he is astonished by the event. The Europe of really-existing socialism is over, the division of the world into two opposed blocs capable of reciprocal destruction has ended, communist parties have—permanently—lost their initiative on the world stage. John Paul II, with some trepidation, but decisively, draws the consequences of this revolution for the Church: what should the Pope do, what should Catholic and Christian forces do in a world that is, once again, *one*—that is, when the obligation to rally against the world of the *infidels* has been exhausted? Who are the new infidels today? What can Christianity say that is "positive" when the "negative" compulsion to defend the Western world and religious freedom is gone? What can the Church propose today to human society?

The exceptional answer that John Paul II gives to these questions is: the Church must, in this situation, raise up again the flags that the workers' movement has allowed to fall into the mud; the Church must ally itself with the workers' movement. Who then, is the infidel? Communists, obviously (they, however have ceased to be a threat), but above all savage capitalism and the imperialist world market. The Church is the ally of the poor in capitalist countries, it is the ally of the States in the countries that are coming out of socialism, it is the ally of the masses in Third World countries. In the global unification of the economic and political market, John Paul II carves out for the Church the possibility of recapturing its medieval vocation. The Church is now, in fact, alone and powerful before the States and before the Empire. It is the sole representative of the poor.

The program outlined by John Paul II for Catholics and Christians is sustained by an interpretation of the genesis of the events of 1989. "The decisive factor which has triggered the changes (of 1989) is certainly the violation of labor law rights"—that is to say, it is not the market forces but the workers' struggles which have determined the crisis of really-existing socialism; within this crisis, the Church has been able to interpret and represent "the spontaneous forms of working (class) consciousness" and to elevate them to the struggle for democratic renewal. This direct encounter has avoided ambiguous alliances at the top between Marxism and Christianity (here "liberation theology" is, in passing, once again condemned). This encounter has occurred at the grass-roots level and has acquired "universal importance": once a communist alternative has disappeared, the theme of liberation can only be interpreted by a

Christian workers' movement, which resumes the critical analysis of alienation without yielding to the Marxist program of violence against exploitation. With these statements John Paul II clearly plans to emphasize that the ideological crisis of Marxism has not eliminated the realities of social injustice and class oppression; and if exploitation can no longer be addressed in Marxist terms (but isn't the situation in Third World countries still the same?) the alienation nonetheless persists. The struggle goes on: the Church must give sense and direction to the spontaneity of the struggle.

While presenting itself as the representative of labor, the Church does not reject the notion of private property. But private property is not an absolute right: it is ordered and limited by the principle of the "universal destination of worldly goods," even when these goods are objects of private appropriation. We must add that today private appropriation (that is, the principle of property and free market) is less and less important. Work, in fact, which is the principle that legitimizes appropriation, is more and more "work for others and with others," the social work of knowledge and technology, an ever broader and more autonomous entrepreneurship, all of which assumes as its productive base not only nature and capital but humanity itself, human reason and the ability to cooperate (did John Paul II perhaps read and learn from the *Grundrisse*?). Well then, property and the market are subjected to a double limitation: that which is established by a "principle of solidarity" and that which is established by a "principle of subsidiarity" (that is, by the assertion of a free process of social self-organization, which must be accepted and sustained by the State—how many transfigurations the medieval corporatism of the Church can undergo!). The associative movement of workers, which embodies by itself these two different principles, must represent the essential transformative lever of society, leading it beyond capitalism.

The political inspiration which animates *Centesimus Annus* manifests itself, finally, in its appeal to volunteerism and militancy. The circle of pontifical thought is complete. With the reconstitution of a Christian social movement, the Church presents itself as the sole bulwark of social justice and as the exclusive representation and mediation of society against the State, of the poor against the rich and of the worker against the capitalist; and it further delegates the practical setting-up of this program to individuals and associations—thus it entrusts charity and piety to become the operating virtue, the subjective militancy of the multitude.

What should we add? It is obvious that by highlighting some of the elements of the Encyclical, we have tried to avoid the grossest contradictions that run through it (the attempt at harmonizing Leo XIII, Pius XI and Pius XII, as well as John XXIII, is pitiful) and the grotesque statements that we find in it (the most absurd of which deems class struggle to be "polemogenetic" in an imperialist sense). We also have tried not to attack the philosophical aporias, anthropological foolishness, and opium scent that flavors the Encyclical (it develops an opposition to communism based on the theory of "original sin"!). These things (contradictions, grotesque statements, idiocies) belong to the realm of faith; we are lucky enough not to possess this faith and therefore we move within the realm of philosophical and political realism. It is in this realm that the intelligence of the Roman Pole impresses us, and the speed and liveliness with which he has responded to the events of 1989 arouses our envious admiration. Together with a bit of dazed astonishment. Is it ever possible—we wonder—that there can be no candidate other than a Pope to raise up again the flags stuck in the mud of a Waterloo of the labor movement? Is it ever possible, discounting the defeat and also the current giant processes of renovation, that a Pope, better than any trade unionist, can understand and disseminate the concept of the intellectual and cooperative nature of the new productive workforce? Is it ever possible that only a Pope, in a climate of generalized conformism, can level, albeit with great caution, a heavy critique against capitalism when no other social-democrat (enlightened by the other event of 1989) by now dares to complain about exploitation? And that only a Pope cheers on an alternative organization against alienation and exploitation? Is it ever possible that, given the relentless barbarization of our times, a wizard can tell more truth than those who make themselves out to be scientists?

One would be tempted to conclude, at this point: if this is our miserable state of affairs, let us put our trust in the wizard—not without promising to the cowardly secular and to the social-democrats the revenge which they so well deserve by virtue of their irresponsible impotence. Honor does not allow for this conclusion. But let us be careful. After a hundred years of solitude, the social doctrine of the Church presents itself as the only alternative to the defeat of the labor movement, in a mystified but no less effective manner. Let us be careful: perhaps we shall never again have the strength to use the vicar Gapon in the new insurrectional demonstrations of the community yet to come ...

12

The USA and Europe after the Gulf War and the Los Angeles Riots

Let us talk about the United States of America. About the crisis of its political system and the catastrophe of its social relations, about economic decline, and the new techniques of control, as well as the mystifying ideologies that America offers us. Let us also tell about the despair and power of revolt. But by talking about America aren't we also talking about Europe? Aren't our destinies now bound together more than ever? Don't the effects of an American crisis reverberating throughout the world, projected threateningly upon a newly designed "world order," affect more than ever our economic, social and political life?

In Europe the political and constituent discussion on the perspectives of our continent is open. In France, in September, there will be a vote on the Maastricht Treaty. What can we say about European unity if we look at it from the point of view of the American "superpower," which is as militarily and politically hegemonic as it is economically and socially in a state of crisis? And what can we say about Europe if we look at its process of unity from the point of view of democracy and of the interests of the exploited social classes, here and in the rest of the world?

We need not dream: the Los Angeles riots are not the beginning of a new cycle in the American Revolution. These riots, however, are extremely important because they highlight a crisis of political legitimacy in the United States. We are familiar with the figures of this social malaise, with the quantitative series of productive decline and economic hardship, the perversions in the way of governing and the violence of the overbearing system—cultural, journalistic, media—that sustains it. But it is always wonderful to see the reaction coalescing into the event of a riot and into a protest movement which questions "the American Republic." Police and judges, the representatives of government: none of the powers of a State that deems itself democratic and federalist is spared by the Los Angeles revolt. A police force worthy of the worst of "apartheid"; racist judges; a representative political cast (Clinton no less than Bush) incapable of a single jolt of generous reflection on the riots and subjugated to the asphyxiating influence of the "moral and silent majorities" that infect the shriveled American public life; a government—above all irresponsible and inept at even imagining a progressive and reformist answer to the rebellion of the poorest and solely capable of persevering in its structural repression. The New Deal engineered by Roosevelt and Ford was a Welfare State that up to the time of Lyndon Johnson's presidency had managed to provide, against all odds, a dialectic of social development that included the participation of the working class and "Blacks" by mixing lines of class and race; none of this has survived Reagan's destructive fury. Such is the origin of the crisis, the fact that the American Republic is irrevocably Reaganite. In order to destroy the counter-power of the working class and of the subaltern classes, neoliberal power and Reaganite populism have turned economic development to mechanisms for the redistribution of wealth, of freedom, of knowledge and of well being worthy of a colonial society. The undermining of production and of democracy have gone hand in hand. The Los Angeles riots were born at this juncture and they unveil, simultaneously, the profound dimension of the undoing of social ties and the impossibility, within this political regime, to answer for it. "No Justice, No Peace": it was not simply the application of the rule of law that the rioters were demanding in Los Angeles; it was justice in the form of distribution of income, of freedom, of the possibility of work and of wealth. They were asking for hope. The American political system, predisposed (even in its most progressive periods) to an oligarchic virus and now corrupted during the last ten years by Reagan's populism, will not, in the deepest phase of social degradation, manage the task, by now impossible, of joining freedom to equality, of producing democracy and work. "No Justice, No Peace," far from being a loud expression of rage and indignation, points to the long trend of the structural crisis of the American political system.

This ongoing crisis of the political system bars the way to an isolationist tendency and leads, conversely, the US political establishment towards imperialism. The "new world order" will be the space within which the American crisis is compensated and rebalanced by the economical and political results of an imperial action. In this phase of the reconstruction of a "new world order," the United States has well proven what it is capable of. From the great crowning "Shock-and-Awe" which was the Iraqi war to the recent statement by the Supreme Court regarding the legal legitimacy of kidnapping enemies outside of territorial boundaries, the right to imperial intervention has become banal. Even international law is subordinate to *Polizeiwissenschaft*, to the structural, preventive and repressive contingencies of a police action aimed at control and power. But even more dangerous than the right to intervene is the tireless action of international pro-American powers to develop a plan of diplomatic, military, political, and monetary destabilization of entire geographic areas in Easter Europe, in Central and East Asia, and in Western Africa. This policy of "divide and conquer"— pushed to its extreme in its support of any initiative aimed at the disintegration of the old order—is monstrous in its goal to export crisis and to impose new hierarchies in the political and economic market useful to American domination. The resulting political and moral costs already go beyond any sense of proportion. The forms of Western imperialism, established after World War II and renewed in the process of decolonization, appear like relics of nostalgic appreciation when compared to the upheavals provoked by the current *Lebanization of continental spaces*. As far as Soviet and Stalinist imperialism is concerned—God willing, we are not going to be forced to reappraise its merits in our search for that honest value which is peace in international relations! The war in Yugoslavia, and the ones taking place or about to happen in the former Soviet empire, are already knocking at the doors of Europe. At this point, the imperial exporting of the American crisis is for us not only an approaching concern, but an immediate one. European and American interests no longer clash on simple issues of agriculture, policies of scientific research or business competition—these issues would be, perhaps not easily, surely negotiable—they are intertwined with pressures, blackmail and immediate threats, all articulated within a woof which it is not premature to define as strategically alternative. One thing is certain: the "new world order" (as stated in a recent document of the US Defense Department, refashioned but never denied) cannot allow for the emergence of a State apparatus of European proportions, one which would be necessarily in competition with the United States. The making of a "new world order" clashes with the unification of Europe in all circumstances: such is the decided conviction of the imperial government under crisis in the United States.

It is said: Maastricht is the Europe of big capital. What else has Europe ever been since the Treaty of Rome? It is said: Maastricht's Europe will evolve into a monstrous bureaucratic structure. In truth, the creation of a bureaucratic apparatus characterized by a large democratic shortfall is in the planning stages (the supervisory power of the Parliament in Strasbourg is close to zero); but we are dealing with a curious bureaucratic apparatus which is extremely open in its hybridization of the federal and con-federal elements that characterize it, and yet is frail in the face of the current adminis-trative structures of its nation States. In fact, when these critiques are leveled against Maastricht's Europe, it is a way of ignoring the central and essential element which dominates the current building project: that is, Maastricht's Europe is essentially a French-German revolutionary attempt, from top to bottom, to create an alternative political pole of stability and of power upon the horizon of chronic instability and unilateral plans for domination which are brought about by the new American imperial order. From this point of view, it is a matter of not splitting hairs on the nature of power in a new Europe: it is self-evident that it is a capitalist power struc-tured around bureaucratic forms—but nothing changes in our opinion of what is really new in the creation of Europe, unless we are sidetracked by the illusion of 19th century Republicanism or, worse yet, by a desire to stick to lurid nationalist ideologies, be they fascist or Stalinist. On the other hand, the question, the only question which we need to address in the current phase of Euro-pean building, is the following: is it in our interest to have a Europe that is opposed to the "new world order"? Our answer is affirma-tive. The new European public pole which is taking shape among inter-imperialist contradictions does not change one bit the nature of the *economic* exploitation suffered in Europe by the subaltern classes, but it does offer to these subjects a *political* space within which the plans and struggles for a radical transformation become (not existing but) possible. Is there anyone among the current "leftist" opponents of Maastricht's Europe who thinks it is possible (what are we saying? merely conceivable) to have an initiative of radical democracy within the present borders of nation States? On the other hand, it is not the first time in the long history of the struggles of the subaltern classes that the inter-imperialist contradictions offer new spaces for mobilizing political initiative. And today this generic remark takes on critical importance. A project of liberation becomes newly viable within the context of opposition to the American imperial plan.

Los Angeles and Europe are very far apart. Not far enough, however, not to be able to recognize, both here and there, the same enemy lurking behind its different masks: "the new world order." We do not know what course the American proletariat will pursue against that enemy, by means of and beyond the riots. And we have no advice to give. We do know, however, what needs to be done here in Europe, in order to defeat the same enemy. Precise goals and plans of mobilization are opening up in the new Europe. The goal is to overcome the democratic shortfall of the current project of unification, consolidating what will be created by this phase of ratification and referendum and going well beyond it; the goal is to develop a cultural, social and economic integration which is well balanced and connected to the needs of a Europe of regions and no longer of nation states; the objective is to establish a true State of distributive justice against the "present state of things," thus re-instituting the "social question" (opened by post-Fordism and by the crisis of the Welfare State) which is at the core of the political struggle. At the same time, it is necessary to re-address the issue of North versus South in radically new terms, both in terms of immigration policies and in terms of debt. The acceptance of immigration and the undoing of a politics of unequal and loan-shark style exchanges are at the top of the list! With whom can we accomplish this? With a left which is presently toppling its own republican and/or nationalistic myths against the very possibility of a united Europe opposed to the "new world order"? Could the rioting youths of Los Angeles count on a left of this kind more than they can count on the "bosses" of the American system? The issue of the creation of a new European and radically democratic political force which can replace the unfit and inept left is as much alive in Europe as it is in Los Angeles. And in the face of the same enemy.

PART FOUR

CHRONICLES OF THE SECOND REPUBLIC

The Italian Transition as Seen by an Exile

Political Statements II

1

The Constituent Republic

1. "To Each Generation Its Own Constitution"

When Condorcet wishes that each generation will be able to produce its own political constitution, he evokes on one hand the
constitutional norm of Pennsylvania (which tends to return constitutional law to common norm and provides for one single method
for creating constitutional principles and new laws); on the other
hand, he anticipates the revolutionary Constitution of 1793: *Un
peuple a toujours le droit de revoir, de réformer et de changer sa
Constitution. Une génération ne peut assujettir à ses lois les générations
futures (art. XXVIII)*. [A people always has the right to review, to
reform and to modify its Constitution. A generation cannot subject
future generations to its laws].

On the threshold of the concurrent development of society and
of the State (as they are determined by revolution, science and
capitalism) Condorcet understands that any predetermined restric-
tion of productive dynamics, any limitation of freedom which goes
beyond the pressing needs of today, will necessarily have despotic
effects. In other words: Condorcet understands that, in the moment
when the establishment of the Republic is in the past, a fixation on
the Constitution becomes reactionary in a society founded on the

development of economy and of freedoms. Customs, the "elders," or an ancient idea of order will not legitimize a Constitution. On the other hand, only life that renews itself can establish a Constitution; it can constantly test it and evaluate it, and always move it toward appropriate changes. From this standpoint, Condorcet's suggestion "To each generation its own Constitution" harks back to Machiavelli, who wanted each generation (in order to elude the corruption of power and the *routine* of administration) "to return to the principles of the State"—a "return" which is the establishment of a set of principles, which is not a legacy but a constant renewal of one's roots.

Must our generation establish a new Constitution? If we think of the reasons behind the urgency with which the old constituents set themselves to the task of renewal, we are forced to picture the entire panoply being present today. But the corruption of our political and administrative life has reached such a degree that the crisis of representation has never been as dire as it is today, and our democratic disillusion has never been so radical. When we say "crisis of the political apparatus," we are actually saying that the democratic State is broken and that, furthermore, it is irreversibly corrupt in all of its principles and organs: division of powers and principles of security, individual powers, one by one, and rules of representation, the unitary dynamic of powers and functions of legality, effectiveness and administrative legitimacy. If there is an "end to History," to which we must say goodbye, it is certainly the end of the constitutional dialectic that we had been tied to by liberalism and by the late capitalist State. Let us be more concrete. Beginning in the Thirties, a constitutional system had started to come into force in the Western capitalist countries, one which was defined as a "Fordist Constitution," or as the labor Constitution of the Welfare State, which is now in crisis. The reasons for this crisis are totally obvious when we look at the changes in the individuals who had agreed on the principles of this Constitution: on one side, the national bourgeoisie, and on the other, the industrial working class, organized in labor unions and in socialist and communist parties. The liberal-democratic system was then subjected to the demands of the development of industry and of the partitioning of global revenues among these classes. The formal constitutions could be more or less different but the "material constitution"—the fundamental agreement for the partitioning of powers and counter powers, of labor and revenues, of rights and of freedom—was essentially homogeneous. National bourgeoisies renounced fascism and were guaranteed in return their power to exploit, within a system of partitioning, the national income which was providing for the creation of Welfare for the national labor class: the latter renounced revolution.

With the crisis of the Sixties which resulted in the emblematic event of 1968, the Fordist constitutional State itself entered into a crisis: the individuals involved in the fundamental constitutional agreement have, in fact, changed. On one hand, various bourgeoisies have become internationalized, establishing their power in the financial transformation of capital with abstract representations of power taking shape; on the other hand, the industrial working class (following the radical transformations of production: the triumph of mechanization in industrial labor and the computerization of social work) transforms its cultural, social and political identity. A financial and multinational bourgeoisie (which sees no reason for carrying the weight of a Welfare nation) is matched by a socialized and intellectual proletariat—a proletariat as full of new needs as it is incapable of maintaining continuity with the articulations of the Fordist compromise. With the exhaustion of "really-existing socialism" and the resulting catastrophe entering the pages of world history at the end of 1989, even the symbols (already generally worn out) of proletarian independence within socialism have definitively fallen apart.

The judicial-constitutional system based on the Fordist compromise, propelled by the constituent agreement between national bourgeoisie and industrial working class, and over-determined by the conflict between the two super-powers (symbolic representations of the two parts in conflict on the scene of each nation) has now reached its end. There is no longer a lingering war between the two blocs at the international level within which civil class warfare can be mitigated through immersion into the Fordist constitution and/or organizations of the Welfare State; there are no longer, within the individual countries, individuals who can constitute that constitution, who should have legitimized its expressions, symbols, even new concepts. All has radically changed.

What, then, is this new Constitution that our generation must create?

2. "Money and Arms"

Machiavelli would say that a Prince needs "arms and money" in order to build a State. What arms, then, and what money are needed to build a new Constitution? For Machiavelli, arms are the people: productive citizens who in the context of a city democracy become people bearing arms. What kinds of people are available today for the making of a new Constitution? Which generation is open today to a new institutional compromise that goes beyond that of the Welfare State? And how does this generation make itself available to organize and "bear arms" to achieve this goal? As far as "money" is concerned, what is happening today? And if this generation is available, in what way is it available?—is the financial multinational bourgeoisie willing to enter into a constitutional and productive compromise that goes beyond the Fordist compromise?

In the post-Fordist social system the concept of people must and can be redefined. Not just the concept of people, but that of "people bearing arms"—that is, of that segment of the citizenry who, by working, produce wealth and thus allow for the reproduction of society as a whole. This segment can demand that its hegemony over social work be constitutionally recorded.

Great strides have been made in defining the post-Fordist proletariat. This proletariat is made up of a mass of workers restructured by processes of computerized and mechanized production, processes which are centrally handled by an ever larger intellectual proletariat which is directly and more than ever engaged in computer work, in communications and in vocational training. The post-Fordist proletariat consists of the sector of the social workers which is traversed and constitutes by the constant intertwining of technical-scientific activity with the hard work of producing goods, by the entrepreneurship of the networks within which this intertwining is distributed, and by the ever more intimate combination of the redefining of work schedules and forms of life. Simply in order to introduce the discussion, here are some elements of the new definition of the proletariat which point to the new fact that this proletariat, in all of the segments that make it up as a class, is essentially *mass-intellectuality*. With the addition—and this is essential—of another element. Within the scientific subsumption of productive work, within the growing abstraction and socialization of production, post-Fordist work is more and more based on cooperation and autonomy. Autonomy and cooperation mean: *the entrepreneurial power of productive work is by now completely in the hands of the post-Fordist proletariat.* The evolution of productivity provides for the greatest independence of the proletariat, as an intellectual and cooperative base, as a form of economic entrepreneurship. Is it also a political entrepreneurship and a political autonomy?

The answer to this question can be provided only after we address what happens to "money" in the context of this historical evolution. And that means what happens today to the bourgeoisie as a class, to the productive functions of the industrial bourgeoisie. Well then, if what we have said with regards to the new definition of the post-Fordist proletariat is true, it means that the international bourgeoisie has at this point lost its productive functions, that it is more and more parasitical—a kind of Roman Catholic Church of capital. This bourgeoisie functions only through financial control, that is, a control which is totally disengaged from the demands of production, "money" in the post-classical, post-Marxist sense of the term, "money" as estranged and hostile universe, "money" as Bible, holiness and miracles—the opposite of work, intelligence, immanence of life and of desire. "Money" no longer mediates between work and goods; it is no longer a numerical rationalization of the relation wealth/power; it is no longer a quantified expression of the wealth of a nation. In the face of the entrepreneurial autonomy of the proletariat, which had enveloped, through materiality, even the intellectual forces of production, "money" is the false reality of a despotic, external, empty, capricious and cruel power.

And here we discover a "new" fascism, a postmodern fascism which has nothing to do with Mussolini's allegiances, with ideological Nazi syndromes or with Pétain's cowardly arrogance. *Postmodern fascism* attempts to adjust to the post-Fordist cooperation of labor and at the same time to express its upside-down essence. Just as old style fascism used to ape socialism's forms of mass organization and used to attempt to transfer proletarian collective tendencies to nationalism (national-socialism or Fordist constitution), so postmodern fascism endeavors to discover the communist needs of the post-Fordist masses and to transform them, one at a time, into the cult of difference, into the glorification of individualism, into the search for identity—always a search for overbearing and tyrannical hierarchies which must place differences, uniqueness, identity and individuality against one other, at all times, tirelessly. While communism is the respect and synthesis of singularity, and as such it is sought by those who love peace, the new fascism (adequate expression of the financial rule of international capital) brings about a war of everyone against everyone else, brings about religiosity and wars of religion, nationalisms and national wars, corporate selfishness and economic wars.

Never have so many crimes been committed in the name of democracy. Never so many wars. Never has no much "nonsense" been produced. Let us consider two "new fascisms" which are typical of our era, Yeltsin in Russia and Perot in the United States: the first will tell you that his is a democratic State because he delivers to all of his citizens pieces of paper on which appears the word "action"—what he seems to be proposing is truly a "communism of capital"!

As far as Perot is concerned, he goes beyond democratic representation—and his is also a claim of communism: he is having his electorate play today (and tomorrow, perhaps, the citizens) a computer game, where the expression of the will and participation of the people are reduced (or cannot but be reduced, at best) to an opinion poll ...

Let us return now to the "arms" of the people, thus to the question of what kind of Constitution must be drafted by the new generations. Which is like questioning power relations, compromises that the new post-Fordist proletariat and the new multinational masters must materially institute in order to organize the next productive cycle in a class struggle. But if what we have been saying is true, does this question still make any sense? What type of constitutional compromise is, in fact, possible at this point in a situation where the greatest proletarian cooperation is juxtaposed to the greatest external and parasitical rule of multinational capital? Is money opposed to production?

Does it still make any sense to wonder how rights and duties can be reciprocally calibrated when the productive dialectic no longer allows workers and capital to mix in the management of the productive relation?

We can probably all agree that this question no longer makes any sense. "Arms" and "money" no longer combine to form a State. The last event in this history of agreements between those who rule and those who obey has its origin, if we trust Machiavelli, in the "dualism of power" established by the Roman plebeian Tribunes vis-à-vis the Republic; it is probably that of the Welfare State. Today everything changes in political science and in Constitutional doctrine: in fact, if those who once used to be subjects are now more intelligent and better "armed" than monarchs and masters, why should they seek a mediation with them?

Surely there is a real horizon along which arms and money, production and control actually clash: it is the horizon of communication. If the issue of a new constitution, in the traditional sense of the term, still has some meaning, we can find it in this horizon. But here, actually, we do not have to solve a new problem as much as we have to return to a theme that the proletariat had, let us say, put aside in the course of other compromises. And on the other hand, how shall we constitutionally resolve the issue of communication? The issue of communication is the issue of truth: how is it possible to reach a compromise on the truth? How is it possible to have two different commercials expressing opposing and contrary views on the same product? How is it possible to reach a compromise within the realm of images and symbols? And then there is the objection that the constitutional issue of communication has impact only indirectly upon the issue of truth, while it has impact directly upon the means of expression—and thus, in this realm a compromise is possible, just as power relations are—well, this objection is only relatively valid, or rather it is valid until we enter a phase of civil war. And since in the postmodern era everything leads to civil war, we do not understand where we can reach a compromise on communication.

3. Forms of the State: What "Constituent Power" Is Not

From Plato to Aristotle and, with some variation, up until the modern era, the theory of the "forms of the State" has come down to us as an unavoidably dialectical theory. Monarchy and tyranny, aristocracy and oligarchy, democracy and anarchy, exchanging roles, are thus the sole alternatives within which the power-cycle unfolds. At some point in the development of the theory, Polybius, with unquestionable common sense, proposed that these forms not be considered alternative but complementary—alluding to the constitution of the Roman empire, he showed, in fact, that these various forms of the State could not only avoid being in opposition to one another, but could even work side by side: they could be branches of government. The theoreticians of the American Constitution, just like the theoreticians of Stalinist democratic-popular Constitutions, have all identified with Polybius! Classical and contemporary constitutionalism, happily paraded about by all whores of the rule of Law, is nothing but Polybian in nature! Monarchy, aristocracy and democracy make up, together, the best of republics!

But such greatly exaggerated scientific value of this dialectic of the forms of the State does not go far beyond that of the famous and ancient parable of Menenius Agrippa: a parable as reactionary as many others, which implies a conception of power that is oligarchical, motionless and brutal, when it asks of the various social classes that they create, together, an animal-like functionality. Is there no scientific value then? Perhaps. However, it is not worth insisting on this nonentity, other than to see it as the century-long continuity of tradition, its historical efficacy; the contemporary inertial effectiveness of these theories is here to remind us, at any rate, of the power of mystification.

The very ideology of revolutionary Marxism has asserted the validity of the theory of the forms of the State, while simultaneously overturning it. The Leninist echoes of "extinction of the State" assume a concept of the State as found in bourgeois theory, while this theory is assumed to be the extreme point of confrontation with the reality of the State. What I mean to say is that the concepts of "transition" and of "extinction," of "peaceful life" and of "popular democracy," of "dictatorship of the proletariat," and of "cultural revolution" are bastardized concepts because they are imbued with a conception of the state, of its sovereignty, of its dominion, and because they are considered to be the necessary means and the inevitable pathways in the seizing of power and in the transformation of society. The mystifying dialectic of the theory of forms of the State has been turned inside out and has become the negative dialectic of the extinction of the State: but the theoretical nucleus remains, in the strength of the absolute, as a reactionary affirmation of the State: "All the same old shit," as Marx used to say.

It is time we got out of this crystallization of absurd positions—elevated to a value of truths by their extremity alone. It is time we asked ourselves if there is, from a theoretical and practical viewpoint, a position which avoids being engulfed by the murky and terrible essence of the State. It is time we asked if there is a point of view that, by giving up the perspective of those who mechanically establish the Constitution of a State, succeeds in maintaining the thread of a genealogy, the strength of a constituent praxis in its range and intensity. This point of view exists. It is the point of view of a daily opposition to authority, of continual resistance, of constituent power. It is rupture, denial, and imagination as the basis of political science. It is the acknowledgement that it is presently impossible to mediate between "arms" and "money," "people bearing arms" and the multinational bourgeoisie, production and finance. We are leaving behind a Machiavellian point of view and yet we are fully convinced that Machiavelli would be on our side. We are leaving behind the curse that forces us to think of politics in terms of domicile. What we are questioning here, thus, is the very form of dialectics, of mediation as the content of domicile in its various forms. For us dialectics is once and for all in a state of crisis. It is a question of being able to think politically beyond the theory of "forms of the State." Going back to Machiavellian terms, we must therefore ask ourselves: is it possible to ponder the establishment of a republic based on the arms of the people and without the money of the Prince? Is it possible to entrust the future of the State solely to popular "virtue" and not to "fortune" as well?

4. Establishing a Soviet Mass-Intellectuality

We have now entered an era which is dominated by the hegemonic tendency toward immaterial labor and characterized by the clashes engendered by the new relation between the organization of productive power and multinational capitalistic control. The issue of a Constitution presents itself, from the point of view of mass-intellectuality, as one of stipulating how its Soviets are to be established.

In order to narrow down the issue, let us begin by reviewing some of the conditions we have presupposed up to this point.

The first of these conditions derives from the widespread hegemony of immaterial labor and, therefore, from the proletariat's ever more significant reappropriation of technical-scientific knowledge. On this basis, technical-scientific knowledge cannot be assumed to be a mystified function of control, separate from the body of mass-intellectuality.

The second condition stems from the already emphasized end of any distinction between work life, social life and individual life, between production and form of life. In this predicament, politics and economy become two sides of the same coin. The old misery of bureaucratic distinctions between trade unions and parties, between mass movements and avant-garde movements, and the list could go on forever, appears to be vanishing. Politics, science and life all work together: and it is within this framework that the real produces subjectivity.

The third point to consider is, consequently, that in this realm an alternative to existing power is found positively, through the expression of power. The annihilation of the State can only be conceived of through a concept of taking possession once again of its administration. That is to say, of the social essence of production, of the instruments that enable us to understand social and productive cooperation. Administration is wealth which is consolidated and placed in the service of control. It is fundamental to re-take possession of it—to re-take possession of it through the exercise of individual work placed within the perspective of solidarity, through cooperation in administering social labor, in order to have accumulated immaterial work reproduced ever more richly.

The Soviets of mass-intellectuality appear here. And it is fascinating to notice how the objective conditions of their onset perfectly intermingle with the historical conditions of antagonistic class relations. In this realm, we have emphasized this point before: no constitutional compromise is any longer possible. Soviets will therefore be defined by the fact that they instantly express power, cooperation and productivity. Soviets of the mass-intellectuality will endow the new social organization of labor with rationality and they will equate rationality with the universal. The expression of their power will be without a Constitution.

The constituent Republic is not, therefore, a novel form of Constitution: this Republic is neither Platonic, nor Aristotelian, nor Polybian and perhaps, not even Machiavellian. It is a Republic that comes before the State, outside of the State. The constitutional paradox of the constituent Republic lies in the fact that the constituent process is never over, that the Revolution does not end, that constitutional norm and common law are brought back to one single source and developed as one in a single democratic procedure.

Here we reach, finally, the core issue from which everything originates and toward which everything strives: the task of eliminating separation, disparity, the power that reproduces separation and disparity. Now, the Soviets of mass-intellectuality can tackle this task by building, outside of the State, an apparatus within which a democracy of the everyday manages active communication and citizens' interactivity and, at the same time, generates ever more liberated and complex subjectivities.

Is all of this preliminary? Is it all too general and abstract? Of course.

It is essential that we begin again to talk about communism—in this form—that is, as a program which in all of its aspects goes beyond the miserable reductions which we have witnessed in History. And if this is preliminary, it is no less realistic. Mass-intellectuality, the new proletariat formed in the struggles against capitalist development and for the expression of constitutive power, must start acting as a real historical subject.

The historical event, the obsolescence, the *Angelus novus*—when they arrive—arrive unexpectedly. Our generation can therefore draft a new Constitution. It's just that it will not be a constitution. Perhaps that historical event has already taken place.

2

Legal-Illegal:
Corruption, Judicial Power and Political Power

The principle of *legality* is, from the standpoint of juridical tradition, above all the principle of the preeminence of the law. But it is not only that: it is also the principle of the "formal compliance" of all the acts of administration and of jurisdiction to the constitutionally guaranteed legal code. From this point of view the distinction between legality and *illegality* is absolutely simple: on both the objective and subjective side of the legal code, legal is that which complies with the law, illegal is that which is dissonant, legal is that which is allowed or solicited from the subjects, illegal is that which is not allowed or is repressed.

The modern principle of legality—as distinct from that of *legitimacy*—originates with the political evolution of bourgeois success. First and foremost, it coincides with the claims made by Parliaments to intervene—before the sovereign—on matters of taxation. This intervention evolves, in European constitutional history, in such a way as to extend to the control of the entire executive branch of the State when this branch deals with "fundamental rights." Eventually Parliaments establish the principle of *supremacy* of the law as being the supremacy of their judicial decisions. *Exclusivity* follows supremacy: with the onset of democratic-constitutional regimes legality becomes, in fact, the source of exclusive juridical decision-making and it assumes universal authority and validity, imposing the principle of "formal conformity" on the entire administrative and jurisdictional activity of the State. Without this historical force of expansion of the principle of legality it would be impossible to describe the genesis of the *Rule of Law* and the history of its extension and stabilization.

Any modern principle of illegality should be compared with the characteristics that we have been identifying for legality: it should consist of the negation of exclusivity and supremacy, as well as of the centrality of law as source of rights; furthermore, it should assert the positive juridical value of breaching conformity and legality and of proclaiming the spontaneous production of social norms. But not even this is sufficient to establish the principle of illegality. Modern institutionalists have taught us that there is no substantial difference between the right of the State and the right of un-codified or even criminal societies. The difference can only be found in the moment when different legal codes, instead of competing as would be allowed by the homology of their structure, radically clash with all points of the norm. That is to say, the principle of legality is not only exclusive of other sources, but also of other contents: it is therefore ontologically determined.

Our discussion must therefore go back to the realm of contents. When the principle of legality is reduced to the sole concept of conformity or formal rationality (as Max Weber and the sociologists that he has inspired would have it) we run the risk of losing sight of or weakening the historical significance of the concept—which is actualized, in fact, as the product of a specific transition in the organization of the modern State, as the supremacy of the law over any other legal source of rights, as the triumph of the *bourgeoisie*. The contents of legality are therefore closely associated to the principles which sustain bourgeois social and productive order. Karl Marx has proven with much elegance and sophistication how even the purest of rights are a function of the interests of the sociopolitical classes which were managing wealth accumulation and directing the division and hierarchization of labor: modern sociologists have just confirmed the Marxian hypotheses. In the principle of illegality, therefore, even when we are dealing with crimes wholly connected to the form of bourgeois life, there is something that breaks away from such life. Legality is always an asymmetrical concept; that is, in the legal realm the values of the bourgeoisie prevail even when the values or experiences of proletarian life have a place in the legal realm and are protected by it—by contrast, illegality points to asymmetrical inversion: even when denying or breaking the legal code have no proletarian modality, they are still anti-bourgeois in nature.

In its most recent phase, some of the presuppositions which used to underlie the principle of legality and its force within the context of executive and jurisdictional activities seem to be fading away. While administrative activity (let us consider, for the time being, this aspect rather than jurisdictional activity) had been enormously growing, legislative power did not keep up with it well. The formal validity of the principle of legality does not resolve itself without leaving its residue upon the effectiveness of the code. Its results are the expansion of the executive and administrative activity of the government to the detriment of the sovereignty of Parliament, the multiplying of activities of intervention which have nothing to do with legal control, the weakening of separation of powers, in sum, the *crisis of the Rule of law*. In this situation it might appear that the concept of legality has become something very abstract, substantially ineffective—almost a transcendental principle that we can turn to but which is incapable of concrete consequences within the code. In reality, this is not the case. The crisis of the rule of law does not eliminate legality; rather, it points to its complex and articulated genesis. That is to say, in the midst of crisis, legality, far from being the exclusive source, the solitary matrix of the legal code, has been forced to open itself up to elements *external* to its own self-production. This happens in the moment when legality is established, in the States of advanced capitalism, as the mediation and conclusive synthesis of elements deriving from the plurality of the social issues of production of the law, rather than as the expression of State monism. From this viewpoint *illegality* is not simply that which the principle of legality cuts out and excludes from itself: illegality is also paradoxically implicated in establishing the principle of legality, and it is completed in the articulation of the social issues that produce the law.

Better yet, we can perhaps say that legality today, in the midst of a crisis of the rule of law, far from establishing a realm of formal self-sufficiency, has become an *instrumental element* of social life. Unlike what Max Weber used to believe, the principle of legality does not surpass, nor exclude, that of legitimacy; rather, it is functionally folded into legitimacy's semantic and practical frame-work. On the other hand, the *principle of legitimacy* asserts its superiority by strongly distancing itself from traditional defini-tions and from the shapes it has assumed during varying historical periods: far from defining itself as a transcendent or transcendental principle in whose name obedience is required, it presents itself as a double, effective principle which thrives on the synthesis of at least two pairs of opposites, that which is vertical between power and consent and that which is horizontal between the monism and pluralism of juridical production. Legality is forced into this shape of legitimacy. Legality is the outermost boundary in the refinement of the tensions which circle around the formation of a legitimate horizon.

Let us look, for instance, at the *Party-State* as a type of State which has replaced and modified the form of the Rule of law, endowing parties (and therefore the dynamic participation that parties organize in massive terms) with all of the expected functions of constitutional mediation. In this case we should define legality as the legitimacy of the organic competitive movement which the parties derermine in taking possession of the State. Power is constituted in this case in a legal code *outside* the realm of strict legality, through parties: it then displays its reconstructed figure as legality. What should we say, at this point, about illegality? In this framework illegality appears to be, rather than an alternative to legality, an element which partially and functionally constitutes legitimacy: it will be, in fact, the prerogative of the parties to select those mechanisms of illegality which, time after time, can be assumed into the Constitutional functions of the effective legal code. Is this a strength or a weakness of the principle of legality? It is apparent, in any event, that the Party-State has not yet succeeded in generating a principle equivalent to legality: an answer to the question we have posed is therefore impossible. Ambiguity lingers on.

Ambiguity lingers on and deepens when we consider situations of *emergency* in the life of the contemporary State. In this case, the topic of the relationship between legality and illegality which seems so convoluted in the event of the crisis of the Rule of Law, is definitely and without much difficulty, resolved in the context of the legitimacy of resorting to extraordinary repressive measures. Illegality, as a necessary tool of the State, is legitimized. But the topic of emergency is not solely connected to a political ot institutional crisis: the life of contemporary late-capitalist States is, in fact, an

indissoluble mass of juridical and economic, ethical and communicative elements. Crisis can affect with intensity each of these
couplings of power and determine at this juncture emergency outcomes. Recourse to forms of legitimate intervention *outside* of
legality becomes legitimate even in realms which have little to do
with the supreme needs of reproducing the state machinery. The
concept of *raison d' État*, in the last century, has become banal: the
regimes of *secrecy* and of *exceptional intervention* have become so
frequent and notorious that they set up a kind of *social Machiavellianism* for the benefit, at least, of all levels of judicial and economic
administration. Hence a strange paradox: that is, at the very
moment when the principle of legality seems to be most questioned and replaced by other administrative protocols, the
principle seems to expand its sphere of application. I repeat: at the
very moment when its logical potential and its validating intensity
weaken. To restate it with the words of an Italian jurist, the range
of the principle of legality is not such "that it can control every
activity of the executive administration"; it functions, rather, "by
way of a whole possible series of intermediate shades and grada-
tions which give the impression of an administration, rather than
actually shaping it." In fact, legality is, at this point, only a horizon.
Illegality is in the same way retained as the formative element of
legitimacy; illegality here referring to some aspects of the activity of
the State and of the main players in the activity which the State
unleashes, from parties, from sections of capital, from great
administrative, ideological bodies, etc. As far as this legitimacy is
concerned, it is easy to say what it is: it is the result of the mediation
between the different functions of state control; it is the go-
between of a continual process of adjustment; it is the instrument
which regulates and expands the political cycle. Legality is illegality;

they are therefore interchangeable in the realm of the concrete reproduction of the system.

Of particular interest, within this framework and based upon our premises, is the function of administration and judicial activities. In the crisis of the Rule of Law and in the process of establishing a State of legitimacy, *judicial power* assumes two functions. The first is the traditional function of repressing all forces which attack the material Constitution of the State and, therefore, threaten its reproduction. The second function is that of intervening in determining the internal balance of the executive class. In the first function, the judicial power applies the law; in the second, it *administers corruption*, it contributes to the creation of legitimacy, it bends legality to legitimacy. The "neutral power" defined by Montesquieu as guarantor of institutional balance reproduces its own function in a context where neutrality has nothing to do with transparency. Judicial power is, conversely, more and more grounded in the structure and machinery of the reproduction of power; it is consistent with these goals and, in functioning in this way it defines in a new manner the very meaning of its own function, of its corporative figure.

Let us turn, briefly, to the other aspect or result of this transformation in the relation between legality and illegality. *In the social realm* the watering down of the difference between legal and illegal corresponds to profound phenomena which have an impact on both economic production and social reproduction. When the line demarcating the difference between legality and illegality becomes thin or ambiguous we witness, in the social realm, the establishment of organizations which turn this in-distinction into a productive element. In this regard, our era has confronted us with imposing phenomena. The submerged industry, the industry which operates in illegal work markets, the industry which does not pay taxes, the relations between big industry and the great normalized services and the conglomerate of illegal, even criminal, productive and service activities, the laundering of money earned through illegal activity and its introduction into legal financial cycles, etc.: these large scale phenomena, in relation to which we have been able to identify the economic boom of entire continental areas, make their way into the current state institutionality of late capitalism. They even represent lines of strategic development. Here they are simply present in order to indicate that the discussion on the relation between legal and illegal and on the new constitution of the principle of legitimacy is not abstract: instead, it belongs (and finds a semantic place) within the enormous dimensions of social and political transformation.

3

Subversion from Above:
Notes on Bribesville

Once the Berlin Wall had fallen and the Yalta Era was over, capitalist strategy tackled the issue of dismantling every social compromise between capital and labor. The requisite for achieving this goal is a strong State, a Parliament as a place where any antagonisms of the subaltern classes are not represented, a Government capable of handling permanent exceptionality. During the last year, we have been witnesses to subversion, from above, of the constitutional structures of the First Republic, subversion used in a way which is suitable to the goals laid out by the strategy of capitalism.

Three forces have mobilized.

A social-democratic faction, strongly supported by big capital, which is in power in the government and in the highest institutions of the State, which generates with a powerful rhythm of anticipation and provocation the measures needed to tidy up the economy of the relation among classes. This faction is relentlessly playing the game of devaluation and inflation, cuts in real wage and dismemberment of the Welfare State, repressive politics vis-à-vis social disorder, with the goal of solving the emergency.

Secondly, Magistracy has become a *task force* of the capitalist government of society. Certainly the magistrates, with their actions, seem to attack both the corrupted and the very form of a corrupt operation within any capitalist parliamentary democracy. And this is why magistrates have the enthusiastic support of the people. But we cannot forget that capitalist democracy is always an ordering of corruption and that each new incarnation of democratic capitalist government cannot but be a different or equivalent form of corruption.

As long as capitalism survives, democracy will be corrupt: the Magistracy knows this, but individual magistrates pretend to ignore it.

The third power-player is "referendum-based." It is a direct descendant of Confindustria;[1] it is the product of the political transformism of the layers of "notables" of the old party structure and it faces many difficulties, but with the substantial support (up to this point) of the new populist factions (above all, the populism of the Northern Leagues). The goal of this third movement is to guarantee, within the new constitutional order of the Second Republic, the transformation of Parliament into the organ of the "notables" (through a uninominal voting system) and the conservative power of the government.

The contradictions which, at the moment, pit different forces against one another, must be understood occasionally, but not insignificantly, as the basis for working out a mass political alternative to the project which is unfolding. The most apparent contradiction is represented by the actions of the Magistracy. The Magistracy acts *super partes* (above partisanship) and attacks—as if they were small time crooks—important representatives of big capital. But we know that this contradiction is only superficial: the Magistracy, in its political actions, is perfectly in unison with the reactionary project of big capital. The actions of the Magistracy will dismantle the traditional parties and the old corrupt ways of handling public life: on the other hand, no Board of Directors of big capital will be dissolved. Bark and bite remain

---

1. Translators' Note: Confederazione generale dell'industria italiana, the Italian Association of Industrialists.

separate things. Perhaps what we should emphasize is another aspect of this situation, that is, the fact that embracing once more this function of direct representation of capitalist interest (as in endless other instances: from the bloody repression of the post-war strikes to the silence in reaction to the carnage during the years of terrorism—"the years of lead"—just to recall the most flagrant instances and to avoid talking about the connivance in Mafia business, about previous instances of corruption, about repression of autonomy, about the barbarization of society in the last fifty years) the Magistracy reveals itself as a tumor produced by the First Republic, a disease which has now become the cause of death of an infected and abused democracy. Other conditions are at play. It is without any doubt, for example, that within the movement of the Leagues progressive forces which want to regain hold of the administration are mingling with fascist forces which foster programs like those of the Balkan insurgents or the Serbian nationalists; there is no doubt that within the social-democratic government fundamental contradictions exist from time to time (and we have seen this above all with regards to privatizations), contradictions concerning the very concept of democracy, of political citizenship (can the latter be separated from the right to public ownership of the means of production and of production control?), of civil rights (abortion), of the issue of immigration, etc. And more contradictions could be emphasized. But these contradictions are not essential. What is essential is the ability of big capital, national as well as international, to reign over the process, to be in charge of the contradictions, to propel the Italian constitutional destiny into an autocratic Second Republic.

The Mainstream Press, the network of mass communication, is the fundamental organ of big capital in this subversive experience: it is its unrelenting and direct instrument. As happened in other instances, the enterprise of the Magistracy would not have been possible without the support of the Mainstream Press, without the direct intervention of this new (and old) big form of corruption in Italian public life.

The Media are the AIDS of the First Republic, an anti-immune system that the First Republic has produced, just as the Magistracy is the other deadly disease. If this is evident in the "Clean Hands" operation, it is even more grotesque when it comes to the advancement of the Referendum movement and of the characters that are at its forefront. Segni, the son of the first coup leader, would never have become a Presidential contender in the Second Republic without the shameless support of press and big capital. The same holds true for Mariotto, the lap dog of Boards of Directors all over Italy. And so forth.

We couldn't care less if the First Republic dies of the diseases it has created. We are glad every time a representative of the *Ancien régime* is exposed for what s/he is, a rogue to her/his fellow citizens (even if we are still disgusted by the San Vittore prison!). But we are completely and absolutely opposed to the capitalist project which is behind all recent events. For years many of us, too many, have fought against the First Republic. In this struggle we have had to endure prison and exile, but we have discovered, above all, the joy of democratic subversion, of grass roots subversion, intended to give maximum power to those who have always been victimized by it. We believe, therefore, that we can oppose the subversion from above caused by big capital with grass roots subversion and democratic rebellion.

The Second Republic, the New Constituent Assembly and Grass Roots Subversion

We want a Second Republic. The old left which keeps guarding the First is nothing but the pathetic, vulgar and cruel residue of the old politics of Togliatti's Communist Party.

We want a Second Republic. But Segni and the referendum movement will not concede it to us, grant it to us. They are even worse than the others. With their movement, their referenda, and their arrogance they want to reject the possibility of something new growing out of the crisis. But something new must grow out of the crisis. We do not want fascism any more. We want a new Constituent Assembly.

We do not have any illusion that a new Constituent Assembly can stop this process in any substantial manner. But we all know that the contradictions within which the capitalist project is exposed with impunity can be exalted and dismissed within a process through which, finally, social subjects are invited to express themselves more freely. These institutional contradictions are nothing but a smokescreen behind which deep-rooted contradictions and real needs, as well as actual desires for renewal, manifest themselves; so here we are again, ready to express our reasonable optimism. We want a Second Republic, but we want it as the product of democratic subversion. The Constituent Assembly, the battle for a Constituent Assembly, the inauguration of a process where everything old is obsolete and the new mass forces can work out new associations and new unities: this is the only project that workers and social autonomy can and must bring about, in order to find a radically democratic solution to the residual problems of the First Republic, to the crisis we have been denouncing for years, to the miseries inflicted upon so many people, to the hopes that the new, wealthy generations are capable of producing. There's no illusion here, just room to have a mass debate, to create a mass movement galvanized by democratic and radical objectives which can become even more radicalized in the discussion, in the clashes, and in the struggle.

It has always been the goal of the labor and proletarian autonomy to inaugurate a movement and to keep it going.

Demanding a Constituent Assembly, bringing this demand to the streets, fighting for public spaces in which new political associations can form and express themselves: this is the field of battle that the "Clean Hands" operation leaves open, if we just embrace it, for the "clean brains" of autonomy. It is a matter of breaking through, together, where the constitutional breach of the First Republic has given way. Not simply against the Amato government, not simply against the referendum movement, but simply against corruption, in favor of a Constituent Assembly, and within the realm of the battle for a Constituent Assembly, for a form of radical direct democracy within which corruption is no longer an option, within which there is neither the highhandedness of the masters nor the hypocrisy of magistrates, nor the shameful behavior of politicians and traditional parties. We must pursue the constitutional breach in order to open up political spaces together with public spaces, in order to regain control of the administration, to reconstitute radically democratic political subjectivities.

Grass roots subversion must and can respond to subversion from above.

Let us recall Gramsci's analysis of the onset of fascism (although his understanding came after the fact). Our intelligence is mobilized before the catastrophe occurs and it would be morally bankrupt, in addition to being politically irresponsible, not to show everybody that—as History goes—it is a capitalist contradiction, once again, that is arming us with a fundamental weapon: that of uniting us from the grass roots to achieve mass subversion and liberation.

4

Laboratory Italy (September 1993)

The framework of contradictions in which the so-called "Italian revolution" is engulfed is narrowing down increasingly. The net gets entangled and becomes a knot: somebody will have to cut it off eventually.

Banal conclusion. But what has occurred to this point is not in the least banal. Just the opposite. Once again, Italy is ahead of the rest of Europe, as in the Twenties and Thirties with Mussolini's dictatorship, as with the constitutional compromise between the populist Atlantic right and the socialist Soviet-leaning left which composed and recomposed itself in all possible configurations, from the post-war period to the fall of the Berlin Wall. And today: Italy is a laboratory of forms of government that capitalist power can/must create for itself in an international context which is no longer over-determined by a dual model of opposed regimes (USA–USSR), but is managed by a single imperial structure, the laboratory of new forms of administration for an imperialist power of medium size.

As we know, the "Italian revolution" originates with the appearance, concurrent to the dissolution of all international duties of a cold war context, of a protest movement against the corruption of the political parties which have dominated Italy since 1945 and the appearance of demands of political participation strongly rooted at the local level, mistakenly expressing both democratic aspirations and separatist, racist and federalist tendencies. At the base of these movements we find the fundamental role of the productive strata of the scattered labor of small and medium sized companies which have come into existence since 1968, especially in Northern Italy. In an extremely short time the Leagues of small owners take the lead within the movement and upset the political landscape in the regions of Lombardy, Piedmont and Veneto, that is, in the "European" regions of Italy. After 50 years of socialism, Milan has a mayor affiliated with the Lombard League.

Since its inception, the protest movement is correctly interpreted and directly challenged by an alliance which is heterogeneous, but nonetheless powerful, an alliance which unites big industry (and the entire system of media and press that it controls) and some "clean" departments of the big State administration (essentially the Treasury and the Justice System). The courts, in strict collaboration with big time press, are charged with the task of solving the issue of corruption: they have no trouble doing it by restarting the instruments of emergency-state legislation and by availing themselves of a generalized climate of informants. It matters very little if this legal operation totally destroys the traditional party system, forces to its knees the corporative democracy and the Welfare State: this is the price to pay for renewing the political structures of the country, for isolating the Leagues and their unfocussed protest, for establishing and regulating a new capitalist democracy. While delegating full powers to the Magistracy, the great bosses (employers) and the other power groups seek to impose, by way of referendum, an electoral reform for a uninominal majority based vote, by means of which they can control the renewal of the political class, forcing it to gravitate around a perfectly malleable social and economic "center."

On the basis of the establishment of a new centrist political force they could start contemplating a reform of the system in the sense of a presidential regime.

If everything stopped here, we might even be able to smile at the possibility of an Italy-laboratory, which we advanced at the beginning of this essay. In fact, the recourse to a uninominal and majority based electoral system and its evolution into a presidential regime represent something that is all too common in European constitutional history to merit any great interest (each time serious social and political crises had to be overcome, this is what happened), were it not for the ever unique circumstances in which the political process unfolds. But it does not end here, or rather, the situation has become more complicated since 1993, when the normality of the model was radically upset. To state it more clearly, even though everything had unfolded between 1989 and 1998, as was required by the alliance of restoration forces, the situation was redefined from 1993 onward in totally new terms by two seemingly insurmountable obstacles and a series of growing and irreversible contradictions.

The two insurmountable obstacles have been revealed: a) by the fact that the battle against corruption, led by the Magistracy, has collided head first with more and more big Italian capitalists and has started to encroach upon certain great central administrative bodies (Defense, Health, Foreign Trade, Industry, etc.); b) by the fact that the new electoral system, once it was put to the test, instead of electing a new center coalition, has swept away any illusion of such and has radicalized the presence of the various Leagues and of a leftist coalition of mixed composition which has remained substantially under the hegemony of the old PCI (Italian Communist Party), today re-named the PDS (Democratic Party on the Left). As far as the contradictions which appear on the horizon are concerned, they are contradictions which are pitted against each other in ever-growing proportions: multinational industry, organically bound to financial capital and speculative markets, and a small, very dynamic industry bound to the international market but also strongly rooted in its own specific territories, capable of representing various strata of a new kind of autonomous labor, scattered and decentralized, within the context of a new political-territorial partnership.

This contradiction emerges in conjunction with nearly all issues of national politics, whether they are tax-related issues, issues of industrial policy, labor practices, service related issues, etc. These contradictions, furthermore, have been strongly accentuated by the crisis in Europe: it is apparent, in fact, that the solution presented by the "Italian revolution" as it was conceived, to be an alliance between big capital and the central the administration of the State, relied on the indispensable and absolute condition of a European dynamics within which regionalism and federalism could become compatible through an advancement in the levels of control.

Let us review the elements at our disposal thus far.

The "Italian revolution" has reached a point which is, perhaps, dramatic. The mechanism was initiated by certain strata of the state bourgeoisie (industrial and administrative) in order to address the new protest movements (which, without being very revolutionary, grew out of the new international situation, out of real changes in the industrial and productive structure, out of a displacement of power and administrative relations, out of the emergence of new needs and demands for new services, etc.). This mechanism had the function of reabsorbing the crisis and is now fraying and exhausting itself into a series of vicious circles. With its independent action, the Magistracy has, in fact, provoked the crisis of some parameters in the exercise of power and in its legitimization: the parameters grounded on the authority of big industry, that is, on the only power player which had caused in Italy an authentic perspective of modernity between the Risorgimento and the Fascist period, and later during the First Republic. As far as the political solution which had been anticipated is concerned, which should have caused a redefinition of a "political center" at a higher level, both within the area of constitutional forms and within a new political context beyond Europe—well, not even this solution is any longer working. The uninominal majority-based electoral standard, instead of exercising pressure in favor of centrist convergences, has propelled political representation towards extremes and, as far as Europe is concerned, for the first time in Italy, just referring to the uninominal majority-based electoral standard begins to provoke more division than unity. What is going to happen?

For the time being, we cannot really envision a solution to the problem. During the summer of 1993 we heard only the threatening sound of bombs: this sound reminds us that at the end of the day there is a power which decides over life and death, and which reappears whenever it is time to handle the difficult thresholds of Italian "democracy" and to guarantee the continuity of the State, in spite of those who claim that in Italy there is no State! If we scratch slightly below the surface, behind big industry, behind the Priests of the Economy and the Justice System, we discover State terrorists. They act with the blessing of the imperial hegemonic power, with total impunity. Between 1969 and 1980 in Italy about twenty massacres took place: no one responsible for those massacres has ever been brought to Court. It is obvious, however, that the present problems cannot be solved with bombs: bombs intended to impose respect and to remind any and all of the authority of the State. But how can we begin to find a solution to this problem?

I believe that for the first time in years, the situation must be looked upon with reasonable pessimism. First of all, this pessimism is related to the very destiny of the nation and is bound to the possibility that the confrontation between the "Milanese Croats" and the "Roman Serbs" will become radicalized and will pave the way to extreme alternatives. Secondly, if this should happen, we cannot envision who would be able to oppose the potential authoritarian shipwrecks of the crisis. For too long now, the left no longer exists. In the clash among the various traditions which have characterized the PCI, the PDS has inherited a bureaucratic conformism and an opportunism void of principles which make it akin to the administrative lobbying proto-Masonic sects of the former Socialist states, as opposed to the socialist democracies of central Europe. The old secular and liberal center does not exist anymore, having been unraveled by corruption; and, as we can observe on the other hand, the appearance of "centrism" is rather problematic. By now, Catholic populism is out of breath. The people in the Leagues, drunk on success, are speeding up the crisis, persuaded that they can, in any case, ride the wave. Should we be confronted with extreme alternatives, who would stand where? Who would be willing today, in Italy, to fight for unity and who for division? Italy is not Yugoslavia; Italy is a rich, cynical and dispassionate country: no one would, in reality, fight and risk her/his own hide or wealth. But on this side, before open war, everything is possible, above all, an authoritarian solution to the crisis. After all, if we really think about it, this is the least costly solution. The people dressed in black who plant the bombs know this and tell us this with a certain skill at making themselves understood. This is what all political commentators clearly emphasize.

Of what, then, can this authoritarian solution of the crisis consist? It consists fundamentally in keeping the crisis going and in exacerbating it until a new political center has been consolidated. The State wants to mold its very own new political personnel and does not want anybody else to choose this personnel. We can rightly anticipate that, at least in the two years to come, elections will be held one after the other, and that the political parties, from the Leagues to the PDS and through to whatever remains of the Christian Democratic Party and of the secular centrist groups, will be called upon to demonstrate their availability to occupy the center. The process of renewal has taken shape in such a way that, through all the contradictions, beyond obstacles and vicious circles, the State redefines itself as the only possible center of political life—and therefore the State demands of the parties, new and old alike, not to represent the interest of the people ahead of the State, but the interest of the State ahead of its citizens. Behind the political issue there is an economic issue. From this perspective, it is urgent to mold the dynamic of scattered production and of autonomous labor to the rules of financial globalization. The new world order does not concern solely Iraq, but also the small independent producers of the Plains of the Po River ...

Thus we arrive at the answer to the first question posed in this article. Why does what is happening in Italy represent a prototype? Why can we, again, talk about an Italy-Laboratory, as in the Twenties or in the Fifties? Here is the answer: in Italy, as far as medium sized capitalist powers are concerned, the new order of the world Empire is endeavoring to become actualized. It is a dramatic endeavor, because in Italy the crisis of leaving the old dual system established by Yalta has been due to the very particular history of class warfare in this country, something absolutely dramatic. This endeavor anticipates conditions and situations, crises and contradictions, which will concern all medium sized capitalist powers.

Nobody should believe that they will be able to elude these issues. And yet, we do believe that the other medium sized capitalist powers that are today affected by the crisis will, perhaps, be able to avoid the situation which is current in Italy. In the Twenties, in this country, we sought a solution to a problem of social modernization in the face of the Bolshevik challenge: fascism, however, was not a good answer even if we must not underestimate its modernizing effectiveness. In the Fifties, in Italy, we sought to incorporate the workers movement into an alliance dedicated to the reconstruction, within the framework of Fordism; but Italian style corporative, *compromise-based* democracy became a cancer that destroyed the energies of the country, corrupting the class of entrepreneurs itself and degrading the productive energy of the working class. In the Nineties, within the framework of US hegemony over the world market, we are now searching for a new form of politics: but the center of authoritarian power with which we are faced is not a good answer. It brings with itself the vocation of big capital to subordinate itself to the American center and to choose a path of violence against the productive classes which do not want to accept this arrangement.

Is it possible to do something to oppose the direction adopted by the "Italian revolution" or, better, by the counter-revolution? We cannot know this. It also does not appear that there are, at a European level, new political subjects which exude the necessary maturity to address these issues. The Italian counter-revolution foretells in reality the temporal framework of the issue of the globalization of the economy and of the processes of political and democratic legitimization as they have been perceived lately by the other medium sized capitalist powers. The Italian counter-revolution challenges political subjects on this terrain and ridicules the new nationalist options, the ones that are denied at the level of the old nation states as well as at the European level. The Italy-Laboratory works well: it is a laboratory of reaction; it is (in whatever form we contemplate it) a formidable realm of experimentation of the "new world order." We are not able to outline an operative and political alternative which is effective in the face of this involution. We only know that it is imperative to resist: that we must resist without any illusion, without reminiscing about a previous time, without thinking that there is something worth salvaging. The only advantage presented by this laboratory of reaction is that it works within and together with material conditions that are utterly new. There lies its interest for our inquiry and for the struggle of those who do not love the new world order and its applications to the medium sized capitalist states throughout Europe.

5

Techniques for a *Coup d'État* (November 1993)

Three *coups d'État* are currently taking place in Italy.

The first *coup d'État* is that of the *League* which alternates between threats of territorial secession, efforts to incite generalized fiscal disobedience, and promises to create a separate parliamentary power and a Northern government. In the League we discern a sophisticated repetition of forms of early fascism, which find expression in populist (at times plebeian) attack initiatives, which are ignited within communal forms of proximity. *Gemeinschaft* against *Gesellschaft*, community against society: never has a more apt definition been proposed.

The second is that of the *PDS* with its implacable Stalinist march through the institutions, taking over, in addition to the magistracy and the Anti-Mafia Police, other administrative public sectors and influencing a large number of the instruments which shape public opinion, newspapers and television media.

The third *coup d'État* is that of the "State center," of the *elite ranks of the State administration* which unites large strata of bureaucratic, Mason-like organizations, and expresses itself through demonstrative terrorist actions, embracing an authoritarian presidentialist project as the antidote against the infiltration into the current power structures by a new treacherous personnel controlled by the PDS.

Each of these lines of attack and of the anti-democratic conquering of the State relies upon specific economic and social forces.

— The League leans upon small industries which are widespread in the North and integrated into the global market, industries which refuse any compromise with State structures which are dominated by parasitical big industry. Localism and liberalism are the dark flags of a California-style ideology.

— The PDS interprets the corporate interests of big industry and of the hegemonic elites of the liberal bourgeoisie, as well as the interests of the residual labor corporations: it has transformed itself into the Italian version of European social-democracy. The Italian progressive block echoes the foolish certainty, on the part of European social-democracy, of the end of all ideologies; like its European counterpart, the PDS displays a cynical predisposition to repress class conflicts.

—The State center expresses its own needs for survival and reproduction by gathering together in this project wide groups from the bureaucratic middle class, by finding in fascist-leaning protest a mass base and by using the residual ideological structures of the parties of the *Ancien régime* as its cultural foundation.

How did we arrive at this situation? How did we come to exemplify a rough reproduction of the Weimar crisis and an apocalyptic anticipation of a new fascism—however this situation might develop, *rebus sic stantibus*—for the 21st century?

The explanation is not difficult. The Italian political forces became, in the Eighties, totally removed from social development and from the modernization of the Italian civil and productive system, after the members of the avant-garde, who had been the main players of this innovative modernization, had been repressed during the Seventies. The cancer of Italian democracy is produced in the period of the "historic compromise." The so-called forces of the progressive party cannot forget this today: they are themselves at the very source of this physiological corruption of the constitutional and democratic system, since the moment when they accepted to put an end to their opposition and to collaborate with a crippled, rotten, Mafia-infested leadership. This was something worse than a Chilean style threat and today it is clear to everybody!

What is scandalous is that today—in a way that would make Stalin, the subtlest of mystifiers, envious—the destroyers of the alternative political class which originates in the post-1968 struggles present themselves as the only forces capable of guaranteeing the life of the Republic. We need to go back to the Seventies to understand how such hypocrisy can be the cause of death.

And today? What is to be done?

At this dramatic juncture, before a threat which has been blown out of proportion, we do not believe that we can say: the hell with you, this is what you asked for! And we shall wait, as you deserve, for your corpses to float before our very eyes on the river of History ... Not at all. We do not believe that passivity, even with an honest and theoretically wise conscience, can be part of the game.

Not at all: we believe that we do not have to dirty our hands, at this dire moment for the subaltern classes, for the sake of the new forces of productive work, for all honest people.

We too, therefore, must begin to discuss a way to re-start a democratic struggle: a path that is as subversive as the one of the three techniques for a *coup d'État* which we have described, but one which contains, unlike the others, a strongly embedded goal at its core: the goal of liberation from labor, the goal of a democracy of all and for all. Never, like today, has this utopia been at the core of discussion, because it points to, in Machiavellian style, a "return to principles" by way of which, alone, democracy and liberty can be rescued. And our principles are those of 1968 and of the Seventies: struggle against wage labor, development of material and immaterial productive forces, social cooperation and destruction of capitalistic subordination, guaranteed wages and massive reduction in work week, democratic self-management of economic development, women's liberation, reappropriation of the administration and creation of a free public space ... It is not a utopia: we all know that each of these formulations can be organized and made to work, better than the decrepit forms of the Liberal State and of the dirty capitalist market. We all know that, in past years in Italy and still today in many other countries, these desires seek, massively and powerfully, a form of expression. A new charter of human rights is emerging from History. After the fall of really-existing socialism, after the fall of the illusion that capitalism could still embody freedom (or simply "more" freedom), millions of citizens are now addressing again this theme of reflection and of action.

Our "*coup d'État*" must lean technically upon this awareness.

Recomposing the elements of resistance and of attack, directly re-appropriating segments of the administration, forcing into demystification the forces (the three forces: Californian, corporate and bureaucratic) of the incumbent fascist restoration, elaborating and re-enlivening clusters of a subversive program: is it really impossible to play the tune of grass-roots subversion and of real democracy?

6

Cloning (December 1993)

Administrative elections, dramatic pantomime. Comic actors comparing themselves to one another. Alessandra Mussolini and Antonio Bassolino, Fini's double-breasted suit jacket (draped over his shoulder) and Rutelli's double-breasted suit jacked (draped over a Vespa).

Behind the scenes: Scalfari and Berlusconi, the two men who own the media, enter directly into the field to play the two souls of the farce, megalomaniacal puppets with heroic missions … The result: everything must be done over again. That is to say, a progressive block (self-styled but extremely fragile) that wins some big cities while the League is rampant in provincial areas, and the neo-fascists, for the first time, present their candidacy on the political marketplace as the mass base of each conservative strategy.

After the elections: the powerless cawing of everybody against everybody. Certainly, the idiocy of *Il Manifesto* ("Call to arms! They are fascists") will remain unequalled—but what more compliant incitement to the union of the forces of the left toward the center could there be? Well, then, everything must be done over again, the "center" does not exist yet, it needs to be invented, everything must be sacrificed to the redefinition of the idea.

The great accusation: the center does not exist yet, we must create it. New political, national elections, soon, very soon: to construct, to discover a center. The circle closes, the script of the future has already been written. Everybody agrees: we need a center. League, fascists, Berlusconi, Craxi's men and a great part of the Christian democrats, "new" men from industry, and on and on …

Here is the new center. It could not be any newer! And if we do not have this center, we will find *another*: this is what is guaranteed by Scalfari, Occhetto, La Malfa, Jr., Craxi's men who are not on the side of Craxi, Christian democrats who are not with the others because they like Rosy Bindi, the "old" men of industry, and on and on. This "new" center calls itself a progressive block. *New* center, then, against an*other* center. Segni and Ciampi, cloned and often confused, wait for their presidential destiny: in the *new* or *other* center, or the other way around. Trilussa, eternal Roman plebeian, or someone else in his place, can make up effortlessly another miserable story, a grotesque one even, of servants and masters, opportunists and crafty devils. In Italy, under our beautiful sun which burns through the shadows, political history is never a tragedy, nor does it repeat itself like comedy: it is farce the first time around, and it becomes coarse at a later stage.

In the meantime, financial reform has been passed: it was voted in by the old (so to speak) party system, together with the PDS which is even older, and with an abstention from the League (neoliberalism *oblige*). All together, then, on important matters: *less money to the workers, more powers to the administration, new world order executed.*

The Republic goes on. The old doofuses of the First Republic, the Bobbios and the Modiglianis, honored witnesses of a Resistance which has lost its honor, introduce the Second Republic and applaud the balancing of financial sheets—privatizations, savage reductions of the deficit, dismantling of the welfare system, reduction in pensions, tampering with all the rules of the Welfare State, and on and on. And just like them, together with them, how many others?

Civil society is cancer-ridden. The platforms of parties and party associations for the next elections resemble one another to such a degree that they are interchangeable. The left with the right, the right with the left and the center, obviously, with the other two at the same time. Our heads are spinning, the Merry-go-round goes wild, Bobbio and Modigliani believe they are in the First Republic while they are already in the Second Republic, the constitutional and monetary orders are exchangeable with much more fluidity than was thought possible. The political market fulfills itself not only as exchange but as law of exchange. It is not just Segni and Ciampi who are cloned, but the First and the Second Republics as well, the right and the left, progressives and conservatives, grandma and aunt. Michele and Giovannino. Italian history is cloned: Vittorio Emanuele and Garibaldi, Crispi and Giolitti, Statace and Bottai, De Gasperi and Togliatti, Resistance and Second Republic, Bobbio and Miglio, Modigliani and Andreatta … All cloned, all clowns; long live Italy!

The circle closes, yes, and in the worst possible way, in a reactionary manner. This Italian revolution is not a revolution, but a "devolution." An event poisoned by a plan which is, without any doubt, fascist in nature, even though the word is no longer, and rightly so, fashionable (too many gizmos have changed). It is better to say, using an old, solid expression, a *tyrannical design*. Because this is what the Second Republic is offering us: a world as flat as a newspaper ad, a choice as open as the programming choices of Fininvest or the pages of *La Repubblica*.

A tyranny without cruelty (except toward the poor), without melancholy (who wants to be free any more?), without joy (not even the shabby types from the years of Resistance and of Autonomia).

The Second Republic—New World Order. A tyrannical design, permitted and encouraged all over the world: a two-speed society, with its clocks regulated inside the society of the rich; a fringe society of a global capitalism which is becoming vertical and hierarchical: if you want a place in it, you must acquiesce; postmodern society, where productive articulation becomes the soft articulation of the present state of things, while exploitation is blown out of proportion as it travels through intellectual realms and intellectual labors, uncertainty of the future and frailty of income. The Nineties are a repetition of the festive Eighties, enacted against the infinite multiplication of the riotous, within a global tyrannical framework. In Italy, at least.

7

The Italian "Revolution" and the "Devolution" of the Left

Nothing was more predictable than the victory of the right in the recent Italian elections. It is not just Berlusconi who has won: before he did, the right had already won. In the summer of 1993 we had written: "In Italy it is the right which is capitalizing on the crisis of 1989, for its own benefit (in spite of the fact that the PCI has hastily changed its name and openly revealed that, for a very long time, nothing communist remained in its conscience)." But, and this is far more important, the right has not just capitalized on the fall of the Berlin wall: it has triumphed because it has grasped the deep changes in the Italian productive framework and has understood the role of communication in contemporary societies. When Berlusconi suddenly entered the stage in last month's electoral campaign, he put the communication industry at the disposal of the party of small and medium sized entrepreneurs who are transforming the anti-tax, anti-bureaucracy and anti-state revolt that they had led in previous years into political victory.

Berlusconi can do this because he is one of them. He shared in the adventure which enabled new energies in the industrial districts of the North to get rid of all old disciplines, and which enabled Italy—based on the productivity of the new Small and Medium Sized Businesses—to become the fourth or fifth industrial power in the world. What Benetton is to the field of textiles, Berlusconi is to the realm of communication: a gathering point of scattered labor. But communication is not textiles. In post-Fordism communication is the political form of productive control, just as in Fordism the political form of control was shaped in the great Taylorized factory, in Mirafiori, in the great car, steel and chemical plants. Berlusconi has replaced the Agnellis in the hierarchies of industrial power in Italy. Here is the novelty: Agnelli in the Senate and Berlusconi in the government. Berlusconi brings to the government the new productive networks, and with them the neoliberal incontinence of the small, narcissistic, pushy entrepreneurs, who are organically introduced into the culture of productive communication and frantically driven to exploit this new territory.

By recalling these simple ideas we have cleared the field of some of the simplifications and false images which have been circulating in Europe concerning the Berlusconi phenomenon. Because, first of all, Berlusconi is not the diabolical function of a nightmarish machine of television power. These eschatological images vulgarly parrot the situationist accusations leveled against the society of spectacle, without grasping the significance and the specific violence of the new character of power. No, really, Berlusconi is not a "tele-fascist": Berlusconi is a master, a figure of collective capitalism, a function of capitalist control of society, because in his person communication and production are the same thing. Secondly, Berlusconi is not a fascist: he is not a fascist, just as much as his god-parents Thatcher and Reagan are not. But we can certainly amuse ourselves by using the fascist metaphor to describe Berlusconi, as we have often done to describe all the great captains of industry and capitalists ravenous for exploitation. I am saying that we, old and unrepentant subversives, can amuse ourselves by doing it, just to be provocative: but how can those who until yesterday requested the modernization of capitalism, and a chance to hitch themselves to its wagon, do this? How can those who, allied to Agnelli or De Benedetti, having lost the election, do this? It is said that neo-fascists are members of Berlusconi's majority and that Europe refuses to recognize all that is reminiscent of the era of totalitarianism ... What hypocrisy! Is there a single European liberal regime which has not flirted with the metropolitan plebes in order to organize them in national-populist terms? Is there a single economic liberalism that has not sought out the support of popular populism? No, Berlusconi is simply a neoliberal: it's just entertaining to hear that he is accused of being a fascist by those who in the last twenty years have felt that they were crushed and/or attracted by the refrains of neoliberalism and who have repeated in unison that privatizations were necessary, that the Welfare system is too costly, that wage deflation is crucial for straightening out the productivity of the system ... What a pack of lies! And now they are trying to reshape those lies by appealing to the inflation of the term "fascist." Watch out! No one ever said that too much of crying wolf is useful when the wolf actually appears.

And the real wolf is there, waiting for the right moment to appear. The "subversion from above" of post-Fordist capitalism has only just begun in Italy. Italy is still not familiar with the monstrous hierarchy of social labor which has already been experimented with by other European rightist movements. Italy barely knows what a society with two speeds is and can barely see the abyss which separates them; up until now Italy has had only a few grotesque experiences with capitalist postmodernism: drugs and Craxism, "historical compromise" and "weak thought," circus shows and corruption, mafia and repentants ... The best is yet to come.

The real wolf is there waiting. But let us not confuse, again, that which is fascist and that which is not. It is not an act of fascism to renew the republican Constitution of 1948 and superimpose upon that a presidential machinery for that liberal-representative system: it is just Gaullism. It is not an act of fascism to extend and broaden local regional autonomies: this can, at most, become an act of egotism. It is not an act of fascism to stage, from the point of view of the majority and by way of institutional pressures, reactionary campaigns against the emancipation of public customs (against abortion, against homosexuality, etc.): this is just clericalism. All of the above, certainly, will be realized by a Berlusconi government: but this is not fascism, it is just the social, economic, cultural and political right. Berlusconi interprets, constructs, renews and exalts a reactionary community; he develops and perfects a new postmodern and communicative capitalism, showing Italian society what Italian society has already become in the past twenty years: a banal society in which left and right have become indistinguishable; in which thought has been either "weak" or incarcerated or neutralized; in which the union of factory councils has been transformed into the union of corporations, just as happened with all social counterforces: a society in which the enormous corruption that implicated entrepreneurs and politicians was nothing compared to the corruption which took over the mortal conscience of the multitude.

This, the Italian "revolution," is only a reactionary operation (not fascist, but reactionary) in its political contents and in the constitutional forms that it assumes, but it is a reactionary operation conducted at the level of the present development of capitalism, and suitable to the transformation of the organization of industry and of control over work. Berlusconi owns an industry of communication which has become the political leadership of a political society (of communication). In this sense, the reactionary revolution is also, paradoxically, an operation of the truth.

But the left does not want to acknowledge this truth. Having been defeated in the elections, the left does not want to understand the reasons for its defeat, and it unloads the responsibility on nothingness, with immaterial rhetoric and an obsession with fascism. The left, alone, is responsible for this defeat:

1) because it did not succeed in understanding the social transformation that had taken place in Italy; and it persevered in seeing corporations as means of representation;

2) because it did not keep in check, better yet, it did not even fathom, the new productive order of communicative relations; consequently, it has entered the realm of the media, cynically and irresponsibly partaking in the reactionary banalization of the media;

3) consequently, the left has lost any ability to represent the productive sectors (material and immaterial) of society. In Italy today there are two parasitical societies: one is the Mafia and the other is the left, with its entourage of trade unions and cooperatives ... But perhaps this is an exaggeration: the left, in fact, does not even have the criminal dignity of the Mafia; it's just the walking dead ... As we have seen, when faced with a reactionary victory, the heroic answer on the left is to scream out fascism. In reality the left is like a dazed boxer, sleepwalking. In all likelihood, the only thing left to do is to trip over this zombie. [...]

8

Italy, the Nineties:
Crisis and Renewal of a Constitutional Model

1. The events which have characterized Italian history in the Nineties are, without a doubt, revolutionary events: they have had a radical impact on the structure of the Republic, its leadership, its constitutional form. Let us now address the modifications of the "material Constitution" of the Italian Republic.

In defining the idea of "material constitution" let us follow the teachings of Carl Schmitt and, in the case of Italy, the teachings of Costantino Mortati, who was a student of Schmitt and one of the authors of the Italian Constitution of 1948, that is, of the Constitution (as it is called today) of the First Republic. Schmitt and Mortati define the *material* constitution (to distinguish it from the *formal* Constitution) as the tacit and structural codification of a set of political power relations which gives meaning to the rules, to the language and to the goals of the Constitution. Being the material constitution of a normative event *par excellence* is the historical condition which provides the foundation, the *Grundnorm* of the system. The material constitution defines the spirit of the formal Constitution and sets its limits.

Well, then, the formal form of the Constitution of 1948 presupposed a democratic constitutional regime of republican nature. But its material base was made up of the programmatic alliance of Catholic political forces together with social-communist ones. The constitutional contract excluded all forces, fascist or not, which were nostalgic of the past: the antifascist sentiment which had animated the Resistance against the enemy, internal and external, became the basis of the Constitution. The social program outlined in the Constitution of 1948 (better yet, by the forces which were guaranteed by the Constitution) was that of a capitalist democracy with strong "reformist" leanings (today we would call it a Fordist social policy), that is, a democracy open to those reforms which would have granted special active citizenship to all workers.

Further concerning the material constitution of 1948, two other elements must be considered. First, the special character of the process of legitimization that is contemplated in it; second, the international over-determination acknowledged by the constitutional process.

A double model of legitimization is enacted by the Constitution of 1948—a legitimization achieved through practical representation and a second process of representation of organized interests (above all unions of workers and farmers, and corporations of business owners). It is with this double system of legitimization that the State powers have to contend; and the actions of the State powers must always achieve the miracle of balancing, in parliamentary, administrative, juridical action, the interests of the parties with those of organized social forces. It is clear from this overview that the Italian State was configured, since 1948, as a *constitutional State* (of reciprocal checks and balances among various political and social forces) rather than as a *Rule of law* (where the dominion of abstract and generalized law is absolute).

The international over-determination of the 1948 Constitution was established by the inter-allied Conference in Yalta. In the division of the world into blocs, Italy was to participate in the Western bloc and was not to be able to decide otherwise. This norm of international order is internalized by the constitutional process. The Italian constitutional system would be built on an "imperfect bipartisanism." "Bipartisanism" because the system was based on two forces, the right and the left, which would be opposed to one another and predisposed to keeping each other in check and—theoretically—to alternating in government. But this bipartisanism was to remain "imperfect": in the sense that international circumstances would prevent, *on principle*, a theoretical alternation from becoming real. As the leadership of the PCI was to repeat incessantly, even if the party had obtained 51% of the ballots, an alternative to the DC would have been impossible.

To assure the functioning of this baroque, and yet democratic and constitutional system, a series of *ad hoc* institutional posts and suitable procedures was established. Some especially crucial procedures made it possible to create a permanent *con-sociation* of parliamentary political forces for the management of the State: for instance, the working protocols of the parliamentary commissions which allowed for wide ranging and ongoing legislative bargaining, or the system of corporate regulation of conflicts of interest—which permitted the development of wide ranging procedures for the participation of the bargaining units in the setting of the political agenda for economic planning and redistribution of income.

What was important, lastly, was the creation (agreed upon constitutionally) of those institutional posts (from the Presidency of the Republic to the Highest Council of the Magistracy, without counting the multiple institutions for economic regulation) whose goal was that of channeling, through them, the duplicity of the representative frame of reference and, consequently, of softening the possibly perverse effects of "imperfect bipartisanism."

This governmental system would last from 1948 until the beginning of the Nineties. As long as the international conditions which had presided over its genesis remained, this type of government could not be changed. The very same international system that imposed its prototype on this type of government (and its limits and shortfalls), guaranteed its own tenure.

This is demonstrated by the fact that the successive crises which that system was to experience from 1948 to the Nineties would renew the spirit of the material constitution of 1948. There are in fact, during the forty years of life of the Constitution of the First Republic, various critical moments: in its early period, these critical moments are caused by the right (in 1953, with the attempt to impose a majority electoral system; in 1960, the attempt to include the extreme fascist right in the government); they were caused by the left at a later time (above all during the first half of the Seventies, which were characterized by a violent break from corporate agreements on the subject of work and of a radical critique of the very procedures of planning). In any event, the political elite renewed the original constitutional contract. In the Sixties the crisis was to be be resolved with a slight balancing of the constitutional axis toward the center-left. In the Seventies there were attempts at new alliances among parties, within parties, which would follow one another, generating several more or less "historical" compromises, and at times reaching out even to the extreme left of the parliamentary line-up. But whatever the shape of the parliamentary line-up was, its constitutional axis could only be in the center: "imperfect bipartisanism" and material constitution were unavoidable. The left could be welcomed into the center, but the center was the steadfast target of all political operations, the destiny of post-war Italian democracy.

2. The crisis of the above described material constitution begins, however, to become increasingly more apparent beginning in the Seventies.

What makes up the crisis? It is the fact that the political forces which were at the basis of the agreement of 1948 are themselves in a state of crisis. The agreement does not change, *cannot change*, as we have seen, but the parties which had entered into it are becoming extinct, or better, they are kept artificially alive by the operations of the formal Constitution. The relation between material constitution and formal Constitution is reversed: the first, which had to give to the second Constitution a story-line and strong vitality, became exhausted; constitutional life becomes nothing more than a formality: it is the life of a dead man.

Today, all of this is clear. But for those who wanted to see it, this crisis was already apparent in the Seventies. The system would reproduce itself automatically, without a soul that would permeate it, without a spirit that would renew it, which was already a horrifying prospect. Only international conditions keep together a system in which all other conditions have collapsed. But we are still in the middle of a Cold War, in the period before 1989 and the fall of the Berlin Wall … Well then, what takes place during all these years? What has happened to the Constitution of the First Republic between the Seventies and the Nineties?

On the right, the old political elite, half Catholic, half capitalist (big Fordist capital), finds itself in contradiction with its own base. During these years, in fact, the Italian productive framework changes—changes with great speed. Powerfully challenged by the workers' struggles at the end of the Seventies, big capital withdraws onto the financial field and begins to move its productive capabilities onto the international stage. On the other hand, small and medium sized enterprises become more and more organically rooted in their traditional territories and offer an alternative to the ambitions of the social control of big capital. In this phase of great industrial changes, which were provoked by particularly intense workers struggles between the end of the Sixties and the beginning of the Seventies, new kinds of enterprises begin to have success—especially in the North—and new workforce pools and territorial networks of small and medium sized enterprises begin to take shape. Industrial power changes appearance, the highest points of productivity move from big Fordist enterprises to territorial networks of scattered labor which is increasingly "immaterial labor." It is in the Seventies that we find the foundations for the industrial "boom" which will explode in the Eighties.

This profound and gigantic productive transformation does not even come close to the old political elite of the center right or the center left. This transformation of production is not even suspected. The country's government continues to act within the old terrain of the Fordist State: it supports big companies in crisis while it does nothing in terms of offering even the most basic but essential services to the thriving small and medium sized enterprises. The old political elite is totally incapable of inspiring those synergies (between territories, enterprises, services and training) which are required for the new industrial reality. The old political forces on the right and in the center remain unmoved by this earthquake. The conflict between the political elite on the right and its base becomes explosive.

Immobility issues forth also from the forces on the left. Those forces also are blind to the changes in production and to the social transformations they have caused. They trust big industry labor corporations in order to persevere the Fordist politics beyond which they cannot see. Already in the Seventies leftist forces waver between an exaggerated defense of union interests and compromises, with no principles, with the government forces. The great march through the institution which they had promised to their base becomes the stroll of a drunk who has lost any sense of direction.

Other insurrectional impulses and movements of armed struggle which last in Italy from the end of the Seventies to the beginning of the Eighties add on to and enhance the disorientation of the left. The fact is that new generations of intellectuals and of workers demand that the left take political charge of the direction of the movement of productive and social transformation which the right was incapable of leading. It is with the refusal of the left to pronounce the First Republic dead that resistance, rebellion, and armed struggle are unleashed. The left, then, in first person, assumes the commitment of repression. A horrible, painstaking, hard job: unforgettable. The disenfranchising of the left from its (worker and intellectual) base would not be characterized simply by blindness in the face of the transformations of production and by foolish loyalty to an already exhausted constitutional contract: the detachment of the left from its base would be marked, above all, by those deeds with no return which are betrayal, Stalinist repression of struggles, the illusion of being able to earn the dignity of government at this price.

And the left actually joins the government in the Eighties. But it has become, by this point, an empty box. After having materially participated in Italian political life in a subordinate role, for the long four decades which span from the Forties to the Eighties, the left formally joins a government system which has lost any social mandate. The Constitution of 1948 was thus exhausted, but the left not only had not realized this, but did not even want to know about it. Watch out, though: when Constitutions end they are either replaced or they become something to be shared, the ground for corruption; either a new constituent spirit is unlocked or everything is dragged into the putrefaction of the old one. The State had become a piece of property to be divided up and spent: the left plays along. The game of corruption. A necessary and inevitable corruption, active and passive, because where the spirit of democracy does not breathe and representation is inexistent, the only relation between government and civil society is that of the *lobbies* which corrupt politicians, and the associations which are corrupted by the politicians. In the Eighties the participation of the left in this perverted machine of corruption is intimate and profound. The highest index of this participation can be seen in the fact that for the first time the left does not denounce the corruption of members of government and of political life. In the Eighties the left's ability to understand and criticize approaches zero; its capacity for corruption and repression is nearly infinite.

In 1989, with the fall of the Wall, the Italian Constitution of 1948—the material constitution which had become exhausted— also collapses formally. The set of social relations which it presupposed had already collapsed; its ability to represent movements or real political subjects had already ended. Now even the pretense disappears. The King is naked. The crisis is apparent. The big pot which was boiling on its own is without a lid. Here the "Italian Revolution" begins, the questioning of the Constitution of 1948, in its material and formal aspects. Here the possibility for a Second Republic opens up.

Between 1989 and 1993 all sorts of games are played. Let's look at this schematically:

First game: President Cossiga and the high State bureaucracy attempt an authoritarian maneuver to keep in check a crisis which— rightly so—they believe to be inevitable. This maneuver is blocked by other State bodies.

Second game: at the same time, the Leagues aggressively appear on the scene and have huge appeal (and above all they are capable of building new alliances which run across the political spectrum). The Leagues represent, at times in a grotesque but no less effective manner, the new productive forces of small and medium sized enterprises which have been successful in the North—that is, in one of the richest productive areas in Europe. The affirmation of the Leagues takes on a subversive form with revolutionary effects. The Leagues expressly propose the end of the First Republic, a new federalist Constitution, and, for the first time, extreme economic liberalism. The entire political establishment realizes that it is impossible to put a stop to this League-led insurgency without operations of radical renovation.

Third game: a new center is formed in opposition to the first and second projects. This center consists of, by way of alternate events, an alliance which includes some big State departments (above all the treasury and the justice System), some reformist Catholic groups and the left. The Amato government and then the government of Ciampi (a former director of the Bank of Italy) assume a role of leadership in this line up which has two goals: the moralization of public life, giving free reign to the Justice department to prosecute and destroy the political forces involved in corruption (the "Clean Hands" operation); the dismantling of the Welfare State (that is: a heavy handed politics aimed at balancing the State deficit is put into action by freezing wages, by waging a campaign to privatize the totality of public patrimony, by dismantling all structures of assistance—equated with the figures of corruption—and a new monetarty policy which is extremely restrictive). This "third game" wants to pull the rug from under the feet of the League, by way of a campaign of moralization and the launching of liberal minded policies: this game attempts to diffuse the subversive potential of that movement.

At the beginning of 1994 this "third game" (that is, the new center) appears to be winning. A so-called "progressive" front, guided by forces made up by big administration, by the center and by the entire left, and led by the Ciampi government, is winning. Except that:

Fourth game: a big capitalist, Berlusconi, steps into the political arena, backed by his television networks and his print empire, and he presents himself as the point of convergence of the new liberal right and the old regime forces which do not identify with the progressive front. For the first time since 1989, and the appearance of the Leagues, the issue of representation for the new productive classes (who see themselves as the outsiders of the Constitution of 1948) is posed in general terms which are politically adequate to the weightiness of the transition which is taking place. In a very short time this new force becomes organized and wins the elections. Berlusconi becomes prime minister.

3. A new "material constitution" is taking shape as the foundation of the new power structure in Italy. What characterizes it? Which fundamental forces shape and limit it, sustain and guarantee its vocabulary, goals, and rules?

The fundamental element of the new material constitution is the *centrality of the enterprise*. And when we speak of enterprise, we mean, in this case, the entrepreneurial function within the capitalist organization of production and of circulation of goods. Production and market legitimize authority, that is, the exercise of power on the entirety of the conditions of social reproduction. Organization and hierarchy, the positioning of subjects in order to maximize the productivity of the "Italy enterprise"—this is what gives shape to the vocabulary and goals of government, and upon this ground we find consensus building elements offered and consolidated. An immediate negative consequence derives from this: the organization of the work force which, in the Constitution of the Fordist period, was fundamental to the process of legitimation of the State, is now eliminated.

The work force, in the entrepreneurial State, is no longer viewed as a collective unit but as a set of consumers, as mobile and flexible elements of capital.

What follows is a radical modification of the concept and practice of political representation. In the Fordist Constitutions, as we have seen, fundamental value was given to the representation of interests: this organizational model would often dictate the shape of bargaining in terms of the redistribution of income. Now, representation of organized interests, especially those of the subaltern classes, is excluded from the political representational processes and—when this is not possible—it is subordinated, nonetheless, to the latter. Second, political representation is, whenever possible, removed from the organization of political parties. In the new material constitution the role of the parties is heavily modified by voting procedures—which not only penalize proportionality but become, with ever greater determination and coherence, personality driven (a majority, personal or uninominal voting system, without any run-off vote). The political party goes back to being a product of the electoral game rather than being a subject, a mass actor in the democratic organization of the State, as the Welfare State saw it. The entirety of social procedures of legitimation (above all in the realm of economics) and of mediation between political citizenry and social citizenry is thus cancelled out.

If the State models itself on business, the government is a government of business. Executive power regains, in this way, a preeminence which, in the last fifty years, had been challenged. The new preeminence of executive power gives a new shape to the other powers of the State. The parliamentary function is the first to be affected by these changes: the Parliament is called upon to exercise a function of control rather than being a legislative structure in the proper sense. As far as the Magistracy is concerned, great pressures are exerted upon it in order to limit its independence and to rein it back to a role subordinate to the growth of the enterprise (be it either an individual business or business-firm Italy).

These changes in the fabric of the State and this reshaping of the architecture of powers unfolded within enormous controversy, as reported by the news in recent years, which often reached the breaking point. But it is clear that this line of development is accepted both on the right and on the left. The problem upon which all the clashes are galvanized is no longer constitutional; it is simply political; it does not concern the structure of the State and the new arrangement of powers, but the formation of the new political and administrative classes.

But we do not want to bore our readers here by continuing to insist on a series of modifications of the formal Constitution which, in great part, presidential regimes already encompass—and which, also in Italy, are setting the stage for a presidential transformation of the political system which is very, if not extremely, near at hand. This transformation is perceived in all of its urgency because the central power must, by way of strengthening the presidential (if not federalist) function, compensate for those processes of decentralization and regionalization which are taking place. While they are adequate for the articulation of the entrepreneurial State and for the need to establish new relations within the organization of the larger European market, the processes of decentralization must be led back to a central control.

We would not want to continue on this path. What happens behind and through these modifications of the formal structure of the Constitution is much more important. It is, in fact, in the realm of the material that similar or even identical formal structures differentiate themselves. Business-firm-Italy, which is headed for a type of presidential regime, is not, thus, like any other presidential Constitutional Country. What is unique in Italy is the force (shall we say violence?) of the transformation. The Welfare State comes through this transformation beaten black and blue. Deregulation goes hand in hand with a process of privatization of State property which has a substantial impact on the balance of power between the classes and on the framework for the redistribution of wealth. From this standpoint, what is taking place in Italy is closer to what happened in the countries of "really-existing socialism," rather than to what neoliberalism has imposed on the welfare-structured Central European countries. Once again, as happened in previous centuries, but with a different level of social complexity, the bourgeoisie identifies with government, the country is reduced to a business and the management of this business is a one-dimensional capitalist venture.

Now—and here the extremely new is piled up upon the already new—this direct reappropriation of power by the bourgeoisie and the transformation of the material constitution are conditioned (as we recalled at the beginning of this article) by the new style of production—and by the new productive system—which have taken shape in these last few years. Berlusconi and his allies are authentic and legitimate representatives of the post-Fordist industry which has used as the basis of its own activity the fields of communication and of immaterial production through networks. The "subversion from above" of the old constitutional structure thus finds a real base in the new strata of the scattered entrepreneurship which was created by the capitalistic reforms of the Seventies and Eighties. The "subversion from above" is, in this case, also a direct appropriation of the political structures by a new political stratum of the bourgeoisie. Berlusconi was very effective in bringing together new post-Fordist entrepreneurs and the new bourgeoisie of communication. He was also quite capable of containing the controversy that these new entrepreneurial classes leveled against big Fordist and financial capital, just as he was successful in reconstructing a unitary front once the power relations internal to the line-up were modified in favor of the entrepreneurs. The so-called Italian Revolution is thus not only neoliberal: it is neoliberal but also, and above all, post-Fordist; it is neoliberal but also, and above all, capable of organizing a new mass consensus on communication and production. The Italian Revolution is thus the *new* formula of a *reactionary* government of the bourgeoisie in a communication-based post-Fordist society. Let it be clear: we insist both on the term "new" and on the term "reactionary." We are totally disinterested in those analyses of "Berlusconiism" which reduce this phenomenon to a reproduction of old fascist behaviors.

In reality, in Berlusconiism there is none of the old fascism, and even less of the new material constitution of the Republic. Some groups on the left which are leveling these accusations are blinded by the rage of their defeat. Berlusconiism is, instead, a new form of the domination of collective capitalism, a form of domination and of exploitation which is suitable to a society in which production and communication are blended together. And in this framework, by accepting the postmodern determinations of our analysis, we can invent suitable alternatives and organize our sabotage of this system of domination.

Sources

Part One: Inquiry Workshop

New Social Movements and Political Realignments: "Nuovi movimenti sociali e riallineamenti politici," in *The New Statesman*, London, February 14, 1988.

Worker Restructurings in Europe. Analysis of the Cycle of Struggles in the Eighties and Nineties: "Ricomposizioni operaie in Europa. Analisi del ciclo di lotte tra gli anni Ottanta e Novanta," in *IM' Media*, Paris, September, 1989.

Social Struggles in a Systemic Setting: "Lotte sociali in ambiente sistemico," in *Futur Antérieur*, Paris, January, 1992.

Peugeot: Restructured Factory and Production of Subjectivity: "Peugeot: fabbrica ristrutturata e produzione di soggettività," with Maurizio Lazzarato, in *Il Manifesto*, Rome, May 1, 1991.

Toyotaism: The Japanese Model and the Social Worker: " Il toyotismo: modello giapponese e operaio sociale," in *Il Manifesto*, Rome, March 22, 1991.

Productive Networks and Territories: The Case of the Italian Northeast: "Reti produttive e territori: il caso del Nord-Est italiano," in *Les Banlieues*, Spring, 1993.

Part Two: The Decline of "Weak Thought"

What Has the Intellectual Become?: "Cos'è diventato l'intellettuale.," in *El Mundo*, Madrid, June 15, 1991.

Chronicle of a Transition: "Cronaca di un trapasso," in *Diario 16*, Madrid, October 10, 1988.

"Come Back, Sweet Terrible Ghost": Nietzsche Today: " 'Ritorna, dolce, terribile ombra.' Nietzsche, oggi," in *El Mundo*, Madrid, October 10, 1994.

More Marx?: "Ancora Marx?," in *El Mundo*, Madrid, December 2, 1993.

Compassion, Terror and General Intellect: "Compassione, terrore e General Intellect," in *Luogo Comune*, Rome, May 1991.

The Infinite Nature of Communication / The Finite Nature of Desire: "Infinitezza della comunicazione / Finitezza del desiderio," in *Futur Antérieur*, Paris, April 1992.

Understanding Being through Language: "Comprensione dell'essere attraverso il linguaggio," in *El Mundo*, Madrid, September 24,1993.

The Sense of a Distinction: The Right, the Left and Bobbio: "Il senso di una distinzione. Destra, sinistra e Bobbio," in *Futuro Anteriore*, Rome, January, 1995.

Deleuze and Guattari: A Philosophy for the 21st Century: "Deleuze e Guattari, una filosofia per il Ventunesimo secolo," in *Futur Antérieur*, Paris, Winter 1991.

Kaosmos: "Kaosmos," in *El Mundo*, Madrid, August 1991.

Part Three: From the End of Really-Existing Socialism to the Gulf War

Rereading Polybius and Machiavelli: With Regard to "Glasnost": "Rileggendo Polibio e Machiavelli. A proposito di 'glasnost'," in *Diario 16*, Madrid, May 1989.

Euro Disney and Tiananmen: "Eurodisney e Tienanmen," in *Diario 16*, Madrid, July 1989.

Eastern Europe between Capitalist Restoration and Constituent Power: "L'Europa dell'Est fra restaurazione capitalistica e potere costituente," in *El Mundo*, Madrid, November 1989.

We Are All Berliners: "Siamo tutti berlinesi," in *El Mundo*, Madrid, November 1989.

On the Difference between Socialism and Communism: "Sulla differenza tra socialismo e comunismo," in *El Mundo*, Madrid, January 1990.

The Consequences of the "End of History": "Le conseguenze della 'fine della Storia,'" in *El Mundo*, Madrid, September 1990.

The Philosophical Consequences of the Gulf War. Reflections on a War, Which, as I Write This, Has Not Yet Begun: "Le conseguenze filosofiche del Golfo. Qualche riflessione su una Guerra che, quando scriviamo, non è ancora cominciata," in *Futur Antérieur*, Paris, December 1990.

War, Communication and Democracy: "Guerra, comunicazione e democrazia," in *El Mundo*, Madrid, January 1991.

For a Europe from the Atlantic to the Ural Mountains: "Per un'Europa dall' Atlantico agli Urali," in *El Mundo*, Madrid, October 1991.

Nations, Racisms and New Universality: "Nazioni, razzismi e nuova universalità," in *Il Manifesto*, Rome, November 1991.

John-Paul II's Fifth International: "La Quinta Internazionale di Giovanni Paolo II," in *Futur Antérieur*, Paris, October 1991.

The USA and Europe after the Gulf War and the Los Angeles Riots: "Usa ed Europa dopo la Guerra del Golfo e la rivolta di Los Angeles," with Jean-Marie Vincent, in *Futur Antérieur*, Paris, October 1992.

Part Four: Chronicles of the Second Republic

The Constituent Republic: "Repubblica costituente," in *Riff-Raff*, Padua, April 1993.

Legal-Illegal: Corruption, Judicial Power and Political Power: "Legale-Illegale: corruzione, potere giudiziario e potere politico," in *Terminologia scientifico-sociale (Anexo)*, Barcelona, 1991.

Subversion from Above: Notes on Bribesville: "La sovversione dall'alto. Note su Tangentopoli," in *Riff-Raff*, Padua, April 1993.

Laboratory Italy (September 1993): "Laboratorio Italia (settembre 1993)," in *Riff-Raff*, Padua, March 1994.

Techniques for a *Coup d'État* (November 1993): "Tecniche del colpo di Stato (novembre 1993)," in *Riff-Raff*, Padua, March 1994.

Cloning (December 1993): "La clonazione (dicembre 1993)," in *Riff-Raff*, Padua, March 1994.

The Italian "Revolution" and the "Devolution" of the Left: "La 'Rivoluzione' italiana e la 'devoluzione' della sinistra," in *Futur Antérieur*, Paris, Summer 1994.

Italy, the Nineties: Crisis and Renewal of a Constitutional Model: "Italia, anni Novanta: crisi e rinnovamento di un modello costituzionale," in *Pueples Méditerranéens / Mediterranean Peoples*, Paris, April–June 1994.